REVENGE

REVENGE

THE INSIDE STORY OF TRUMP'S RETURN TO POWER

ALEX ISENSTADT

GRAND
CENTRAL

NEW YORK BOSTON

Grand Central Publishing
Hachette Book Group
1290 Avenue of the Americas, New York, NY 10104
grandcentralpublishing.com
@grandcentralpub

First Edition: March 2025

Grand Central Publishing is a division of Hachette Book Group, Inc. The Grand Central Publishing name and logo is a registered trademark of Hachette Book Group, Inc.

The publisher is not responsible for websites (or their content) that are not owned by the publisher.

The Hachette Speakers Bureau provides a wide range of authors for speaking events. To find out more, go to hachettespeakersbureau.com or email HachetteSpeakers@hbgusa.com.

Grand Central Publishing books may be purchased in bulk for business, educational, or promotional use. For information, please contact your local bookseller or the Hachette Book Group Special Markets Department at special.markets@hbgusa.com.

Library of Congress Cataloging-in-Publication Data has been applied for.

ISBNs: 978-1-5387-6551-7 (hardcover), 978-1-5387-6553-1 (ebook)

Printed in the United States of America

LSC-C

Printing 1, 2025

To Catherine, Lester, and Joey

CONTENTS

AUTHOR'S NOTE

This book is based on more than three hundred interviews. I began reporting in February 2023, a few months after Trump launched his campaign, gleaning information in real-time from an array of sources, including Trump aides, allies, donors, senators, House members, and senior Republican strategists. My goal was to capture people's memories while they were still fresh, and to bring readers "inside the room" as Trump embarked on his quest for the White House. I have used quotation marks in instances where either the person making the comment or someone hearing the comment directly has provided the sourcing. When a quote is paraphrased, it is because the person making or hearing the remark did not remember their words exactly as they said them or because information was provided to me by someone who was not present but was familiar with the conversation. When I have related someone's thoughts, they are based on a retelling from that person or someone with direct knowledge of them. In describing every conversation or situation, I have taken pains to corroborate my reporting with the people who were involved. In rare instances where there was disagreement over something that transpired, I have made my best judgment in representing it.

REVENGE

PROLOGUE

Donald Trump huddled with his senior lieutenants backstage at the Van Andel Arena, a Grand Rapids, Michigan, hockey rink otherwise known as the Freezer on Fulton. The clock had just struck midnight. Election Day had arrived.

The former president wasn't one for sentimentality, but this rally, the seventy-eighth of his 2024 campaign, would be his last as a presidential candidate. Trump's trademark rallies had become a cornerstone of his movement, his way of connecting with supporters who saw him as a sledgehammer against a system that had let them down. Trump's first rally in New Hampshire on June 17, 2015, the day after he rode down the Trump Tower escalator announcing his first candidacy for president, had drawn a few hundred people.[1] A month later, five thousand fans packed into the Phoenix Convention Center, where Trump declared: "The silent majority is back, and we're going to take our country back." By August that year, thirty thousand red-hatted MAGAites flooded into the Ladd-Peebles Stadium in Mobile, Alabama.[2] Trump had arrived on the political scene as a bona fide force.[3]

Now, something was coming to an end. He had been reflective all week. "These are going to be the last few campaign rallies I ever do," he'd said aboard his plane.

The choice of Grand Rapids that night had been intentional. It was the last campaign stop of Trump's victorious 2016 campaign, another nod to his feeling of nostalgia. He was feeling good and knew there was a chance he could win the election, but there was a sense of wistfulness.

Thousands of supporters had lined up for hours for a chance to see the former and potentially future president. As Trump waited in his holding room, he could hear the place going bonkers. Trump's loyal aides had gathered around him, and one by one he went around and gave them all fist bumps.

There was one for Walt Nauta, Trump's ever-present body man who had been indicted alongside him in a federal case over mishandling classified documents. There was one for his personal assistant Chamberlain Harris, another for senior adviser Taylor Budowich and one more for his hard-charging spokesman, Steven Cheung. Trump did not say anything as he went around the circle, but his silence spoke volumes. Trump was a demanding, hard-to-please boss, and in the final weeks he'd stretched his staff to their breaking point. Trump's schedule had been nonstop. He was hitting three or four stops a day and was doing tele-rallies during flights and when he got home late at night. In October, his campaign co-chair, Susie Wiles, had sent an email informing staff they were now expected to show up to work from 9 a.m. to 7 p.m., seven days a week. Some aides said they were becoming sick with exhaustion. The fist bumps were his way of saying thank you.

After Trump wrapped up backstage, he walked across a strip of red carpet, climbed a few stairs, and passed through an American flag serving as a curtain. The sounds of Lee Greenwood's "God Bless the USA" filled the arena. His fans needed nearly four and a half minutes to quiet down before Trump could speak. He made his final pitch: "Your paychecks will be higher, your streets will be safer and cleaner, your communities will be richer, and your future as an American will be much better than it ever has been when I get in."[4] He finished up at around 2 a.m., with a call to "fight, fight fight," the same declaration he had made after narrowly surviving an assassination attempt three and a half months earlier in Butler, Pennsylvania, by a mere fraction of an inch.

"That's a wrap," he said to his team when he got backstage. "That's the last one we'll ever do."

Rain pelted Trump's motorcade as it pulled away. Five hours later, he'd be back at Mar-a-Lago. Twenty-four hours later, he'd be president-elect.

━━

Trump's victory in the 2024 election represented the most remarkable political comeback in American history. He left the White House in disgrace nearly four years earlier following the January 6 riot at the Capitol, which he had inspired and for which he was impeached. In its aftermath, he was with few friends or allies, and his once formidable political operation was no more.

The obstacles he overcame in the long campaign that followed would have felled lesser politicians. He dispatched with all his primary rivals, including Florida Governor Ron DeSantis and former United Nations Ambassador Nikki Haley, who had drawn the support of a Republican establishment desperate to destroy him. He was indicted four times. He was found guilty once, for paying hush money to a porn actress. He survived two assassination attempts. He fought not one but two Democratic rivals for the presidency, when Kamala Harris replaced Joe Biden as candidate 107 days before the election, spending $1.5 billion in her attempt to defeat him.

There has been no more polarizing figure in American life over the last decade than Trump. He has split the public between those who perceive him as a threat to democracy and a destroyer of societal norms, and those who celebrate him as a brash insurgent who "sticks it to the man" and shakes up a system that isn't working for them. Following his 2024 win, one thing is inarguable: Trump has proven himself to be one of the most resilient political athletes in American history.

Trump tapped into visceral feelings of anger, resentment, and alienation among a broad swath of the public. His plight, far from being a political weakness, became a strength. Supporters identified with him; they saw him as a warrior against the establishment. After Trump was booked in Atlanta's Fulton County Jail over charges stemming from his effort to overturn his 2020 election defeat, his scowling mugshot became a viral sensation. Old Row, a website owned by Barstool Sports that caters to southern college guys, sold T-shirts imprinted with the photo with the lettering "LEGEND" above Trump's head. After he was shot during a rally in Butler, Pennsylvania, the image of the bloodied former president pumping his fist became iconic. Beer koozies with imprints depicting the immediate aftermath of the shooting, like one reading "IMPEACHED. ARRESTED. CONVICTED. SHOT. NEVER SURRENDER," began to appear on the shopping website Etsy. Trump embraced the idea of being a warrior and draped himself in it. He orchestrated

Saturday night walkouts at UFC events. He campaigned with wrestler Hulk Hogan. "Fight, fight, fight" became the rallying cry of his campaign.

While Trump's 2016 victory was based heavily on his appeal to white voters, he expanded his 2024 coalition to include working-class Black and Hispanic people, and young men of all kinds, each of whom grasped on to the perception Trump was an underdog fighter. They welcomed him into their barbershops, their bodegas, their frat houses. Weighed down by the rising costs of inflation in the wake of a global pandemic, frustrated by immigration, and repulsed by liberal "woke" politics, they turned toward a man they embraced as their soldier. According to exit polls, Trump won 46 percent of the Hispanic vote, an increase of 18 percent from 2016. Among young people aged eighteen to twenty-four, he did 9 percent better than he did eight years earlier, and among Black men 8 percent better. His vote share among urbanites rose by 4 percent.[5]

After being treated like a pariah throughout the 2016 campaign, Trump was embraced this time by an alternative media ecosystem—in particular, mostly male influencers and podcasters who saw Trump as a like-minded antiestablishment force. While Harris was centering her campaign around traditional media outlets, Trump was sitting down with twenty-three-year-old streamer Adin Ross, wrestler-turned-talk show host Mark "The Undertaker" Calaway, and, most significantly, podcast king Joe Rogan. Trump tapped a crew of prankster podcast bros named the Nelk Boys to help register young voters. He invited Tucker Carlson, who launched a top-ranked podcast after being fired by Fox News, to speak at the Republican National Convention.

Trump would make inroads in deep-blue states, too, where voters expressed rising frustration with issues such as homelessness and violent crime. In New York, he performed better than any Republican candidate since 1988. In New Jersey and California, he performed better than anyone since George W. Bush.

Away from the cameras, Trump took other steps to ensure his return to power. After being hamstrung by dysfunctional past White House and campaign operations, he surrounded himself with a group of savvy and disciplined strategists, led by Susie Wiles and Chris LaCivita, who had no appetite for backstabbing, leaking, or chaos. He engaged in the care and feeding of the billionaire donor class, like Elon Musk, the richest person in the world. He wielded power like an old-school political boss, pressuring those in his party to get in line. He adopted a successful courtroom strategy aimed at delaying and dragging out the legal cases he was confronting. He exhibited a willingness to break with conservatives when he deemed it politically advantageous to do so. He was patient with his vice presidential pick, JD Vance, despite a rocky launch, rather than impulsively throwing him overboard. Most of all, he demonstrated an intuitive understanding of the power of imagery.

There were missteps along the way. Trump could alienate people in his own party, act impulsively, and make off-the-rails comments. But, in the end voters cared less about Trump's comportment—something they became inured to over the previous decade—than about what Trump *represented* to them.

With his sweeping victory, Trump got revenge—on the legal system he argued was aligned against him, on the media that skewered him, and on the Democratic Party, which had defeated him four years earlier. But Trump's win was not just revenge for himself. It was revenge for his millions of followers who saw him as their vessel—and for half the country, who saw him as the best bet to address the nation's problems.

The story of Donald Trump's comeback was four years in the making, and it is one filled with unexpected twists and turns. It begins one month before the deadly assault on the United States Capitol, on a cloudy December day in Washington, DC.

ONE:
"YOU'RE NOT GOING TO BELIEVE THIS"

DECEMBER 3, 2020

Donald Trump stared dead ahead.

Exactly one month after he had lost reelection—and four weeks before a mob he inspired would wage a bloody, failed attempt to stop the peaceful transfer of power—aides sat silently before him in the Oval Office. The president made clear he was thinking about another race—one that would be taking place four years down the road.

"You know why we're doing this, right?" Trump said. The words hung in the air. After weeks of loudly contesting his loss to Joe Biden, Trump had brought in aides ostensibly to talk about the millions of donor dollars flowing into his legal defense account, which would be used to bankroll the plethora of frivolous lawsuits he had launched aimed at overturning the election.

But the president was steering the conversation in a direction that surprised the suits who had trekked to the Oval. Trump's lieutenants gathered in a socially distanced semicircle around the Resolute Desk, an unspoken recognition that the COVID pandemic was still raging. A Christmas tree stood in the corner, next to a portrait of Abraham Lincoln. A glass of Diet Coke, filled nearly to the brim, sat by Trump's left hand. Trump's son-in-law and senior adviser, Jared Kushner, had taken a break from dealing with Middle East policy to make the meeting, sporting a blue and green striped tie, his hair neatly combed, a pen clasped in his hand to take notes. There was White House lawyer Eric Herschmann, who crossed his legs as he took in the proceedings, a blue-and-white printout in his hands. To Trump's far right was political adviser Jason Miller, who was next to two other 2020 campaign veterans, Sean Dollman and Alex Cannon.

"We're going to pursue every legal challenge we can," the president said, stating flatly that he had won the election. He was convinced it was being stolen from him. But, he admitted, it would be tough.

"If it doesn't go our way, we're going to come back and do this again. You understand that, right?"

It was a stunning declaration. For all his bluster that he had won the election, for all his declarations that he had been the victim of rampant voter fraud, for all the half-baked legal tactics he had used to try to hold on to power, Trump knew he would likely be leaving the White House on January 20. But he also knew something else: By fighting the outcome of the election, he was firing up his supporters, casting himself as the victim, and setting the stage for 2024.

It was the furthest some aides had heard the president go when it came to running again. Sure, Trump had been intimating for weeks another run wasn't off the table. But the seventy-four-year-old Trump would bounce ideas off people all the time, some of which were real, but most of which weren't. Hell, sometimes it seemed he liked to float things just to get a reaction out of people. And sure, a lot of it had leaked to the press, providing endless fuel to the cable news programs that inhaled his wild private musings like crack. But how much of it had come to pass? Not much.

This felt different. Sharper. The president was leaning in. As his White House tenure wound down, it was clear Trump was thinking more and more about his future.

—

Brian Jack made his way to the West Wing from the Eisenhower Executive Office Building. It was January 13, a week after thousands of Trump supporters had laid siege to the Capitol. Earlier that day, the House of Representatives impeached Trump, arguing he had incited the January 6 assault. The riot would be the single event that most defined the president's turbulent four years in office, and its cosmic blast-radius fallout was guaranteed to shape whatever his future looked like.

Jack, a shaggy-haired, low-key Georgia boy who was Trump's White House political director, had been called to meet the president in the private dining room next to the Oval. Unlike other Trump aides who jostled for public attention, knifed their coworkers to a bloody pulp, and built out massive portfolios for themselves, Jack kept his head down, was well liked by his colleagues, and stayed in his lane. While other White House officials gathered after work at see-and-be-seen Washington spots such as Cafe Milano, Jack preferred to dine at Buffalo Wild Wings or P.F. Chang's in suburban Virginia.

He was joined at the meeting by several other senior advisers, including Kushner, Miller, and Bill Stepien, Trump's campaign manager. In the wake of January 6, staffers were fleeing by the day, and as the three men talked, Trump wanted to know who would be sticking with him going forward. He wanted to know about the coming midterm election. And he wanted to know about the ten House Republicans who voted to impeach him—each of whom were now dead to him. At the top of his "shit list" were Wyoming Representative Liz Cheney and Alaska Senator Lisa Murkowski, a member of the upper congressional chamber who had also savaged Trump over his conduct on January 6. Both would be up for reelection in two years, and Trump would have an opportunity to try to take them out.

As he sat in the dining room, it dawned on Jack that Trump was doing something that, as far as recent history went, no defeated ex-president had done before. Had Jimmy Carter or George H. W. Bush considered wading into race after race after they lost reelection? Had they pressed their lieutenants to come up with plans to exact revenge on their enemies? The answer was no. Trump was to hand over the keys to 1600 Pennsylvania Avenue in a week. He had just been impeached for a second time and had thrust the country into a maelstrom over the fate of American democracy—but he seemed as obsessed with the ins and outs of electoral politics as ever.

As Jack shuttled back to his office following the meeting, a thought crossed his mind: This guy wants to maintain control over the Republican Party—and he is not going to fade away.

Trump held on to his rage until his very last day in the Oval Office. Breaking more than a century of tradition, he refused to attend Biden's inauguration. Instead, he addressed supporters from Joint Base Andrews at a ceremony with a twenty-one-gun salute, where he blasted the Village People's "YMCA" on his way out. From there, he flew to Mar-a-Lago, his club in Palm Beach, Florida, once known as the "winter White House" and now his base of operations as he plotted for the future.

By late January, Trump had begun to settle into post-presidential life. Each morning, he woke up, put on a suit with diamond cufflinks, and headed into his office, which had just been converted from a bridal suite. He golfed, took in hours of cable news, and scarfed down well-done steaks prepared by his chefs in the Mar-a-Lago kitchen. But he was also doing something else: stewing. Over Biden. Over the former loyalists who had proven themselves to be anything but. And over the Republicans who had crossed him.

He remained convinced—despite all the evidence proving otherwise—the election had been stolen from him. "If a thief steals diamonds from a diamond store, they have to return them," Trump would tell people.

John McLaughlin, a veteran Republican pollster, pulled up to Mar-a-Lago at around 5 p.m. on February 10. McLaughlin had known Trump since 2011, when the real estate tycoon was first thinking about running for president. He had worked on Trump's 2016 and 2020 campaigns, too, staying in touch with him while he was in the White House.

McLaughlin came bearing gifts. He made his way toward Trump's office and found the former president watching Fox News's coverage of the post-January 6 Senate trial. Democratic impeachment managers had shown graphic footage of the pro-Trump mob assaulting police officers, spewing obscenities, and stampeding the Capitol—interspersed with Trump's speech that day imploring his supporters to "fight like hell."

Trump would be indelibly linked to the violence that enveloped the Capitol. But McLaughlin was convinced Trump still had a political future and wanted him to think long-term. He presented Trump with his latest survey findings, which found the ex-president still overwhelmingly popular among Republicans following the Capitol riot. McLaughlin's thirty-page presentation also concluded that voters overwhelmingly felt Congress should be focused on dealing with the coronavirus pandemic rather than impeaching Trump.

There was more. McLaughlin had also taken a look into the lay of the political terrain, and it showed that roughly two-thirds of Republicans wanted Trump to run again. And, McLaughlin argued, less than a month into his term, Biden was unusually weak for a just-elected president. His poll had found that in seventeen battleground states, more people disapproved of Biden than approved of him.

"When Biden fails, there will be buyer's remorse, and you can win the next presidential election," McLaughlin told him.

It was all music to Trump's ears. He was getting hammered from all directions—congressional investigations, castigations from fellow Republicans—and the numbers reassured him he still had the party in his grip and had an opening for a comeback.

Trump, it was clear, didn't want to let go. If anything, he wanted to grab tighter. He might be out of office, but the midterm elections in twenty-one months' time, he was convinced, were an opportunity for him to maintain his hold over the Grand Old Party.

No ex-president had ever plunged so aggressively into shaping his party after leaving office. But Trump wasn't any ex-president. Trump wasn't just going to sit and watch from the sidelines—he wanted to run the party like a big-city political machine.

He had a model in mind. During his time in the White House, Trump had spoken privately of his affection for Meade Esposito, the late cigar-smoking Brooklyn political boss who in the 1960s and 1970s ruled the borough with an iron fist—cashing in on favors, demanding loyalty, and playing patronage politics unapologetically.

Like Esposito, Trump wanted to crush those who dared to cross him. Just as important, he wanted to stock the party ranks with staunch allies. He started on that mission a few days after leaving the White House, throwing his weight behind Kelli Ward, a fire-breathing election denier who was running for reelection as chair of the Arizona Republican Party.[1] Trump had focused particular post-election ire on the state, fueling off-the-wall conspiracy theories that his loss there—the first for a Republican since 1996—was the result of Sharpie pen–filled out ballots that couldn't be read by voting machines.

Ensconced at Mar-a-Lago, he no longer had the high-end technology to which he had access in the White House, which would allow him to seamlessly cut robocalls endorsing his candidates of choice. For the first few weeks after returning to Palm Beach he was only able to log onto Mar-a-Lago's shared Wi-Fi network, which was also available to other club members. So Trump improvised by calling up Jack, who put him on speaker and recorded him endorsing Ward. The message went out to the state party officials who elected the chair—less official, less polished than Trump was used to, but the deed was done.

Now, armed with McLaughlin's numbers, Trump felt even surer that, despite the arrows from the Cheneys and Murkowskis after January 6, his ironlike grip over the party was intact. He was ready to plunge into the midterms, his first step in his political comeback.

▬

A few months into 2021, Trump was becoming increasingly explicit about his plans to run again.

"I'm going to do this," Trump told South Carolina Senator Lindsey Graham, his old pal and loyalist, during a round of golf that spring.

"Are you sure?" Graham asked.

"Yeah," Trump said. "I have unfinished business."

Graham loved the idea, and told Trump if he won, it would be the greatest comeback in political history.

Trump spent the next year and a half outlining his political future and enjoying the pace of post-presidency life. On the one hand, he would vacillate over when to announce to a nation that had just rejected him electorally he was already planning on running again. It felt impossible for him to be out of the spotlight. Stripped of his White House pulpit, as well as his suspended Twitter and Facebook accounts, he dearly missed the all-consuming attention a sitting president commanded.

At the same time, he appeared content to live life as a non-candidate. For all his complaints that it was he, not Biden, who was supposed to be in the Oval Office, part of him was enjoying the freedom of being out of office. It was a nice existence: golf, cable TV, dinner on the Mar-a-Lago patio at a table encircled by velvet rope separating him from other members. Lather, rinse, repeat. Announce now, and all that would come to an end.

That tension was on full display in mid-August. Trump was scheduled to do an interview with Fox News's Sean Hannity on Biden's then ongoing messy troop withdrawal from Afghanistan. Scenes of chaos were beamed around the world as Americans and Afghans flooded Kabul airport while the Taliban took over the capital. The idea was for the former president to appear live on camera, making him look very much like a candidate for the nation's highest office. But Trump didn't feel like appearing in person and only wanted to be patched in by phone. He was out of office now. Why the hell would he want to be in a suit until late evening?

—

As the midterms approached, it was hard to find a race Trump wouldn't endorse in. He relished taking on the role of Meade Esposito, making candidates kiss his ring, rewarding allies with endorsements, and punishing detractors by backing their primary opponents. He developed an almost encyclopedic knowledge of races in every state and talked about campaigns like fantasy sports fanatics talk about stats. New York Congresswoman Elise Stefanik, the fourth-ranked House Republican, noticed that Trump's familiarity of districts surpassed any of the political consultants she dealt with.

In all, Trump would give his seal of approval to more than 250 candidates—chits that could pay off down the road.

But it would also tie him to the midterm results. Republicans were expected to capture the House and maybe the Senate, riding an expected wave of discontent over inflation, the messy US troop withdrawal from Afghanistan, and overall dissatisfaction they would likely take out on the party in the White House. But if they didn't? Well, that would be a black eye for Trump—and ammunition for the critics inside the Republican Party who were making the case it was time to leave the former president behind.

And then on August 8, everything changed.

—

That morning, FBI agents raided Mar-a-Lago in search of classified documents Trump had brought from the White House, cap-
ping months of federal efforts to get the material back. Trump
was now in serious legal trouble. What's more, a possible federal
indictment virtually ensured that he would be dealing with the
case while he was running for president.

Trump—who that day was 1,200 miles up north, at
Bedminster—had learned of the raid from his son Eric, who had
starred alongside his father in NBC's *The Apprentice*, helped run
the family's business empire, and spoke at the rally that preceded
the January 6 Capitol assault.[2] By that afternoon, aides knew
word of the search was going to leak soon, and it was guaranteed
to set off a firestorm. They scrambled to draft a statement.

That afternoon, senior adviser Taylor Budowich's phone
buzzed. It was Peter Schorsch, a plugged-in Florida lobbyist and
blogger.

"You're going to hate me, but I think I have something big,"
Schorsch said. He knew of the raid.

Budowich, who was in Sacramento, needed to buy some
time. He told Schorsch he'd get back to him. After thirty minutes, Budowich called Schorsch back with a statement from the
former president. Mar-a-Lago, Trump said in the statement, was
"under siege, raided, and occupied by a large group of FBI
agents."

Trump responded to the development with his signature
mix of defiance and grievance. As he saw it, he did nothing
wrong. Trump believed that, as a former president, he had an
absolute right to the documents. The raid, he said in his statement, "was not necessary or appropriate."

"Nothing like this has ever happened to a president of the
United States before," he added.[3]

Within Trumpworld, speculation mounted over who had leaked the news. Some of it centered on Florida Governor Ron DeSantis, who was increasingly looking to rival Trump for the party's 2024 nomination. Stephen Miller, Trump's White House speechwriter and senior adviser, privately complained that attorney Christina Bobb, who had been at Mar-a-Lago at the time of the raid, had allowed the FBI agents onto the premises. "No lawyer should have ceded this ground," Miller griped.

Paranoia reigned. Trump's aides worried their cell phones were being tapped by the feds. Now, when they met with Trump in his office, they left their devices outside.

Trump however, remained oddly calm. The day after the FBI moved on Mar-a-Lago, Trump was to have dinner with Indiana Congressman Jim Banks and other conservative members of Congress. Banks figured Trump would cancel on him, but to his surprise he got word from the former president's team: The dinner was still on.

As Banks dined with Trump that night, he was struck by how undeterred the former president was. Just hours after feds crawled over his estate, Trump was talking politics with lawmakers and taking pictures while flashing a thumbs-up. Banks couldn't believe it.

Budowich experienced the same thing. Shortly after the raid, the spokesman sat with Trump in his office. Trump was staring out the window.

"What are we going to do about this?" Trump asked his lieutenant.

"We're going to fight," Budowich said, "because that's the only thing we know how to do."

"You're right, we're going to fight," Trump said, looking at Budowich. "That's the only thing we know how to do."

—

On the eve of the midterm elections in November, Trump headed to Ohio to lend his support to Republican Senate candidate JD Vance, a rising populist in his own mold. Vance, a former venture capitalist and author of the bestselling memoir *Hillbilly Elegy*, had once been a Trump critic, but when he launched his Senate campaign, he changed his tune and became a full-blown supporter. Vance knew he needed to get on the ex-president's good side if he wanted a shot at winning the primary.

Word began circulating through Trump's orbit that the former president was seriously thinking about using the rally to make a surprise election-eve campaign launch. For the Republican Party honchos, it was perhaps the worst possible scenario. If Trump threw his hat into the ring that night, it would be the last thing swing voters remembered before they went to the polls the next day. Ronna McDaniel, head of the Republican National Committee, was with Pennsylvania Senate candidate Mehmet Oz when she got word of Trump's apparent forthcoming announcement and relayed the news to the candidate, whose fortunes would partly hinge on whether he could turn out the Philadelphia suburbanites who had bolted the party under Trump.

"That would be really bad," Oz said, grimacing.

McDaniel called Trump and tried to wave him off. Trump's team of political veterans, who were convinced Trump would be better off politically if he waited until after the election, were also trying to put the kibosh on it. Aides knew the only way to stop him was to get everyone on the plane, including Trump's family, to do a full-court press.

Trump Force One took off from West Palm Beach en route to Dayton International Airport that evening. Aboard the flight was Donald Trump Jr., the former president's hard-driving, very online eldest son, who had emerged as a key player in his orbit as other relatives like daughter Ivanka Trump and Jared Kushner retreated. Don Jr. publicly threw bombs and served up red meat to Trump's base, but privately, he was a calculated operator. As of late, he had been advising his father that if he was serious about running again, he couldn't just focus on relitigating the 2020 election.

He pitched his father on delaying the announcement.

"It's a bad idea, you shouldn't do this," Don Jr. said, arguing that the timing meant Trump would be quickly overshadowed by the next day's election.

The gambit worked. Onstage, Trump lavished praise on Vance—"I've gotten to know him really well. He's a great guy"—and stopped short of fully declaring his candidacy, instead teasing a "very big announcement" he would make the following week at Mar-a-Lago. He used his speech to call out the "far left lunatics" in the Democratic Party, saying they were "strangling Ohio families with soaring prices and crippling inflation." Trump devoted much of the speech to rattling off the names of the dozens of midterm candidates he had endorsed, a list he had drawn up on the flight over. If they won in the next day's elections, Trump knew he could claim credit and then use it as a springboard for his own political revival.

As the results rolled in the next day, however, it was clear they were disastrous for Trump's party. Republicans fell well short of expectations, failing to take control of the Senate, barely winning the House, and losing in several governor's races they had hoped to win. To top it off, many of Trump's endorsed candidates lost. Fingers were being pointed, almost all of them at the ex-commander-in-chief. Trump's critics argued his brand had

tarnished the GOP, and the disappointing outcome was proof
the party needed to move on.

Trump made it clear to his advisers that, for him, nothing
had changed. He would make his candidacy official on November 15.

—

Trump spent the afternoon of the 15th practicing his speech in
the ornate, wood-paneled Mar-a-Lago library. His team had
planned for the speech to be held late so it would be carried live
during Hannity's program, giving the ex-president access to the
much-coveted Fox News audience. They had brought in supporters, like former House Speaker Newt Gingrich, to offer input. As
Trump practiced his speech off the teleprompter, he edited and
rewrote it line by line, paragraph by paragraph.

Trump waited in a suite before taking the stage in the Mar-a-
Lago ballroom. To one aide who was present, he appeared muted—
not what one would expect from someone about to announce his
candidacy for the highest office. Perhaps, this aide thought, the
party's midterm losses had taken a toll on the boss.

Jubilant supporters crowded the ballroom as Trump finally
made it official, declaring that "America's comeback starts right
now." Trump's words echoed those of his first presidential
announcement seven years earlier. He painted a grim picture of
the country, calling it a "nation in decline" and declaring the
"blood-soaked streets of our once-great cities are cesspools of
violent crimes."

Despite his defeat in 2020 and the party's underperformance
two years later, he conveyed no lack of confidence in the election
that would be taking place two years down the road. "Everybody

will agree with us because everybody sees what a bad job has been done" under Biden, Trump said.[4]

He had pulled the trigger. His loyalists loved it. The party elites? Less so. GOP pooh-bahs, gathered that week in Orlando for the Republican Governors Association conference, were gob-smacked. New Hampshire Governor Chris Sununu, who was toying with a run himself, went around the Waldorf Astoria hotel telling people Trump was getting in at his weakest point. DeSantis used his appearance before the conference to highlight his landslide reelection win just a few weeks earlier—a not so subtle jab at the ex-president. I'm a winner, DeSantis implied. Trump isn't.[5]

With the announcement made, Trump told aides he wanted to go low-profile for the rest of the year. Thanksgiving fell a little more than a week later, the holidays were about to be in full swing, and the country had just endured a long political season, he reasoned.

—

Chris LaCivita, a pugnacious Marine veteran who was Trump's newest political adviser, was at his home in Virginia's Northern Neck with his family for Thanksgiving, building a fire in his out-door fireplace and sipping a glass of burgundy, when he got the call from a fellow lieutenant. "You're not going to believe this," said Susie Wiles, who, with LaCivita, was heading up Trump's campaign.

She had just learned that earlier in the week, Trump had din-ner with Ye, the rapper formerly known as Kanye West, who by then was as well known for spouting conspiracy theories and vile antisemitic rhetoric as he was for his music. It got even worse. Wiles, a no-nonsense Republican strategist whose steely blue eyes could cut through glass, told LaCivita that Nick Fuentes, a prominent Holocaust denier and white supremacist, was also at the dinner.

Trump had long drawn criticism for playing footsie with white nationalists. In 2016, he declined to disavow former Ku Klux Klan leader David Duke. In 2017, he said there were "very fine people" who had participated in a white supremacist rally in Charlottesville, Virginia. During a 2020 debate with Biden, Trump called on the Proud Boys, a far-right extremist group, to "stand back and stand by."

Now, just weeks into his 2024 campaign, he'd done it again.

Trump's aides soon learned that Karen Giorno, a Florida-based Republican strategist who had been replaced as his Florida state director in 2016, had escorted Ye and Fuentes through Mar-a-Lago security. Aides were confused as to how she and her guests made their way to the boss's table. The people Trump had plucked to run his political operation were trying to build a tight machine—as tight as one could be around Trump—and here they were learning just how hard that was.

Ye had been scheduled to have dinner with Trump, and Giorno would later tell *Inside Edition* that while driving to the airport to pick him up, she had gotten a call from one of the rapper's people informing her that a few others, including Fuentes, would be with him. Giorno would also say she didn't know who Fuentes was, despite his prominence in far-right circles. After ushering the two into the club's lobby, she said, Trump approached the group and asked Ye, "Should we go to dinner?"

Ye, she said, then told the president that he'd like the others— whom Ye only introduced by first name—to dine with them as well.[6]

Milo Yiannopoulos, a far-right provocateur who years earlier had made remarks condoning pedophilia and advocating for violence against journalists, would eventually claim credit for arranging the dinner. Yiannopoulos was convinced that Trump was increasingly surrounded by establishment figures, and he wanted to get Fuentes, whom he regarded as a true believer, in front of the former president.[7]

Back in Washington, Steven Cheung, Trump's newly appointed campaign spokesman, knew it was only a matter of time until the media found out about the dinner, and he alerted his war room to be on the lookout for any traffic on social media. Cheung, a combat sports aficionado who once worked for the Ultimate Fighting Championship, was quickly becoming a Trump favorite, thanks to his press savvy, passion for whacking Trump's critics, and formidable physical presence.

"Look at Steven! I wouldn't mess with that guy!" Trump would say. "He's a big guy! He has huge hands!"

Just one week into the campaign, Cheung's well-sized hands were full. The episode, everyone knew, was a reminder of what so many did not like about the former president: the chaos, his tolerance of eccentric people, the lack of guardrails. And, just as precariously, it would give an opening to Republican rivals—like fellow Florida Man DeSantis—to hammer home the message they would deliver Trumpism without the turmoil.

The news broke on November 23, the day after the dinner took place, when Cheung got a call from *Politico* reporter Meridith McGraw, who said she'd heard about the Trump-Ye-Fuentes sit-down. The news was out.

Making matters more complicated was Trump's refusal to publicly apologize. Wiles called and urged him to issue a public apology, but Trump insisted he hadn't done anything wrong and didn't know who the hell Fuentes was. When Cheung got in touch with Trump, the former president said he had brought Fuentes in because he thought it would be nice of him to invite everyone in the group for dinner and not have them waiting outside for him and Ye to finish. He loved to play the role of friendly host, and, in his mind, it was about that simple.

As the media firestorm grew, the president, true to form, doubled down, taking to Truth Social, the social media platform he had founded after being booted off Twitter in the wake of January 6, to lay out his case. He wrote he had generously met with Ye, whom he described as a "seriously troubled man, who just happens to be black," at the rapper's request so that he could "give him very much needed 'advice.'"

Trump's high command realized that if they didn't right the ship soon, Trump's comeback bid could be seriously paralyzed before it even got off the ground. Contributors were threatening to close their checkbooks, members of Congress who'd been prepared to endorse Trump were getting cold feet, and he was getting ripped by fellow Republicans. Mike Pence, Trump's former vice president and future GOP primary rival, called on Trump to apologize and said he "demonstrated profoundly poor judgment" in dining with the pair.[8] Mitch McConnell, the Senate minority leader, said there was "no room in the Republican Party for antisemitism or white supremacy" and that "anyone meeting with people advocating that point of view, in my judgment, are highly unlikely to ever be elected president of the United States."[9]

Trump's team wasn't budging in their loyalty to the candidate; none of the aides were quitting. But they realized they needed something to show donors, activists, and party leaders. Cheung settled on a plan of attack: Trump would do an hour-long interview with Matt Boyle, a reporter for the Trump-friendly

Breitbart News, which would allow the former president to speak more extensively about the dinner and clear things up.

During the mid-December sit-down, at Trump's Doral, Florida, golf course, Boyle asked Trump if antisemites had any place in the GOP.

"No, they don't," Trump said.[10]

It wasn't an apology, but Trump's aides finally had something. They sent the story around to donors, many of whom were repulsed by the dinner—and who, if things continued to devolve, could defect to someone like DeSantis.

The episode was a stark reminder of what the Trump team was in for. The concerns weren't only political. The lieutenants were also trying to tackle a whole other problem the dinner had raised: How to keep possible security threats away from the boss. If people like Ye or Fuentes could get through the Mar-a-Lago gates, then anyone could. One aide wondered if a suicide bomber could have gotten in. Trump had maintained a substantial Secret Service detail since leaving office, and his security apparatus was on alert for everything from a lone gunman to an overhead drone. Within the Secret Service there was ongoing concern that Iranians could target him for assassination in retaliation for Trump's decision in 2020 to order a drone strike that killed Iranian major general Qasem Soleimani. Trump knew the Iranians wanted him dead.

LaCivita had flown down to Florida shortly after Thanksgiving to meet with Wiles and Sean Curran, the head of Trump's Secret Service detail. The Secret Service had looked into what happened and determined that Mar-a-Lago staff and security—which it said was responsible for determining who got in to see Trump—had dropped the ball in allowing Yiannopoulos's posse into the club.

As the year came to a close, the question was whether Trump could be kept from engaging in the self-destructive behavior that was a hallmark of his chaos-plagued administration. He'd surrounded himself with a team of experienced advisers, led by Wiles and LaCivita. But, as was the case during Trump's presidency, it was he—not his consiglieres—who was in control.

Within his orbit, there was no lack of uncertainty about how much damage had been done by the dinner. Among those who remained in disbelief was McLaughlin, the longtime Trump pollster. Shortly after the dinner, Trump had called him.

"What are you doing meeting with this guy? He's a loser," McLaughlin said of Ye. "Kim Kardashian dropped him, that's for a reason."

FEBRUARY 2023

"Chamberlain! Bring in the poison!"

Into Trump's Mar-a-Lago office walked Chamberlain Harris, a twentysomething assistant tasked with fetching whatever Trump needed. She was carrying a basket of goodies the former president couldn't resist: Rold Gold pretzels, Oreos, Lay's potato chips, and mini candy bars.

Trump was meeting later that day with Susie Wiles and Chris LaCivita. He'd had a rocky launch. And it wasn't just the Ye-Fuentes dinner. In December, Trump had taken to Truth Social to call for the "termination" of the constitution in order to overturn his 2020 election loss, infuriating those who saw Trump as a dictator-in-waiting.[1] Trump then announced he would be slinging $99 digital trading cards depicting himself as a cartoon superhero, despite pleas from his advisers not to.[2] The lieutenants were looking to right the ship, and putting out graphics with Trump muscled up and wearing a Superman-like cape, well it . . . wasn't what was needed. ("This might not be the best idea," they told him at one point. His response: "This is going to be big. It's going to sell out, just trust me.")

There were indications Trump was taking a hit. McLaughlin had conducted a poll showing that Trump's support among Republican primary voters had slipped since after the November midterm election.

Within Trump's high command—and among donors, elected officials, and activists—questions were starting to simmer about how serious the boss was about actually waging a campaign. *Ye? Baseball cards? What was going on here?*

Trump had picked a pair of veteran operatives to lead his campaign. Wiles kept a low profile but had a formidable history in Florida politics, having worked for a number of local and statewide politicians over the span of more than two decades. She had been brought in to save Trump's dysfunctional Florida campaign back in 2016 and led it again in 2020. While his reelection campaign had generally been a disorganized mess, the Wiles-run Florida operation had been as smooth as butter.

About a month after Trump left the White House, he summoned Wiles to have dinner with him at Mar-a-Lago. Trump asked her to debrief him on how she'd won the state. After driving four and a half hours from her home in Jacksonville, she walked the former president through an after-action report she had done, which included a rundown of what had worked, what didn't, and what it had cost. Then she made the trek back home.

At the time, Trump had no real political apparatus to rely on. Some operatives had fled after January 6, some Trump was finished with, and others had simply moved on with their lives. Trump generally viewed his previous strategists with suspicion and was convinced they had used him to make a buck and to promote themselves. Wiles, he decided, was who he needed. The day after the dinner, Trump called the sixty-three-year-old Wiles and asked her to run his campaign.

"I don't know if I have any money; I don't know if they're stealing from me; I don't know who's in charge. I don't know what's going on," he told her. "I need you to take over."

Wiles took the job and quickly set out to learn how to manage the ever-turbulent Trumpworld, consulting with Jared Kushner and Don Jr. and reading whatever she could get her hands on. The consensus: You have to be smart, you have to be organized, and, most of all, you have to be good with money. If Trump didn't trust you with his campaign dollars—and he didn't trust many of his past political lieutenants—you were finished. Wiles would slowly begin building out Trump's apparatus and weeded out almost everyone involved in the 2020 race, many of whom Trump still blamed for his defeat.

Wiles was well acquainted with powerful men: Her father just so happened to be the late NFL player–turned–announcer Pat Summerall.[3]

Trump and Wiles were, however, very different people. While Trump was late to bed and late to wake up, Wiles went to sleep early and rose early. While Trump swore a lot, Wiles barely ever did. But their partnership worked. Wiles softened some of Trump's rough edges and was able to shoot him straight without making him feel controlled. He appreciated her aura of calmness and confidence. Wiles didn't tolerate staff drama and had a knack for managing the wild jungle of Trumpworld personalities. She knew how to keep bad actors—the grifters, the psychos, the people who gave Trump nutty advice—at a distance, but just close enough so they were content. Plus, she commanded respect, was someone aides felt comfortable going to when they had a problem, and gave off the vibe of someone you didn't want to mess with.

"She looks like a sweet grandmother," Georgia Congresswoman Marjorie Taylor Greene, the staunch Trump loyalist, told people. But Wiles was a grandmother who wielded a sharp blade, Greene knew, and she was savvy and easy to underestimate. Greene wanted Wiles to help her if she ever ran for a bigger office.

As Wiles built her team, she thought of how Trump had told her to "get me an asshole." She asked people she knew for advice, including Tony Fabrizio, a Republican operative who had served as Trump's chief pollster during his 2016 and 2020 presidential campaigns. Fabrizio suggested LaCivita, with whom he had worked on numerous past campaigns dating back to Bob Dole's 1996 presidential bid, when they first met.

"Will he fit? Will we get along?" Wiles asked.

"You two are going to get along great, trust me," Fabrizio said.

"Will he get along with the president?" she asked.

"I think the president will like him," Fabrizio assured her.

Wiles, LaCivita, and Fabrizio had several dinners together, and the two strategists got to know each other. Eventually, Wiles invited LaCivita to have dinner with Trump at Mar-a-Lago. The meeting went well, though LaCivita had a hard time hearing the former president because he was blasting music on the patio's loudspeakers.

Over the coming months, Trump spoke to top Republicans who sang LaCivita's praises, including Lindsey Graham. LaCivita's ties to Senate Republicans and others in the party establishment—including Mitch McConnell, who had repudiated Trump in the wake of January 6—were a plus, allowing him to serve as liaison to those in the party who were skeptical of the former president. Wiles and Trump tapped him as co-campaign manager.

Trump and LaCivita were a match made in heaven. Trump liked LaCivita's aggressiveness, his refusal to play by the traditional rules of politics, and his endless desire to demolish anything that stood in the former president's way.

LaCivita had worked for a plethora of Republican candidates, committees, and groups over the previous three decades. He had risen to prominence in the 2004 presidential election, when he was chief strategist for the Swift Boat Veterans for Truth, an outfit that ran TV ads featuring Vietnam War veterans who claimed that Democrat John Kerry had exaggerated his military service. Kerry strenuously denied the accusations, but they took a massive toll on his ultimately failed candidacy.

The fifty-six-year-old LaCivita, whose prolific use of four-letter verbiage rivaled Trump's, referred to himself as FNG, or Fucking New Guy, because he was a newcomer to Trumpworld. He was relentless in working the press, shaping stories, defending the boss, and dishing dirt on Trump's rivals. He also had a personal story that Trump loved. He had been a sniper during the Gulf War, where he'd been injured and was awarded a Purple Heart. Before long, the former president was paying LaCivita the ultimate Trumpian compliment.

"You're a killer, aren't you LaCivita?" Trump asked his aide one day.

"Yes sir, I am," LaCivita responded proudly.

As Trump, Wiles, and LaCivita sat in the office—complete with a bronze statue of an eagle, chairs upholstered in Trumpian gold, and a painting of Trump—the ex-president made it clear he was comfortable staying off the trail for the time being. The first Republican primary votes were still a year away from being cast.

It was too early to be out there every day, he reasoned, and he thought the right thing to do was hold off on doing his trademark rallies for a few months. Plus, he was a former president; people already knew him, and he was at the stage of his life where he didn't feel like being out there every day.

So, his team settled on another plan: They would put out a series of videos with Trump talking about what he would do in his second go-around as president, from cracking down on immigration to boosting the economy.

Trump's lieutenants were also thinking about something else: How to squelch the threat his candidacy faced from a Republican Party establishment that, within some corners at least, was determined to keep Trump out of 1600 Pennsylvania Avenue. They didn't want him in the White House the first time. *Another four years?* No thanks.

The biggest obstacle came from four hundred miles north, in Tallahassee.

▬

Ron DeSantis was drawing big interest from the billionaire donor class. He had won praise from conservatives for his laissez-faire approach to the COVID pandemic, when he shrugged off school closures and mask mandates as handling of the virus became increasingly politicized. To top it all off, he had just won a nineteen-point landslide reelection as governor.

It was clear DeSantis had bigger ambitions. He was about to release a book detailing his fight against what he derided as the liberal "woke" agenda and had for months been cultivating a national profile on cable TV interviews.

Trump wasn't quite sold that DeSantis would actually run.
He had convinced himself the Sunshine State honcho was
indebted to him for endorsing him back in the 2018 governor's
race. After DeSantis won, Trump flew down to Florida to hold a
fundraiser for DeSantis's state party, invited him to the White
House, and praised him repeatedly for his handling of the pandemic. The idea that DeSantis would run against him, Trump
thought, didn't make a lot of sense.

But, Trump's aides knew, for the Republicans who wanted
the former president gone, DeSantis had emerged as the person
to get it done. He was Trump but with all the stuff Republicans
liked and without all the stuff many of them did not. He zeroed
in on culture war issues, stuck it to liberals and the mainstream
media, and had an assertive, never-back-down sensibility to
him. But, at the same time, unlike Trump, he didn't flamethrow
on social media, hang out with Nazi sympathizers during
Thanksgiving week, or incite deadly riots.

Sure, there were some questions about DeSantis personally.
He seemed stiff and awkward, and he could be a cold fish. He
burned through staff. He was also insular, a little full of himself,
and weirdly hard to reach. Even Ronna McDaniel, the RNC
chair, often struggled to get hold of the Florida governor by
phone.

But all that was background noise. At the moment, DeSantis
looked like he might be the Godzilla that could topple King
Kong. To many of those in the party's ruling class, that was good
enough.

Trumpworld's disdain for DeSantis was profound. For some,
the source was what they saw as his betrayal of the old man. For
others, it was that they felt DeSantis had manipulated the boss into

endorsing him in 2018. But for many, this contempt went back to what they saw as the governor's brutal and unfair past treatment of Wiles, a figure who was widely respected and engendered loyalty from her staff. Within the campaign, Wiles was seen as a maternal figure; she would call her male staffers her "boys." And Wiles's boys, some of whom had also worked for DeSantis and felt mistreated by him, were going to make DeSantis pay.

The DeSantis-Wiles saga was long and winding. After running Trump's successful 2016 Florida effort, Wiles had been tapped by DeSantis to help lead his 2018 gubernatorial campaign. He exiled her less than a year into his administration, convinced she had leaked information about his political operation to the media, an accusation she vehemently denied.

DeSantis escalated his war on Wiles in the fall of 2019, successfully lobbying Trump to fire her from his reelection campaign. Trump brought her back the following year over the objections of DeSantis, who at one point told Trump giving Wiles credit for the governor's 2018 win was like "giving the batboy credit for winning the World Series."

Now, with the next presidential election approaching, DeSantis and Wiles appeared to be on a collision course.

DeSantis was hopscotching the country ostensibly to promote his new book. But to anyone who was paying attention, it was really just a precursor to an official campaign launch. Trump didn't like it one bit. "Yeah, he's fucking running. Can you believe him? How disloyal," Trump told advisers that spring. "Is Ron really that stupid to run against me? Why doesn't he just wait until 2028?"

Only a bad person, Trump vented, would do what DeSantis is doing.

DeSantis's betrayal touched upon something feral in Trump. As a young New York businessman, he'd had a chip on his shoulder toward the elites who saw him as a fraud. As a politician, he'd similarly felt enraged by the Republican leaders who thought he was a clown. Now, like Judas, DeSantis turned around and became a vessel for the GOP high society looking to take Trump out.

Trump's rage was white hot. He decided to post on Truth Social a story that included a photograph of DeSantis allegedly partying with underage students while working as a high school teacher in the early 2000s. Trump dictated his post to an aide. "That's not Ron, is it? He would never do such a thing!"

The post caused a firestorm, with reporters flooding the campaign with questions. *Was Trump really accusing Florida's governor of grooming children?*

Trump's team shrugged their shoulders. Like so many things with Trump—whether it was Nick Fuentes or NFTs or accusing a soon-to-be primary opponent of grooming underage girls, it was Trump's show, and they were just along for the ride. Was it good for the campaign? Who knew?

"When the bullet has left the chamber, there's no calling it back," LaCivita told fellow aides after the post went out.

Trump was angry to the point of obsession. To anyone who listened, Trump would tell the tale—and who the hell knew how much of it was true—of how DeSantis came to the Oval Office, "tears in his eyes" to plead for his endorsement.

"He was like a beggar," Trump told people aboard Trump Force One in June 2023, as he blasted Sinéad O'Connor's "Nothing Compares 2 U" from a portable speaker, a personal favorite that he kept on his Spotify playlist. "I could have said, 'Drop to your fucking knees, Ron.'"

Betrayal was just about the only prism through which he saw DeSantis. In April, he ordered up a TV commercial describing how Trump had dragged DeSantis to victory in 2018. Soon after, the ad—with a narrator grimly intoning, "Instead of being grateful, DeSantis is now attacking the very man who saved his career"—began airing nationally.

Trump said it was the best political ad he'd ever seen.

Trump's next move was to do what he always did when he wanted to tear someone down. He embarked on a quest to come up with the perfect nickname. One option he entertained was "Meatball Ron," because of the governor's roundish body shape. Another was "Tiny D," which became a fan favorite of the pro-Trump online influencers. "Oh, it's a double entendre," Trump said. Then, one day, he came up with it: DeSanctimonious.

His team wanted to know: Why that one? Wasn't it a little . . . long?

"He is a DeSanctimonious asshole," Trump explained.

To make it all worse, DeSantis had Fox News in his corner.

——

Trump's relationship with Rupert Murdoch was at a low point. The two men had not spoken for about two years. During his time in office, Trump and Fox had had a codependent relationship. Trump gave the network extensive access, turned hosts like Sean Hannity and Tucker Carlson into informal advisers, and OD'd on its coverage. Fox, meanwhile, had a simple reason for being nice to Trump: He was great for ratings.

That all changed the night of the 2020 election. Trump was furious at Fox's early call that Joe Biden had won Arizona, the first indication the then-president was on the path to defeat. His aides and surrogates quickly decamped to the channel's conservative rival, Newsmax. Fox's ratings began to tank.

The truth was, things between Trump and Fox were always a lot more complicated than they appeared, and a lot of it had to do with the long-standing psychodrama between Trump and Murdoch.

Trump had for years seen the WASPish Murdoch as part of the elite club that had long looked down on him, dating back to his days as a Queens-born developer with a chip on his shoulder. It was a club Trump always wanted in on but never entered, even when he was president. Murdoch had always been repulsed by Trump, finding him cloying, overly flattering, and desperate to win Murdoch over. The Australian-born media baron was offended by Trump's personal manner and thought he was beneath him.

So when Trump began running for president in 2016, Fox News flayed him. When he became president, Murdoch saw Trump only as a useful idiot who was good for business. And now that he was out of the White House, the Murdoch empire was more than happy to hammer him. And hammer him they did. When Trump announced his campaign launch, the *New York Post* buried the news with the headline: "Florida Man Makes Announcement."[4]

Trump reacted viscerally.

"That Rupert is such a piece of shit, he's so cold," he said privately. Trump's public comments weren't much nicer, like the time he posted on social media that Murdoch was "aiding & abetting the DESTRUCTION OF AMERICA."[5]

As for Rupert's son, James? "He's a crazy fucking liberal," Trump complained to Tucker Carlson one day.

The Murdoch platforms weren't just trashing Trump; they were also propping up DeSantis. DeSantis had announced his

2018 campaign on Fox News, was given puffy coverage in the
New York Post, and had even been featured on the cover of the
Murdoch family–owned *Times* of London. During his first term
as governor, DeSantis gave many of his interviews to Fox News.
The channel wanted him on all the time. When in early 2023
DeSantis held a donor retreat in Palm Beach, just a few miles
down the road from Mar-a-Lago, Fox News prime time host
Laura Ingraham was in attendance.[6] For the Murdoch crew,
DeSantis was perfect; he appealed to Trumpers and not-Trump-
ers alike, without any of the Trumpian eccentricities.

By early 2023, things between Trump and Murdoch had
devolved into all-out war. Trump's team made clear they were
ready to play hardball. Wiles and LaCivita told McDaniel that
Trump wouldn't commit to participating in the first debate that
summer if the committee awarded Fox News the rights to it. Jason
Miller, meanwhile, met for lunch with two Fox staffers, Kellianne
Jones and Jessica Loker, at the Capital Grille restaurant just off
Capitol Hill and spelled out his concerns about their coverage. The
former president had recently been absolutely savaging Fox, calling it a "group of MAGA hating Globalist RINOS."[7]

As the war escalated, one of the big guns from Fox decided
to step in. The evening before Trump was headed to Iowa for his
first campaign appearance in the state, he interrupted speech
prep with his team to take a call from Sean Hannity. Hannity, a
prominent pro-Trump host at the cable news giant, lived down
the road from the former president and was one of his closest
friends. Now he had a message he wanted to get across.

"Please do not hit Fox, do not hit the Murdoch family. Just
please, for the love of God, please don't do it," Hannity pleaded.

Hannity wanted the two sides to make some semblance of
peace. The host was trying to make the case that things could get

better between the two sides if the former president could just tone it down.

"Mr. President, I'm trying to help you out here with the Fox people here. But you're not making it easy for me by going after the Murdochs. You're not helping me. You're not helping yourself," Hannity said. "If you can just lay off, we can start making some moves and getting back to normal."

Trump was having none of it. The former president held up his iPhone so the aides gathered in his office could hear Hannity's pleading. Trump loved that the Fox bigwig was groveling.

"Sean is trying to do the right thing. But, man, the Murdochs? I don't know," Trump said.

Not having any luck with Trump, Hannity turned his attention to the more even-tempered Wiles, who was among those listening in on the call.

"Susie, are you in the room? Susie, can you talk to the president? For the love of God can you talk to the president?"

"Well, Sean, President Trump is going to do what President Trump thinks is best and fair," Wiles said, refusing to undercut her boss.

Trump, done with Hannity, moved to end the call. "You're a good man, Sean. I've got to go now," he said. And then he hung up.

THREE:
"EMBRACE THE SUCK"

MARCH 14, 2023

Trump saw betrayal everywhere.

Settling in for the three-and-a-half-hour flight to Davenport, Iowa, for his first appearance in the state since announcing his candidacy, Trump made clear to his advisers that he wanted revenge on Republicans who endorsed his rivals. If he went back to the White House, he would campaign against them or find some other way to take them out.

A slew of former Trump administration officials were looking to run against their former boss, including former Vice President Mike Pence and former United Nations Ambassador Nikki Haley. Mike Pompeo, Trump's CIA director and secretary of state, was also considering a run. The former president began derisively referring to Pompeo as "Band Man," because he suspected Pompeo's dramatic weight loss was attributed to lap band surgery.

Trump never feared the former lieutenants now looking to run against him, but he was stung by their disloyalty. Have other presidents, Trump lamented to Brian Jack one evening, faced this kind of opposition from people who served in their administrations?

Jack urged Trump to turn the betrayal he faced to his advantage. Voters like loyalty, Jack argued. And voters understood that if DeSantis and others were disloyal to Trump, voters would come to believe they would also be disloyal to them.

The fact was, there was no shortage of prominent Republican lawmakers, interest groups, and donors hell-bent on stopping him. At times, Trump seemed puzzled by it. He was especially galled by Iowa's governor, Kim Reynolds. After Trump won the 2016 election, Trump appointed Iowa's then-governor, Terry Branstad, ambassador to China, opening the door for Reynolds to ascend to the governorship from her post as lieutenant governor. He then endorsed Reynolds in her successful 2018 and 2022 elections. Trump was convinced Reynolds owed him her job.

Now Reynolds—a popular governor who presided over a critical early primary state—was making it clear she wouldn't be endorsing anyone just yet. She wanted all candidates to feel welcome at Iowa's caucuses in January, and taking sides would tip the scales. In Trump's mind, it was yet another example of a politician who had used him and now wasn't paying back the favor. Would a political boss tolerate such disloyalty? Not likely.

"I just can't fucking believe she would do that. That's just fucking crazy. After everything we did for her," Trump told Alex Latcham, who was spearheading his Iowa campaign, after the aide gave him the news.

For Trump, Iowa wasn't just another state on the primary calendar. He had let it be known to anyone who would listen that it was especially important to him. During the 2016 primary, he lost the state to Texas Senator Ted Cruz. Years later, he still recalled how his daughter Ivanka called to tell him he didn't seem to have any organizers at a caucus site she visited that night. He sure as hell didn't want that to happen again.

Despite Reynolds's insistence she was neutral, it was obvious the governor was cozying up to DeSantis. She had flown to Florida to attend DeSantis's donor retreat, and one of her top political advisers had also joined a pro-DeSantis super PAC run by Ken Cuccinelli, another former Trump administration official.[1]

"Is the governor going to fucking run again?" Trump asked his team one day. "Because you know, if she does, we're going to fucking primary her and take her out."

Reynolds. DeSantis. Fox News. Pompeo. Haley. For Trump, a pattern was emerging: His former allies in the Republican elite were turning against him. It was a stinging rebuke. Much of the GOP hierarchy had never respected Trump, even when he was president. They'd merely used him. And now they were ready to kick him to the curb.

The battle lines were clear. Trump would be running against an establishment class that, since he was a young man rising through the ranks of the New York real estate world, had never respected him and viewed him as a low-rent imitator. He was out for blood.

Earlier that month, Trump had sat down with his team to prepare for his upcoming appearance at the Conservative Political Action Conference. CPAC's transformation in recent years—from a gathering of conservatives and libertarians to one dominated by Trump—reflected the broader metamorphosis of the Republican Party. This year's gathering would feature one of the highest-profile speeches of his campaign yet. As he went over the speech, during which he would rail against the Biden administration over the border crisis and rising inflation, Trump suggested a new line be added. It was edgy, but his team thought it was perfect. The campaign created T-shirts prominently featuring the phrase; they would be available on its online store as soon as Trump wrapped up his remarks.

On a Saturday evening, Trump took the stage at the Gaylord Resort in National Harbor, Maryland.

Before a throng of screaming, red-MAGA-hatted supporters who'd filled a cavernous ballroom, he conveyed in two sentences the thrust of his 2024 comeback campaign.

"In 2016, I declared, 'I am your voice,'" Trump said. "Today, I add: I am your warrior, I am your justice, and for those who have been wronged and betrayed, I am your retribution."[2]

—

Iowa politics wasn't the only thing on Team Trump's mind on the flight to Davenport. Wiles had something important she wanted to broach. As they made their way from sunny Palm Beach toward the chilly Midwest, she gathered her team inside a small conference room toward the front of the plane and shut the door. Chris LaCivita and Alina Habba, one of Trump's attorneys, joined Wiles on one of the gold-colored couches. Jason Miller and Steven Cheung, the campaign's two top press guys, sat on another.

Wiles didn't invite Trump to the sit-down or even tell him it was happening. She was about to drop a bomb and didn't want him to be distracted while campaigning that afternoon.

Trump, Wiles told the group, was all but certain to be indicted by the Manhattan district attorney for allegedly concealing a $130,000 payment to adult film actress Stormy Daniels during the final days of the 2016 election. The twists and turns of the scandal had hung over Trump's first term. Prosecutors had been aggressively pursuing charges related to the falsification of business records and a violation of campaign finance laws, and now they were closing in.

Once the indictment came down, Trump would have to turn himself in at a lower Manhattan courthouse to be arrested, and it was sure to be a spectacle unlike anything in the history of presidential politics. Never before had a president been indicted. The idea of a former commander-in-chief sitting before a judge was hard to imagine.

Habba, a former general counsel for a parking garage company who got to know Trump by frequenting his Bedminster, New Jersey, golf club, told the group charges could come as soon as the following week or two. The Trump team had much to do. They needed to work with the Secret Service to ensure some psycho couldn't shoot Trump while he was en route to the courthouse. They needed to figure out a way to deal with the media circus. And they needed to get legal surrogates on cable news to defend the reality TV star-turned former president.

This wasn't just about the Daniels case. The Trump campaign was entering entirely new territory. As the country continued to reckon with the fallout from Trump's presidency, the former commander-in-chief was facing three other possible criminal indictments. One centered on Trump's alleged taking of classified documents upon leaving office and his ensuing efforts to keep them from federal officials who were trying to retrieve them. Another was tied to his campaign to overturn the presidential election results and his stoking of the violent January 6 Capitol riot. Yet another was focused on his interference in Georgia's 2020 election vote count.

Then there were the civil cases. Trump was being sued for civil damages by the writer E. Jean Carroll, who had accused the former president of sexually assaulting her in a New York City department store in the 1990s and later defaming her. New York

Attorney General Letitia James, meanwhile, had filed a civil suit accusing Trump of engaging in business fraud.

Trump was in grave legal and political jeopardy. Would he be spending the next two years leading up to the 2024 election in courtrooms? Would he be going to prison? And how would voters react?

Who the hell knew?

As he listened to the group discuss the upcoming indictment, LaCivita thought back to his time as a Marine reservist and the Purple Heart he won for being wounded while fighting in the Gulf War.

During his military service, LaCivita had picked up the expression "Embrace the suck." The meaning: Embrace the misery and the challenge that comes along with a hostile environment. Don't run from it. Lean into it and find the opportunities that come from it. Turn it to your advantage.

That, LaCivita concluded, was what Trump should do. The indictment didn't have to be all downside. Trump could use it to raise gobs of money from small givers. He could use it to vacuum up oxygen and prevent rivals like DeSantis from getting traction in the media. And he could use it to rally and solidify his base.

Trump's "I am your retribution" declaration at CPAC a few weeks earlier had been a hit. Now, the former president could take his vengeance-centered campaign to a new level.

Others in the plane's conference room saw it the same way. Trump had his account on Twitter reinstated in November 2022 by the social media company's new owner, mega-billionaire entrepreneur Elon Musk. Musk was turning Twitter into a conservative-friendly platform, using it to promote Republican politicians and the online right's war on liberal "woke" values and in the process becoming a hero of the online right himself.

The time was ripe for Trump to make a grand return to the site, and Cheung suggested Trump electrify his supporters by publishing his first tweet the day he was indicted.

The group also tossed around the possibility of flooding lower Manhattan with supporters when Trump turned himself in. No final decisions were made, but everyone wanted a show of force to underscore the power and durability of Trump's movement.

A few days after the Iowa trip, Trump's team informed him of the likelihood of an indictment. He was initially less optimistic than his advisers that his legal problems could help him politically. During meetings, he would quiz them about what impact it would all have on his poll numbers. But if Trump knew anything, it was the power of television. Like LaCivita and the rest of his team, he understood his legal drama would make great TV. Great TV equaled attention. If he got all the attention, his rivals couldn't get any traction.

If they couldn't get any traction, the nomination would be his.

A few days later, Trump sat down with his team at his Mar-a-Lago office to discuss, among other things, how to maximize the amount of press coverage they could get for the forthcoming indictment. By that point, Cheung, Miller, and Justin Caporale, deputy campaign manager for operations, had been working with various media, from national TV networks to cable stations to conservative streamers, to make sure that in their live programming of the arrest they could broadcast second-by-second camera footage of Trump turning himself in. Cheung and Miller were planning on sending outlets a stream of notes updating them on Trump's whereabouts, from when he was leaving Trump Tower to his movements in the courthouse. There would be shots as Trump motorcaded through the streets of Palm Beach, as Trump Force One took off and touched down, as Trump's security caravan barreled through New York City, and then as he strode into the courthouse. The Trump team would choreograph and time everything.

Cheung and Miller also toyed with the idea of having a press camera poke out of a moonroof of a vehicle in the motorcade to mimic the famous scene in the 2001 film *Ocean's Eleven*. One possibility Caporale raised was getting a flatbed truck to ride at the front of the motorcade, with a camera at its back to capture dramatic head-on footage. The concept was scotched only because they couldn't find a Secret Service agent who was credentialed to drive that kind of truck.

"We're going to make this more insane than O.J. This will be O.J. on steroids. Must-see TV," Cheung said.

Trump had his own ideas about what the coverage should look like. This was, after all, a man who had gone from local tabloid fixture to national sensation thanks to a starring role on NBC's *The Apprentice*. He wanted helicopter shots and multiple TV camera angles along the motorcade route. He wanted to make sure Trump Force One's takeoff was carried live. Trump wanted to know if and where cameras would be situated in the courthouse. And the former president made clear to his team he wanted to make a public statement once returning to Mar-a-Lago. Do it on his own turf. Not in liberal Manhattan.

Trump was happy to coordinate with his team on optics, sharing ideas and discussing what would work and what would not. But Trump was still Trump, and in this life-defining moment, he was also determined to steer the ship on his own—no matter the chaos it created.

The media was exploring every possible scenario for Trump's impending arrest. On the afternoon of March 17, Fox News reported that the Manhattan DA's office was considering hand-cuffing Trump after he turned himself in.[3] Just before 7:30 the next morning, a Saturday, Trump took to Truth Social to declare his arrest was imminent.

"THE FAR & AWAY LEADING REPUBLICAN CANDIDATE AND FORMER PRESIDENT OF THE UNITED STATES OF AMERICA, WILL BE ARRESTED ON TUESDAY OF NEXT WEEK," Trump declared. "PRO-TEST, TAKE OUR NATION BACK!"[4]

Trump's lieutenants were blindsided. No one yet knew the actual date of the expected arrest. LaCivita woke up to see his phone inundated with text messages from reporters.

It was clear Trump had no real evidence to back up his asser-tion he was going to be arrested in four days. But Trump was proud of himself, seeing it as a brilliant strategic move. He'd pre-empted the DA's announcement, generated the kind of media firestorm he relished and mobilized his legions of supporters. It was vintage Trump: Always be on offense.

That afternoon, Trump boarded Trump Force One en route to Tulsa, Oklahoma, to take in the NCAA wrestling champion-ship. It would be his first public appearance since he'd broken the news of his impending indictment. That morning's blizzard of media coverage had been intense, and news outlets were reporting Trump was in dire straits, but Trump soon saw the effects of his preemptive post.

As he made his way into Tulsa's BOK Center, it became apparent to Trump his base was rallying. Trump was about to be arrested on charges stemming from secretly paying off a porn actress. But there wasn't a "boo" to be heard.

Trump was mobbed again during a visit to a UFC event soon after. NFL quarterback Joe Burrow came over to say hello, as did

UFC fighter Jorge Masvidal. Trump spent the night sitting next to boxing legend Mike Tyson and the musician Kid Rock. It was the celebrity status Trump had always craved.

The next morning, Trump called Jack. Trump and Jack often spoke on Sunday mornings about boxing or other fights that took place on Saturday night. This time, Trump was particularly stoked. He'd been embraced in a way he couldn't believe.

"Have you ever seen an atmosphere like that?" Trump asked.

■

On the evening of March 30, Trump got the call from one of his attorneys. It had happened: the forty-fifth president of the United States had been indicted. In just a few days, he would have to turn himself in at the courthouse in downtown Manhattan, a spectacle the entire world would spend the next few days anticipating and scrutinizing.

After the news broke, Wiles, LaCivita, Miller, and Cheung walked into Trump's office to find him watching coverage on Fox News. Trump asked them one by one what they thought would happen to his poll numbers. Trump was ahead of his pack of primary rivals, but he wanted to know how this could impact things. They paused and looked at each other.

"Your numbers are going to go up, sir," Cheung said.

The subtext was clear. Trump's spokesman believed Republican primary voters would rally to Trump. The others agreed.

"They're trying to get me, and I'm just going to fight like hell," said Trump. When the time came, he wanted to walk into the courthouse with his head held high.

The former president flew to New York City on April 3, the day before he was due in the courthouse. The next morning, he sat in his personal office in Trump Tower, an ornate gold-decorated suite overlooking Central Park. Joining Trump were Wiles, LaCivita, Miller, and Dan Scavino, his former golf caddy-turned–social media guru. Trump's son Eric also joined them.

Trump was planning to give a televised statement that night, and dictated to his team what he wanted to say. He would take a page out of the playbook he used during his presidency, when he painted himself as the victim of a deep state that was conspiring against him. The message was aimed at appealing to Trump's formidable base of loyalists, who viewed elites with disdain and had been conditioned to believe that he was being unfairly targeted by the justice system. To them, Trump was a martyr.

Trump did a final once-over to make sure he looked just right. Noticing a wrinkle in his blue suit, he called an aide to come over with a steamer. Helicopters buzzed overhead. Cameramen lined the streets of Midtown Manhattan. Networks were cutting into live programming. The eyes of the country were about to be on him.

The former president exited Trump Tower's gold doors a little after 1 p.m. and stepped into a waiting SUV. The motorcade snaked through the streets of Midtown Manhattan, down FDR Drive to 100 Centre Street. He stepped out of his car and strode into the courthouse. Donald John Trump was officially under arrest.

After being read his rights, Trump entered the courtroom, where he sat submissively at the defense table. When asked by Judge Juan Merchan how he pleaded to the thirty-four counts of falsifying business records, Trump said not guilty. Merchan warned Trump against making threatening posts about the case on social media, as he had been doing in the days leading up to his arrest.

When the hearing was over, Trump stepped back into his waiting motorcade and headed to LaGuardia. The whole affair had taken about two hours.

For most people, getting arrested would be the worst day of their life. But Trump was embracing the suck. He'd managed to turn his arrest into high-octane entertainment, and the flight home felt celebratory. McDonald's was served, and Cheung handed Trump a picture of all the TV networks showing over-head shots of Trump Force One taken before it left. The former president laughed about the attention his plane was getting.

Upon landing, Trump's fleet of SUVs made its way from the Palm Beach airport back to Mar-a-Lago, where the former president delivered a speech to a crowd of supporters gathered in the ballroom, which was also aired to a national audience.

"I never thought anything like this could happen in America. I never thought it could happen," Trump said. "The only crime that I have committed is to fearlessly defend our nation from those who seek to destroy it."

Over the course of twenty-five minutes, Trump called New York Attorney General Letitia James and Fulton County, Georgia District Attorney Fani Willis, who are Black, "racist"; described the special counsel investigating him, Jack Smith, as a "lunatic"; and declared the "radical left" wanted to "interfere with our elections by using law enforcement."[5]

The speech was dark, but the mood at Mar-a-Lago was celebratory. Supporters saw Trump as a hero, and they packed into the club to get a glimpse of the former president, who ate dinner on the patio at a roped-off table with his daughter Tiffany and her husband, Michael Boulos. To one attendee, it felt like Trump's 2016 victory celebration. It was as if Trump was having the time of his life.

The party went past midnight, with Trump playing the role of DJ. He waved his arms as he played some of his favorites, including Luciano Pavarotti's performance of "Ave Maria."

Also on the playlist: the Village People's "Macho Man."

■

While Trump was dealing with an onrush of legal battles, something else was happening: His takedown of DeSantis was working. The Trump campaign's polling had shown the former president narrowly leading DeSantis after the midterm election, and its latest numbers had Trump opening up a thirty-plus point gap.

Trump didn't just want to stop DeSantis from winning the Republican nomination. He wanted to destroy him and make it impossible for him to run for anything ever again. Back in January, a few months after he had entered the race, the former president had spoken with Vance, who had won the Ohio Senate race with the help of Trump's endorsement. Vance had interacted with DeSantis on the campaign trail the previous year and noticed the guy was raising money like a madman, a surefire indication he was getting ready to take on Trump.

Trump told Vance he wasn't messing around: "I'm just going to squash this guy like a bug." The following month, Trump's high command had huddled in the campaign's West Palm Beach headquarters, with one purpose: figure out how to make Ron DeSantis look weird.

The group exchanged alleged tales portraying the governor in an unflattering light—like the time DeSantis shoved chicken fingers in his jacket pocket, the time he clipped his toenails in the back of his security vehicle, and the time he had a bathroom mishap aboard an airplane. There was the story of how DeSantis supposedly drove a golf cart behind his wife, Casey, as she ran around the neighborhood so she would lose weight. Or how, when he was a congressman, he allegedly stockpiled dirty underwear in his gym locker.

From there, the team began shipping out the stories to news outlets and allies on social media. Before long, pro-Trump figures on Twitter were putting together videos of DeSantis wiping his nose with his hand, of DeSantis laughing uncontrollably, of him interacting awkwardly with people.

DeSantis had yet to officially enter the race—he wouldn't do that until May, after the state's legislative session closed. But Trump's operation was already unloading its war chest, looking to further bolster the former president's assault on the governor. At the end of March, the pro-Trump MAGA Inc. super PAC began a $22 million TV advertising campaign highlighting DeSantis's past support for cuts to entitlement programs, positions that could turn off older voters. It was a major gamble. The sum represented more than a third of what the super PAC had in the bank, and spending the money now meant it couldn't be used months down the line, closer to the start of the primary season.

A turning point came that month, when Budowich, over at MAGA Inc., got an email from a fellow operative, James Blair, which included a proposed script for a forthcoming commercial the organization's digital whizzes had drawn up.

"Pudding Fingers" it was titled.

"Oh my god," Budowich texted a member of his team. "What the fuck is this?"

By this point, the super PAC's operatives were aware that the *Daily Beast* was about to publish a story alleging that DeSantis had gross eating habits—specifically, that, during a 2019 flight, he had downed pudding with his hands.[6] The commercial would be based on the forthcoming article and feature a DeSantis look-alike using his fingers to scoop chocolate pudding out of a container and then sucking on them. The commercial reinforced Trump's broader case against the governor: that he was, well, strange.

Budowich's team thought it was a great idea, and they were prodding their boss to run it. He spent a week weighing the positives and negatives. On the one hand, it would spread like wildfire. On the other hand, the operative knew it could come off as low-rent and silly and hurt his prospects of raising big bucks from elite donors.

Budowich in the end pulled the trigger, after editing out some zoomed-in shots of the DeSantis look-alike flopping his pudding-lathered tongue around, which he thought was too much to stomach. He would spend only about $100,000 to air it for one day, a pittance in the world of multimillion-dollar super PAC advertising. But Budowich knew he didn't need to spend more. It would go viral on its own.

He was right. Sunday political talk shows played the ad. Cable outlets covered it on prime time and played it on repeat. TV host Piers Morgan even asked DeSantis about it. "I don't remember ever doing that," DeSantis responded, not exactly denying it. "Maybe when I was a kid?"[7]

For all the criticism the ad received, it was getting attention. And that was the point.

For the most part, DeSantis, still not officially in the race, did not punch back. But every now and then he would poke Trump. Shortly before the former president was indicted, DeSantis criticized the move, but added he didn't "know what goes into paying hush money to a porn star." Trumpworld pounced, with harsh messages on Truth Social and Twitter. Don Jr. led the pack, tweeting that DeSantis was projecting "pure weakness." After days of endless abuse online, DeSantis changed his tune and derided Trump's arrest as "un-American."[8] The Trump machine had roared, and DeSantis had cowered. DeSantis was facing an existential dilemma: How could he beat Trump if he couldn't take him on?

The media covered every Trump attack breathlessly and latched on to the idea that DeSantis was losing steam. "Ron DeSantis may be missing his moment," read one NBC News story published in late March.[9]

Wiles wanted to plunge the dagger. Wiles knew Florida politics like few others, and she also knew DeSantis. The governor, she recognized, had weak points, and one of them was his relationship skills—or lack thereof. She wanted to find a way to spotlight it.

Early in the year, Wiles had spoken by phone with Brian Jack. What if, Jack said, they could get a bunch of members from the Florida congressional delegation to endorse Trump, and then invite them to a photo op with the former president at Mar-a-Lago? Many of the Florida members either were on bad terms with DeSantis or had no relationship with him at all. When DeSantis was a congressman, he was distant and made no effort to establish relationships with them. When he became governor, things didn't get much better.

Now, the Trump advisers realized, if they could get the Florida members to endorse the boss, it would be an embarrassment for the home state governor.

Wiles loved the idea. Before long, the two Trump aides were burning up the phone lines to Florida members. Congressman Greg Steube got onboard and publicly relayed a story about how after suffering a fall earlier in the year, Trump called to wish him well but DeSantis didn't. Nearly a dozen other Florida members also announced their support for Trump. DeSantis, whose team was caught off guard by the Trump endorsement push, would get only one.

In late April, Trump hosted his Florida backers for a three-hour dinner at Mar-a-Lago, where he handed out signed MAGA hats and copies of his newest book with personalized inscriptions. Over steaks and spaghetti and meatballs, the lawmakers told the president, joined by Wiles and Jack, tales about their nonexistent relationship with their governor and former colleague.

Trump was feeling confident. He'd been blamed for the party's poor showing in the midterm election, had been indicted, and was facing a Republican Party hierarchy that badly wanted to retire him. But he was far and away the GOP primary front runner.

Yet Trump's lieutenants, not content with the damage they'd done, were dreaming up another way to paint DeSantis as aloof.

Despite his long-held aversion to germs, Trump's team was increasingly working retail stops into his campaign appearances. He would make appearances at restaurants, where he'd buy food for customers and shake hands. It was a heavy lift: Trump's advisers would spend days planning the stops, and Secret Service agents would have to scope out the shops before the former arrived to make sure it was safe. In February, Trump had visited East Palestine, Ohio, where a train carrying toxic chemicals had derailed. The Biden administration had drawn criticism for its response, which some residents had called sluggish. Biden had yet to visit the town, nor had Transportation Secretary Pete Buttigieg. Trump said the White House had demonstrated "indifference and betrayal," and he had mingled with customers at a McDonald's, where he got burgers for residents and first responders. Trump's team thought the Trump-with-the-Regular-Guy imagery had been powerful and credited the trip with helping to extricate him from his post-Ye slump. A clip of him buying McDonald's meals for first responders had gone viral and underscored Trump's appeal to working-class people who felt ignored and mistreated by Washington.

Plus, the visit had the added benefit of creating an implicit contrast with the cocooned DeSantis.

It was a big change for Trump, who hadn't done that kind of person-to-person campaigning since before the pandemic hit. Trump was dismissive of the visits and wasn't convinced they would make a difference, but he went along with them. "Is the reason we're doing the rope line and taking questions because DeSantis doesn't work the rope line and take questions?" Trump asked Jason Miller.

"Exactly," Miller said.

"Let's do it," Trump said.

FOUR

YOU'RE EITHER WITH ME OR AGAINST ME

APRIL 14, 2023

On a spring night in Nashville, Trump sat down for a two-hour dinner with more than a half dozen Republican lawmakers in a private room at the Four Seasons Hotel. The ex-president, who'd taken up residence for the evening in a lavish suite overlooking the Cumberland River and Nissan Stadium, was in big-city political boss mode.

Senior party figures, powerful lobbyists, and wealthy benefactors had descended on the Music City for a donor retreat hosted by the Republican National Committee. Now, Trump was looking to lock in endorsements from the influential lawmakers at the table with him, including Tennessee senators Bill Hagerty and Marsha Blackburn, whose husband, Chuck, had joined, wearing a red, white, and blue bowtie. One by one, he went down the table and put each one on the spot. Trump reminded them how he'd partnered with them in the past and told them he wanted their support. Their endorsements, he said, would matter in determining who won the primary race.

"Are you with me?" he asked each of them.

In the days that followed, everyone at the table would publicly announce they were, indeed, with him.

Trump was giving Republicans a choice: You're either with me or against me. He could afford to play that game. Republican voters were making it clear they sympathized with the former president. According to a Morning Consult poll conducted a few days earlier, Trump held a massive thirty-three-point national lead over his nearest rival, DeSantis.[1]

Republican pooh-bahs who months earlier had thought they were on the precipice of knocking off the old man were either getting in line with Trump or zipping their mouths shut. *Who the hell would want to get on the wrong side of a retribution-hungry former president who could well be making a return to the White House?* Republicans who'd crossed Trump could be frozen out of his administration, face Trump-backed primary challenges, or be publicly attacked by Trump and his supporters.

Even some of his primary opponents resorted to suck-uppery. After finishing his speech at the National Rifle Association's annual conference in Indianapolis on April 14, Vivek Ramaswamy, a fast-talking entrepreneur who had joined the race for the Republican nomination, poked his head backstage when Trump was waiting to go onstage. Surprised Trump aides knew what was up: Ramaswamy was there to kiss the ring.

The ambitious thirty-seven-year-old was presenting himself as heir to the Trump legacy, and now he was buttering up the former president by telling him that no matter what happened, it would be an outsider in their mold who would win the primary.

Trump listened and then quipped, "If you catch up to me, we're going to have a problem."

Ramaswamy was just as warm to the former president publicly as he was privately: On the trail, the young candidate would
praise Trump as the "best president of the twenty-first century."

Tim Scott, who had entered the primary in May, pulled
something similar after an Iowa Republican Party dinner where
he and Trump both spoke. After approaching a member of
Trump's security entourage, the senator was brought over to
greet the former president.

"Oh, Tim, it's great to see you. Keep up the good work,"
Trump said.

Scott wasn't as cloying toward the former president as
Ramaswamy was. But he almost never took on Trump, something that didn't escape the former commander-in-chief.

"I like Tim Scott," Trump told an adviser aboard his plane
one day. "Let's always be nice to him."

As the primary entered the summer months, Trump's
opponents—whom Steve Bannon had mockingly begun to call
"the Keebler Elves"—often seemed more intent on defending
Trump than on attacking him. Haley had called the Stormy
Daniels indictment a "political prosecution."[2] Pence described it
as an "outrage." Scott labeled it a "travesty."[3]

New endorsements were coming in by the day, and Trump
wanted more. The courtship was intense. Trump invited party
officials from Nevada and Louisiana to dine with him, and he was
working the phones feverishly. Once, as Trump's plane was taking off, he got Texas Congressman Michael Burgess on the phone
and secured his endorsement just before his reception was cut off.

The backing Trump was getting from party elites represented a remarkable shift. After January 6, senior party figures
were ready to cast the former president aside and never deal with

him again. But now, fueled by poll after poll showing Trump's advantage, they were getting back onboard. By the summer, Trump had vacuumed up dozens of congressional endorsements, dwarfing his rivals. Trump had even received support from several House Republicans who'd previously defied him by voting to establish a January 6 investigative committee.

Trump lavished his supporters with goodies like flights aboard the sleek, newly refurbished Trump Force One, which years earlier was used by the Portland Trail Blazers. Trump loved the plane—"Best way to travel!" he would say as he beamed—and had designed its interior himself, down to the golden-glow-emitting light bulbs.

As they stretched out on the plush leather seating and took in the big-screen TV programming, Trump's guests would munch on in-flight snacks. Diet Cokes and McDonald's flowed freely. The scene often resembled a frat party, with lawmakers bantering and milling around the cabin. Seat belts were rarely worn—by the former president or anyone else—even when the plane hit turbulence. And when it came to in-flight entertainment, Trump took on the role himself. During one trip to Iowa, Trump was joined by Florida Congresswoman Anna Paulina Luna and other members of the Florida delegation. Luna, who was pregnant, at one point remarked that she wasn't feeling well.

"If you need a bed to lay down in, there's one here on the plane. If you feel sick and you need to lay there, you can lay on it. Just don't tell Melania. She doesn't like other women on my bed," the thrice-married Trump joked to uproarious laughter.

House Speaker Kevin McCarthy learned the hard way what happened when you didn't fall in line with Trump. Trump aides were steamed that McCarthy was refusing to endorse the former president as the primary got underway. After turning on Trump in the wake of January 6, saying Trump "bears responsibility" for the riot, McCarthy had come around just a few weeks later, visiting Mar-a-Lago to kiss the ring.

Now, he was quiet. Then, during a late June interview on CNBC about the upcoming contest with Biden, McCarthy threw a bomb.

"Can he win that election? Yeah, he can," McCarthy said of Trump. "The question is, is he the strongest to win the election? I don't know that answer."[4]

Wiles, LaCivita, and Miller were furious. McCarthy held the speakership only because Trump had called a small group of insurgent Republicans, including Marjorie Taylor Greene and Florida Congressman Matt Gaetz, to get them to knock off their attempt to block him from getting the votes he needed to win it.

The media was going wild. McCarthy needed to clean it up, and fast. McCarthy finally called the former president and tried to smooth things over. To top it off, he dialed up Breitbart News to declare that Trump was "stronger today than he was in 2016."

That wasn't enough for the Trumpers. That day, Trump aides planted an anonymously sourced item in *Politico* outlining Trumpworld's "fury" at the speaker.[5] Message sent.

—

At the Capitol, Republican lawmakers who hadn't yet climbed aboard the Trump train were starting to get squeamish. Some who had dared to endorse other candidates approached Greene and asked if she could put in a good word with Trump for them. If Trump returned to the White House, they worried he could back their primary challengers and try to kick them out.

Greene had always felt plenty of her colleagues never actually liked Trump, even if they publicly acted like it. When Republicans were pondering bailing on Trump after the January 6 attack, she warned them it would be a dire political mistake.

"The American people are not going to leave him," she told them then.

Anyone who dared work for another candidate was also putting themselves in the line of fire. Trump's aides had begun collecting names—and taking screenshots of social media accounts—of the DeSantis staffers who were shit-talking Trump. If Trump took up residence in the White House, they would be blacklisted from getting a job in the administration.

Well-heeled Republican contributors—a group who'd long viewed Trump with derision and abhorred the idea the real estate mogul was one of them—were also feeling the heat. Trump was calling up dozens of donors, some of whom had refused to get behind him in the past, and putting them on the spot.

Trump's take-no-prisoners approach to the donor class was on display that summer during a conversation with Wiles and LaCivita about Charles Koch, the conservative billionaire. Koch had never been a Trump guy. Before Trump was elected, he had called Trump's rhetoric toward Muslims "monstrous" and later warned that his protectionist trade policies could be "disastrous." Koch's political group, Americans for Prosperity, was funding a door-knocking operation in the primary, and LaCivita showed Trump a video of the organization's staffers trying to dissuade voters from supporting him.

"These fucking people," Trump said.

A promise of retribution was in order. He hammered out a Truth Social post.

"IF YOU GO AFTER ME, I'M COMING AFTER YOU!" Trump wrote.[6]

Trump had long refused to engage in the presidential tradition of cultivating billionaire megadonors, partly because he was afraid of being told no by people whose approval he hungered for. Now, Trump was like a machine. He called people over and over—even those who he assumed would say no. There were people who'd told him they weren't interested, citing January 6 or some policy quibble they had. But he kept calling them anyway. It got his competitive juices flowing. He wanted to get them onboard.

As Trump's lead in the primary grew, he relished the idea of getting these masters-of-the-universe types on the record. He would ask if he could count on their support. Either the answer would be yes or no. "Okay, I understand," he told those that turned him down.

"But when you want to support me, here's my number. Call me."

And, if they didn't end up with him? Well, if Trump returned to 1600 Pennsylvania Avenue, they'd have to live in fear of a commander-in-chief who wouldn't forget who was with him—and who wasn't.

———

If there were any lingering doubts about Trump's hold over the Republican Party, they were all but erased on June 10, 2023.

The previous day, Trump was dealt his second criminal indictment. The Justice Department announced it was charging Trump with mishandling classified documents he took from the White House and obstructing the efforts of federal officials to

retrieve them. The thirty-seven-count, forty-nine-page indictment accused Trump of, among other things, taking documents
that outlined the US nuclear programs, urging lawyers to hide
the papers in their hotel rooms, and even storing some of the
documents in a Mar-a-Lago bathroom.

Prosecutors said Trump showed the documents—including
one describing US military attack plans—to visitors. Special
counsel Jack Smith, the lead prosecutor in the case, warned in
the court filing that the "unauthorized disclosure of these documents could put at risk the national security of the United
States."[7]

The prosecution also charged Walt Nauta, Trump's personal
valet, with helping to conceal the papers. Trump and Nauta
would be turning themselves in the following week at the federal
courthouse in Miami.

Twenty-four hours later, the former president—with Nauta a
few steps behind him—exited his black SUV, gave a thumbs-up,
and climbed the stairs to Trump Force One. It was a Saturday,
and he had a busy day of campaigning ahead of him, with stops
in Georgia and North Carolina.

Two hours after takeoff, Trump's plane dipped below the
hazy cloud cover and began a bumpy descent into the Columbus,
Georgia, airport. Fans were lined up on the side of the road par-
allel to the runway. Some stood atop pickup trucks so they could
get a glimpse of the plane as it touched down. Others waved flags
and held their iPhones aloft so they could take pictures. When
Trump stepped onto the tarmac, he was greeted by a throng of
supporters, some holding signs saying "Witch Hunt."

After a six-mile drive, Trump arrived at the Georgia Republican Party convention and took the stage to thunderous applause
from the red-MAGA-hat-wearing audience. Trump would use

his speech to lambaste the new indictment as a "political hit job." But he also did something else. Early in the speech, he unveiled a list of endorsements from a handful of prominent Georgia Republicans he praised as "patriots."[8]

After a pit stop at a Waffle House, where he was mobbed by fans, it was on to North Carolina. Before taking the podium in Greensboro, Trump spoke backstage with Lieutenant Governor Mark Robinson, a leading Republican candidate for governor. Robinson, a bomb-throwing MAGA fan known for embracing conspiracy theories, told the former president he would back him.

Trump had been slapped with two indictments, and the prospect of two more arrests loomed. Yet he'd just wrapped up a multi-stop campaign swing where he'd locked up the support of powerful Republican politicians.

Beyond all the bluster, though, Trump was feeling vulnerable. Even though he was prospering politically, he knew he was in legal jeopardy. And it was all but certain to get worse. Trump had spent the first year of his presidency dodging a special counsel investigation and had been impeached twice by the end of his term. Yet this was different. He was now facing the possibility of time in prison, and Smith, the ball-busting prosecutor who was also investigating Trump's role in the January 6 Capitol assault, seemed determined as ever.

"Nobody wants to be indicted," Trump told me in an interview on his plane that June day. "I don't care that my poll numbers went up by a lot. I don't want to be indicted. I've never been indicted. I went through my whole life, now I get indicted every two months."[9]

FIVE:
BORIS AND THE HUMAN PRINTER

Trump's operation was more effective than anything he'd ever had before, and it was playing no small role in his domination of his rivals.

While Trump's previous campaigns, and his White House, were marred by brutal knife fighting, damaging leaks, and dizzying turnover, Susie Wiles wouldn't tolerate any of that BS. And whereas Trump's previous operations empowered bootlicking loyalists who only told the boss what he wanted to hear, Wiles had other ideas. Senior advisers knew going in they couldn't control Trump or tell him what to do, but they were encouraged to give it to him straight.

Trump appreciated the relative calmness and effectiveness of Wiles's operation. But that didn't mean he totally gave up indulging the brownnosing and dysfunction that had defined his administration.

Trump's circle included loyalists like Boris Epshteyn, a physically formidable Russian-born lawyer and Republican operative who had a taste for three-piece suits and fashioned himself as Trump's political fixer. Epshteyn had worked on Trump's 2016 campaign, served in his White House, and was a member of

Trump's post-2020 election legal team. He embraced the perception that he was Trump's enforcer and flaunted it, regularly holding court in the front window of DC's powerbroker-fashioned Palm restaurant, in full view of Dupont Circle area passersby.

Epshteyn had spent years on the periphery of Trumpworld. But he'd outlasted others and now had the access to the boss he always wanted. And he used it.

After boarding Trump's plane one day, LaCivita turned to Epshteyn. "Hey, Boris, now that you're on the plane, are you still going to call DJT twenty times while we're in the air?" asked LaCivita, who had a friendly habit of busting people's chops.

As Trump's indictments piled up, Epshteyn—now in charge of the legal effort—would collide with other lawyers who wanted to give the boss their unvarnished opinion free of spin or happy talk. Several would exit because they believed Epshteyn was blocking them from accessing Trump. He burned up Trump's phone with legal advice that ran counter to what the Wiles hierarchy wanted. And in what would become a headache for campaign leaders, Epshteyn himself became a target in the same investigations Trump was facing. Prosecutors were looking at, among other things, Epshteyn's role in Trump's efforts to block the 2020 election certification and in his handling of classified documents. Epshteyn had been in legal trouble before. In 2021, he was arrested after being accused of groping two women at a bar in Scottsdale, Arizona. Epshteyn paid a fine and served probation, and the conviction was later set aside.

The idea that Epshteyn was evading further legal trouble by cooperating with the feds became a running joke. Some would rib Epshteyn by telling him they thought he was wearing a wire. Sergio Gor, a Trump ally who ran the former president's book publishing house, once approached Epshteyn at Mar-a-Lago and patted him down. "I don't know about this," Gor said. People laughed. The fact that Epshteyn would sometimes speak in his native Russian, others would quip, was only more evidence that he was a spy.

And, of course, there were the typical flies that swarmed the Trump orbit and created headaches for Trump's high command. Lots of people had Trump's cellphone number, and it was impossible for Wiles et al. to keep outsiders from calling him. That included Dick Morris, the Bill Clinton confidant-turned-conservative pundit who'd gone down in infamy for once allegedly sucking the toes of a prostitute in a DC hotel. Morris was constantly calling Wiles and LaCivita and trying to offer his advice. Now, he was phoning Trump directly and making the case that he should take part in the primary debates, which contradicted what the Wiles and LaCivita tag team was telling the boss. The Trump forces made clear to Morris that his guidance wasn't wanted.

But easily the biggest migraine for the campaign hierarchy was Natalie Harp. The thirtysomething aide had begun working for Trump in 2022, after leaving her job as an anchor at the pro-Trump One America News. Harp had long been enamored with the former president. During the 2020 Republican National Convention, Harp, who had fought stage 2 bone cancer, delivered a speech in which she claimed that Trump had saved her life because he signed a bill allowing her to get access to an experimental treatment.

Harp was known within the campaign as the "Human Printer" because her primary responsibility was to print out news articles for Trump to read. During flights, she would sit at a laptop and search for Trump news on the internet. She then printed out the articles, scampered up a few rows to Trump, and handed them to him. Other times, she would pass along pictures that she thought made the famously vain Trump look flattering.

"I've got a good photo of you, Mr. President!" she told him after a long day of coverage following one of his indictments.

Harp didn't do well with boundaries. There was the time when a surprised Melania Trump stumbled upon Harp late at night in Trump's private quarters at Mar-a-Lago, an area that was typically off-limits to those outside Trump's family. Harp was there to deliver Trump some documents and didn't want to wait until the morning to give them to him. And she was possessive over him. Harp derisively labeled some women in Trump's orbit—people like Alina Habba, press aide Margo Martin, and lawyer Lindsey Halligan—the "Party Girls," even though there was no evidence that any of them had acted inappropriately.

In another instance, Trump had asked Harp to remove a box of papers. When Nauta, who as Trump's full-time valet often took on such jobs, offered to do it, Harp snapped at him.

"This is my job to take them," she huffed. "He told me to take it."

Then there was the time Trump visited Scotland to celebrate the opening of his new golf club. Trump had wanted to give the course a spin, despite the gray Aberdeen weather. Trump and his security entourage were traversing the winding greens in motorized carts. But Harp, who often trailed Trump at his Palm Beach golf course on a cart with a printer attached to it, couldn't get one. So the determined aide settled on an alternative: She would sprint after him on foot.

Nearby, an aide took in the scene. A black-clad figure was chasing after the former and possibly future leader of the free world. And they were booking it. *Was that Natalie?*

Before long, Trump advisers jokingly began to compare Harp to Alex Forrest, the character played by Glenn Close in the 1987 movie *Fatal Attraction*. Forrest had become obsessed with a married man and, in the film's most memorable scene, broke into his house and boiled the family's pet rabbit.

Even Trump seemed to think that Harp's sycophancy was a bit much. During a flight back from the college wrestling championships in Oklahoma, Trump teasingly began asking the women onboard if they had found any of the strapping young athletes attractive. At one point, he waved Harp over and asked which one she found most appealing.

"None of them, sir," Harp said.

"Seriously, you didn't think any of the guys . . . This was the NCAA championship. You didn't fancy any of them?"

"No, sir."

Trump then turned sarcastic.

"That's one thing I like about Natalie," he said. She "only has eyes for her president."

Trump liked having Harp around. The famously insecure former president always had a soft spot for those who treated him like a king and did whatever he asked. Harp was his Girl Friday. If Trump wanted to publish a flamethrowing post on Truth Social? Natalie was there to send it through. If he wanted to read a fawning but factually dicey story in a Trump-aligned media outlet? Natalie was there to print it out. If Trump wanted to send some random news article to a Republican member of Congress? Natalie was there to text it to them.

As much as those in the senior ranks wanted Natalie gone, they knew she was unfireable.

Before long, Harp was acting like a boss and busting through the Wiles-established org chart. The press team at one point confronted her about going around them and talking to reporters. At another point, she reached out to the campaign's TV ad maker, John Brabender, to ask for changes to be made to a commercial in the works. When LaCivita found out about it, he blew his fuse.

"If you take her edits one more time, if you take one more goddamn phone call without telling me, I'll find somebody else to do your job," LaCivita told Brabender.

During the White House years, aides had tried to manage paper flow to control what got to Trump's desk. Now, it was Natalie who determined what he saw. The articles she delivered to him with gold paper clips could be weeks old and culled from anywhere on the internet.

Aides began to notice a pattern. When something bad happened on social media, Natalie was often at the helm. When Trump published a Truth Social post with an image of him holding a baseball bat next to Manhattan District Attorney Alvin Bragg's head, it was Natalie who had sent it out. When Trump published a statement on the platform over a Jewish holiday weekend attacking "liberal Jews," it was Natalie who had posted it.

At the same time, she was prickly with her coworkers.

"What do you want?" Harp snapped when answering a phone call from Wiles one day. She had apparently been on another golf outing with Trump. "I had to leave the golf course to take this call," she huffed.

Harp even collided with one of Trump's namesakes. The young aide had angered Eric Trump by back-channeling with Eric's employees at the Trump Organization. Eric told Harp that she was unprofessional and asked her not to go behind his back anymore.

Harp's behavior over time grew more erratic. Harp had jumped into her car after deplaning from Trump Force One at the Palm Beach Airport one evening, floored the gas, and then slammed into a parked Secret Service SUV. Harp got out of her vehicle, threw her hands up in the air, and asked a few aides who'd witnessed the accident what she should do. Was it bad? Did anyone else see it happen? Should she leave a note?

Natalie's behavior was increasingly drawing attention. Particularly concerning: The Secret Service had obtained handwritten letters Natalie had given Trump in which she came off as obsessive, adoring, and desperate for his approval.[1]

In one, Harp apologized to Trump for her behavior "on the course in Scotland."

I want things to always be right between us. I also know I've been distracted all week (forgetting to eat throughout the days, and even forgetting to sleep, and only catching a couple hours at a time) . . . I started letting the remarks of people who haven't bothered me before, get to me—not because I care what others think, but because I see myself being lowered in your eyes and good opinion. That is the fear you see, because I never want to bring you anything but joy. I'm sorry I lost my focus. You are all that matters to me. I don't want to ever let you down. Thank you for being my Guardian and Protector in this Life . . .

She concluded the letter: "I will return a better person. I have to sign off now, as the cars are leaving. See you soon. With all my heart, Natalie."

In another letter to Trump, Natalie wrote about how the trip had given her time to reflect on her work for him.[2]

"I need to reunite my past self with my current into a better version who will make you proud," she wrote. "And please, when I fail, will you tell me? You have the absolute right to cuss me out, if need be, when I deserve it, because no one knows or cares about me more."

SIX:

"IS THAT LADY FROM THE RNC GONE YET?"

SEPTEMBER 2023

Ronna McDaniel knew by the summer of 2023 that Trump would be the Republican nominee. The only question was what it meant for the party she chaired and for its prospects of winning back the White House.

McDaniel—perhaps just as well as anyone else—was attuned to Trump's ever-changing moods, his impulses, his tics. She knew his considerable political strengths and his just as considerable weaknesses. And she knew where the Trumpworld bodies were buried.

Few Trumpians had been as long-lasting or as central to the former president's inner circle as McDaniel. She had been operating at a stratospheric level in Trump's orbit since 2017, a virtual lifetime in Trump years. Trump churned and burned through top aides and allies, but because McDaniel knew how to get along with him—he saw her as loyal, levelheaded, and not out for her own personal gain—she had survived.

Trump had handpicked the Michigander to be RNC chair after he won the presidency, and they'd been close ever since.

Her office at party headquarters overlooking First Street South-
east was filled with Trump tchotchkes—a signed MAGA hat,
pictures of McDaniel's family with the boss, tickets to Trump's
2017 inauguration. Trump at one point had suggested to McDaniel she be his White House chief of staff. She dismissed the idea,
telling him she wasn't qualified for the job.

For the last seven years, she'd gotten calls from him when
she was on flights, when she was on the treadmill, when she'd
retired to whatever hotel room she was staying at. When it came
to their topics of conversation, not much was off-limits. At one
point during the primary, he'd called to excitedly tell her about
the new nickname he'd come up with for Nikki Haley, his former UN ambassador–turned–rival.

"Ronna, I called her 'Birdbrain.' Did you see it? It's all over
the news," he said proudly.

The two were so comfortable with one another that when
they were once backstage at the Republican Jewish Coalition's
Annual Leadership Summit in Las Vegas, Trump told the party
chair that her hairdo wasn't working.

"Honey, I need to fix this," he said, grabbing his ever-present
bottle of hairspray and showering it on her. When McDaniel
took the stage after, her now helmetlike 'do didn't move.

But the truth was, McDaniel was over the job. She was now
the longest-serving RNC chair in modern history and had spent
the last six-plus years in the middle of a tug-of-war between
Team MAGA and Team Establishment. The Trumpers thought
they owned the party committee and wanted her to perfectly
align herself with the former president. The party elders wanted
her to see Trump as an existential threat to the GOP and be independent of him. As for the party's mixed electoral record, she

was being blamed by both sides. She was sick and tired of being the punching bag. Who needed this?

By fall, McDaniel began picking up on something else: Her relationship with Trump was breaking down.

Trump was becoming convinced that McDaniel wasn't raising enough money, that her get-out-the-vote operation was weak, and that she hadn't done enough to fight the outcome of the 2020 election. More than that, he was angry that McDaniel was hosting primary debates. By now, there were nearly a dozen people in the race. Trump had refused to participate in the televised events because he thought it was beneath him to be onstage with the jamokes running against him. It infuriated him that these guys were getting airtime.

"The RNC is not doing its job," he badgered her. "You're distracted. You need to get rid of these debates."

The conversations were ugly. McDaniel tried to explain to Trump that, as was typically the case in an open primary, the RNC chair was expected to be neutral and hold debates, regardless of the fact that he was a former president and was leading by a wide margin. He wasn't having any of it.

"People are turning on you, they're mad at you," Trump warned her, referring to his hardcore fans. "I don't know if I could stop them."

Now he was coming up with other demands. He pressed her to cancel the primary entirely and to move the Republican National Convention, scheduled for July, from Milwaukee. He thought the city was a dump. Democrats had picked a first-class city, Chicago, to have their convention, Trump thundered. Why couldn't he have that? He wanted a city like Las Vegas, something with flash and sizzle.

McDaniel, who found Trump's behavior on the calls to be incendiary and hurtful, didn't budge.

During an October phone call, McDaniel conveyed to Trump that if he wanted her gone once he became the presumptive nominee and took over the party's operations, so be it.

"You deserve to have the chair you want, and if you are the nominee and want me to step down, I will." He demurred.

The stare down revealed something central to Trump's nature: Either you acceded to his demands, regardless of how unrealistic they were, or you were out. This time McDaniel wasn't giving in. And she was about to meet her downfall.

▬

Trump was pissed about debates and Milwaukee, that was clear. But things were looking up for him politically.

A *New York Times*/Siena College poll released in early November showed Trump leading Biden in five of the six swing states most likely to determine the outcome of the election.[1] They were auspicious results for Trump and ominous for Biden. The president, it was becoming abundantly clear, was sinking. The poll found that voters overwhelmingly felt the eighty-one-year-old incumbent had done a poor job of managing the economy, with inflation higher than it had been in decades, and was too old to serve.[2]

"Our numbers are higher than they have ever been," Trump boasted at one rally. "We are beating them so badly in the polls."[3]

As the Iowa caucus approached, Trump knew he didn't just want to beat his rivals there; he wanted to decimate them—and to telegraph to the remaining Republican Party dissenters he was the party's standard-bearer and they had no choice but to get behind him.

For months, polling had shown Trump with wide leads in Iowa and the states that followed. Brian Jack had delivered a presentation at an all-staff meeting in early December in which he estimated that, based on the survey numbers, Trump would become the presumptive nominee by March 12 or March 19. During the 2016 primary, when Trump was facing formidable opposition from the likes of Texas Senator Ted Cruz, he didn't lock up the nomination until May.

But Iowa wasn't going entirely smoothly. Trump had dominated the endorsement game in every state—except there. Even though Trump was running far ahead of DeSantis, he had far fewer endorsements from the state's political class. DeSantis had racked up the support of Governor Kim Reynolds, prominent evangelical leader Bob Vander Plaats, and dozens of state legislators.

The Trump team had theories for why the Iowans weren't onboard with the old man. Maybe the DeSantis team was paying off his endorsees. Or maybe the Midwestern nice crowd didn't mesh with Trump. Whatever the case, Iowa's Republican elites weren't with Trump, and he didn't like it.

"This is the hardest state," Trump said privately. "I don't understand it."

Trump was especially fired up over Reynolds. During a July flight on Trump Force One, the itchy-fingered Trump had told advisers he wanted to pound out a Truth Social post ripping into the governor. Wiles talked him out of it, noting that she was popular and that it wouldn't be good to alienate her supporters. But then, after returning to Bedminster, Trump fired off a post, bellowing that when Reynolds "fell behind" in her race, "I ENDORSED her, did big Rallies, & she won."[4]

Trump wanted to cut off the Iowans who crossed him. In September, he had attended the Iowa—Iowa State college football game, a perennial matchup that was a regular stop for White House hopefuls. While Trump was taking in the game from a private box, his Iowa guru Alex Latcham was getting asked by local Republicans if they could see the ex-president.

One of those doing the asking was Eric Branstad, the son of the state's former longtime governor. Problem was, the elder Branstad hadn't yet endorsed Trump. Trump made clear he had no interest in letting Eric, or anyone else who wasn't backing him, into his booth. Screw that, Trump said. These people just want things from me, but they give me squat in return.

Now, he wanted to show them who was boss. Polls had Trump up by historic margins in Iowa and other primary states, and blowout wins would create an aura of dominance. The truth was, he was sensitive to anything that even resembled vulnerability. After appearing at another college football game in South Carolina just after Thanksgiving, *The Hill* had published an article saying there was a "smattering" of boos directed toward the former president.[5] Egged on by South Carolina Senator Lindsey Graham, who had joined Trump on the flight back home, Trump had spoken by phone with a top official from Nexstar Media Group, which owned *The Hill*, to vent.

The story was unfair, Trump complained. How could the reporter write that I was getting mixed reviews? Were they not at the stadium? Total BS. Trump couldn't stand it when journalists undersold him, and he kept close track of which reporters were "good" to him.

As the caucus approached, Trump's lieutenants wanted to lower his expectations. Trump had been boasting at rallies that polls showed him leading in Iowa by between twenty and thirty points. Trump's aides were trying to convey to him that his winning margin could be smaller. No Republican candidate, they told him, had ever won a contested Iowa caucus by more than twelve points. They knew if the boss finished by less than the polls showed, he would be majorly disappointed—and potentially take it out on them. Latcham, for one, worried it could result in Trump telling him, "You're fired."

Trump was leaning into a central theme of his campaign: He was the victim of, as he put it during one rally, a "weaponized" legal system that was "after" him. McLaughlin wanted to put an exclamation point on it. In January, he sent a memo to the campaign's leadership proposing that on the day of the caucus, which fell on the Martin Luther King Jr. holiday, Trump would hold a rally where an image of MLK being arrested would be shown on a screen. The picture, the pollster suggested, would then "dissolve" into an image of Trump.

The troll, McLaughlin wrote, would "blow the media's mind." (The idea was never executed, and Trump took to comparing himself publicly to Nelson Mandela, who had been imprisoned over his opposition to apartheid in South Africa.)

There was a last-minute wild card as the day of the caucus approached: the weather. It was mid-January, and temperatures were bone-chilling. Snow blanketed the state. Trump flew into Iowa on a Gulfstream jet lent to him by Steve Witkoff, a wealthy real estate executive and friend, because Trump Force One was getting repaired. When he landed in Des Moines a few days before the caucus, the windchill was around negative forty degrees

Fahrenheit. Aides struggled to get their footing on the tarmac and latched on to each other as they tried to get into cars.

Trump was relying partly on first-time and other less experienced caucus-goers, and the weather might deter them from turning out. At an event the day before the caucus, he had told rally-goers to turn out even "if you're sick as a dog." "Even if you vote and then pass away, it's worth it," he said.

The former president didn't like to appear concerned about anything, but now he was coming pretty close to it. Trump—the crowdsourcer-in-chief—wouldn't stop asking aides which candidate the weather helped or hurt. Hunkered down in a conference room at the Hotel Fort Des Moines, Trump called organizers across the state to pick their brains. What did this mean for him?

On the evening of January 15, Trump made a final pitch to caucus-goers at the Horizon Events Center in Clive, Iowa. His speech was to be short and designed to project an air of spontaneity. As he spoke, the reception in the room was decidedly muted. His team began to worry. Everyone knew Trump would romp, but the optics of a former president talking to a silent group of Iowans weren't great.

Soon, that wouldn't matter. While Trump was speaking, LaCivita's phone rang. It was CBS News political director Fin Gómez. We're calling the race for your guy, Gómez said.

LaCivita was shocked. It was about 7:20 p.m., mere minutes after caucusing had begun.

Trump's team told him the news once he left the stage. He was just as surprised as they were. He knew he would win, but he certainly didn't expect it to be this early. Whatever concerns Trump had about his margin of victory were erased. The returns were showing him lapping Haley and DeSantis.

After a fifteen-minute motorcade ride, Trump arrived at the Iowa Events Center, where his team had rented out a space. It was before 8 p.m., when the victory party was to start, so the ballroom was virtually empty. But in a nearby high-ceilinged conference room, the mood was pure elation. Four TVs were tuned to different networks, and Trump snapped pictures with guests.

"Great job," Trump told Latcham, shaking his hand. "You can celebrate for only two minutes. You've got to get to New Hampshire."

To Wiles, he joked: "You get to keep your job for another week."

Speechwriter Vince Haley gave the boss a victory speech, but Trump didn't want it.

I'm going to riff, he said. Once onstage, he sounded a conciliatory note, saying the party was now going to "come together."

The celebration continued on the flight to New York City. Trump was due in court early the next morning to attend the E. Jean Carroll defamation trial—a case that, if he lost, could result in millions of dollars in penalties. But there was no shuteye to be had that evening on the plane. McDonald's was once again served. Music videos were played. Some of Trump's lieutenants had been booked to stay at the wrong hotel that evening—in Flushing, Queens, about forty-five minutes away from Manhattan—but even that didn't dampen the mood. The plane landed at LaGuardia Airport at around 3:30 a.m., and the former president finally made it back to Trump Tower forty-five minutes later. Yes, turnout in Iowa had been low. But Trump still viewed his win as a major accomplishment. Eight years earlier, he'd finished second place to Cruz. This time, he was on top.

Trump had left the White House almost exactly three years ago, on a cold January morning that he would never forget. The Republican Party had deserted him in the wake of the Capitol riot, and he had returned to Mar-a-Lago isolated and cast aside. Now, 1,090 days later, he'd won Iowa and was on his way to clinching the GOP nomination. The Trump comeback was underway.

———

A few days after Iowa, as the Trumpians got word that DeSantis was about to exit the race, LaCivita placed a call to DeSantis lieutenant Phil Cox and made an offer. Would the governor be interested in us flying him up from Tallahassee to campaign with Trump in New Hampshire? The Granite State's primary was two days away. Just putting it out there, LaCivita told him. No expectations. We know it's raw.

It was a turning point. The Trumpians had thoroughly disemboweled DeSantis—questioning his manhood, deriding him as weird, and even accusing him of wearing high-heeled boots to make himself appear taller. Now, they were trying to get him on the same stage as Trump.

About an hour after the call, DeSantis released a video in which he announced he was withdrawing and endorsing Trump. As for LaCivita's overture, DeSantis just wanted to be done with the whole thing. The idea of schlepping up to frigid New Hampshire wasn't appealing.

Whatever the case, Trump was finished with DeSantis. Trump told aides that he would have endorsed DeSantis as his successor if the governor had waited another four years to run for president. But DeSantis had burned the relationship down and destroyed his political career, Trump concluded.

"Now nobody wants him," Trump said. "He's done."

For Wiles, whom DeSantis had exiled and unsuccessfully tried to crush, it was a sweet moment. She'd had fun kicking the crap out of DeSantis. And, she told people, her press guys weren't necessarily done using "the rusty knife" on the governor. Trumpworld's treatment of DeSantis going forward, she would say, would depend partly on whether he played nice with Trump. If DeSantis attacked the former president going forward, Cheung et al. could always slice and dice him.

For now, though, Wiles was content with a rare public victory lap. "Bye bye," she wrote on X, the platform formerly known as Twitter. Wiles almost never posted. But she couldn't resist.

The field was thinning. Mike Pence and Tim Scott had dropped out before Iowa when it became clear they weren't gaining traction, as had Chris Christie. Vivek Ramaswamy met with Trump privately on Iowa caucus night and told him he was withdrawing and endorsing him, which made sense given that he'd run as a Trump Mini-Me. The two had become quite friendly. Trump had called Ramaswamy right before the first debate and wished him luck and gave him a piece of advice: Stay loose. Ramaswamy later called it the best advice he'd gotten before taking the stage.

That left Nikki Haley as the last rival standing. The Trump team had anticipated this outcome for some time. At a December all-hands strategy meeting about six weeks earlier, the group had concluded that it would be she, not DeSantis, who would last longer. While the Florida governor was hanging on for dear life financially, Haley had become the favorite of Republican establishment donors who were determined to stop Trump. She was militarily hawkish, opposed Trump's policy of imposing tariffs on imported goods, and wanted to finance Ukraine in its fight against Russia. And unlike DeSantis, Haley was trying to win over moderate-minded independent voters who were allowed to participate in the New Hampshire GOP primary.

Trump aides were worried. The former president himself freaked out when a public poll was released in December showing Haley dramatically closing the gap. In the days after Christmas, McLaughlin's private numbers showed Trump beating Haley in a head-to-head matchup by only one or two points.

In his memo, McLaughlin outlined a series of steps that should be taken to down the rising Haley. They included doing away with Trump's chosen nickname for her. "'Birdbrain' doesn't work,'" McLaughlin wrote, suggesting Trump instead call her a "fool." (A few days after the memo was sent, Trump assailed Haley as a "globalist fool.")

Trump wasn't afraid to get down in the muck with Haley, an indication he saw her as a threat. He resurfaced a decade-plus-old rumor that Haley had cheated on her husband prior to becoming South Carolina governor. Aides suspected he got the idea from Laura Loomer, a pro-Trump social media provocateur who brought up the allegations while on Trump's plane one day. On Truth Social, Trump also began referring to Haley as "Nimrada" and "Nimbra," intentionally misspelling her birth name of Nimrata Nikki Randhawa. (The American-born Haley was the daughter of Indian immigrants.) The campaign had even drafted a speech in which Trump was to use the "Nimrada" label, but McLaughlin put the kibosh on the idea.

On the evening of the January 23 primary, Trump and his team huddled at the Sheraton hotel in Nashua, where aides had set up a war room with four TVs. Scott and Ramaswamy, former rivals–turned–Trump VP wannabes, were on hand, as were Eric Trump and his wife, Lara, along with donor friends Steve Wynn, a casino mogul, and John Paulson, a billionaire investor. Aides worried that Trump's expectations were too high. While public polling had shown Trump beating Haley by twenty points or more, McLaughlin's private numbers had shown him only leading by eleven.

As Trump took in the returns, it became clear the campaign's numbers were the right ones. Trump worried that a closer-than-expected margin would allow Haley to claim an upset victory of sorts, à la Bill Clinton in 1992, when the young Arkansas governor dubbed himself the "comeback kid" after his eight-point loss in the Granite State.

Before Trump knew it, Haley took the stage at her election night party, vowing to stay in the primary.

"This race is far from over!" she said to cheers.[6]

It didn't take a genius to realize that Haley was trying to spin her defeat. She'd ended up losing by eleven points, so it wasn't exactly close. Plus, Trump had now won the first two primaries, and McDaniel was planning on going on TV later that night to essentially declare him the presumptive nominee.

Trump was visibly annoyed. It had infuriated him that Haley refused to drop out of the race, and that he would need to spend more time and money trying to wrap up a nomination that by now should be his. He couldn't believe Haley spoke before he did—allowing her to somehow cast herself as the winner—and briefly lashed out at his team for it. He was done with her. In recent weeks, Trump had been privately floating the idea Haley could be his vice presidential pick, raising the prospect she could help him win over women and suburbanites who had spurned him in the past. Now that was out.

Before Trump addressed his supporters at the Sheraton ballroom, he chatted backstage with Wynn, his old casino billionaire pal. Wynn had served as the Republican National Committee's finance chair after Trump took office, reflecting their close relationship. While Wynn had some establishment sensibilities—former George W. Bush strategist and Trump punching bag Karl Rove was a top adviser to him—they remained close. Just go out there and be civil like you were after Iowa, Wynn urged him. Trump allies like Wynn believed Trump needed to unite the Republican Party—including Haley's supporters—in order to compete in the general election. Antagonizing them would do no good. Yes, Trump was pissed. But, this time, he needed to stuff it.

I got it, Trump said.

But he apparently didn't. When Trump took the stage, he said Haley would be "under investigation" by the press for "stuff she doesn't want to talk about." He insulted how Haley had dressed that evening, saying she was wearing a "fancy dress that probably wasn't so fancy." And he mocked her performance in the primary, assailing her for giving a "victory speech" when she "had a very bad night."

Wynn, watching from the audience, was horrified. What was going on?

▬

With the nomination all but locked up, Trump prepared to take over the Republican Party infrastructure. The first step: ousting his old ally, Ronna McDaniel.

Trump had been unhappy with McDaniel for months. He'd been hearing complaints from allies about her, too. A few months earlier, Trump had held a fundraiser at the 22,000-square-foot,

$125,000-per-night, two-story penthouse suite at the Post Oak Hotel in Houston. During the dinner, Trump had gone around the table and asked each of the donors what they thought of the RNC. One by one, the fat cats said they lacked confidence in the committee and were reluctant to fund it. McDaniel's organization, they agreed, was a dud. The committee's fundraising was piss-poor, they said. It had a lackluster turnout operation. And McDaniel had taken a Switzerland-like approach to the primary and had insisted on hosting pointless primary debates.

The dinner reaffirmed to Trump it was time to force McDaniel out. He was sick of absorbing criticisms about the committee.

"Is that lady from the RNC gone yet?" he vented one day.

As Iowa neared, LaCivita had begun drawing up plans for a Trump-led takeover of the RNC and a complete overhaul of its operations. LaCivita, like other Trump lieutenants, was deeply worried about the state of the committee. McDaniel's organization was starting out the election year with a paltry $8 million in its piggy bank, a fraction of what its Democratic counterpart had. The Trump team worried that unless there were changes, they would be vastly outspent by the Biden machine.

Trump, meanwhile, began asking an assortment of people if they'd be interested in replacing McDaniel. Before long a front runner emerged: Michael Whatley. Trump had heard that Whatley, as the North Carolina Republican Party chair, had been laser focused on combating "voter fraud," as Trump called it. And that was good enough for him. Trump was obsessed with the idea the election would be "stolen" again, and he wanted to turn the organization's focus toward that threat. Trump supporters felt the RNC had fallen short in its legal efforts four years earlier, and they wanted to deploy lawyers and poll watchers across battleground states. It didn't hurt that Whatley knew Susie Wiles from his time volunteering for Trump's 2016 campaign in Florida, where he did everything from parking cars to planning rallies. When Whatley ran for North Carolina chair a few years later, Wiles drove up to Raleigh to support him.

Trump had sat down for lunch with Whatley in a private room at 801 Chophouse in Des Moines the day of the caucuses. Eric Trump joined them, as did a handful of aides, including Wiles and LaCivita. Steak, Caesar salad, and crab were served. Trump lavished praise on Whatley. The former president liked that the North Carolinian had aligned himself with the "Stop the Steal" movement. Whatley had defended Trump over the January 6 siege and the ensuing impeachment, and he had agreed with Trump's belief that elections were vulnerable to fraud.

"You've done a great job," Trump told Whatley. "We've got big plans for you. You're going to be happy. You're going to be excited."

Trump envisioned an RNC led by his staunchest allies— people who would ensure that the committee would do exactly as he wanted. Trump's campaign and the RNC would be effectively the same organ. Lara Trump, the ex-president's daughter-in-law and another North Carolina native, would be RNC co-chair. The forty-one-year-old former TV producer was married to Eric Trump and had been active in the 2016 and 2020 campaigns. LaCivita, meanwhile, would become the committee's chief of staff. Going forward, the strategist would split his time between the RNC's offices in Washington and Trump HQ in Florida.

The former president's decision to install LaCivita at the RNC reflected his growing trust in the adviser. Trump admired his pure aggressiveness, his rough edges, and his eagerness to demolish opponents. There was one story the former president particularly liked. LaCivita had left a Palm Beach restaurant one evening and was confronted by a guy wielding a metal pipe. Before he could be hit, the Marine veteran picked up a chair on the sidewalk and smashed the dude with it.

McDaniel had always anticipated Trump would eventually cast her aside; there was bound to be a disagreement between them at some point that would end things. But she was upset about how he was doing it. While Trump was largely keeping his mouth shut about McDaniel publicly, his allies, including Matt Gaetz, Charlie Kirk, and Vivek Ramaswamy, weren't. The latter had called on McDaniel to resign during a debate, saying the GOP had become a "party of losers" during her tenure. McDaniel suspected that Ramaswamy had coordinated the assault with the Trumpers, something they denied.

Classic Trump, McDaniel thought. *Get your friends to do the dirty work so you don't have to.*

McDaniel was increasingly thinking of life after the RNC. She had spent the last seven years crisscrossing the country, pleading with donors for checks and dealing with Trump chaos. Now she could make some money, become a TV news talking head, and spend more time with her husband, Pat, back in Michigan. It would be an easier life.

On February 6, shortly after the New Hampshire primary, McDaniel flew down to Mar-a-Lago to meet with Trump. She knew this was the end. By that point, she had decided the job wasn't worth fighting for. The conversations with Trump had become too painful, and she knew he wanted a change. (She'd almost quit in December, as the tension between her and Trump had intensified, but decided against it.) Trump had said in a pre-recorded Fox News interview that had aired a few days earlier that "there will probably be some changes made" at the RNC. Trump aides had told the McDaniel team they were going to ask Fox to edit out that part of the interview, but it aired anyway. McDaniel thought the Trumpers had lied about trying to get it stripped.

After arriving at Trump's estate, McDaniel went to Trump's office to meet with him and Wiles. McDaniel wanted the door shut. A few Trump aides were outside the office, and McDaniel didn't want them hearing the conversation. The chair got down to business. She would step down shortly after the South Carolina primary, which was at the end of the month.

"You did a great job," Trump told her. "I'm going to say nice things about you when it's the right time."

McDaniel left after about three hours. She had assumed the meeting would be kept private, so she was shocked when later that evening the *New York Times* reported, citing anonymous sources, she would be leaving her post. Trump, McDaniel believed, had leaked it himself.

Trump, it turned out, was in a hurry to get his takeover underway. McDaniel was in New York on February 12 when she got a call from Wiles. The former president, Wiles told her, wanted to put out a press release in which he announced he was putting Whatley, Lara Trump, and LaCivita in charge of the RNC. The announcement would make no mention of McDaniel.

McDaniel pleaded with Wiles to wait. There was no need to rush this, she protested. It could wait a few weeks, closer to when she would be making her departure official.

"He's made up his mind," Wiles said.

After the call ended, McDaniel sat in her car. She was about to appear at a get-out-the-vote rally for a Republican congressional candidate on Long Island, whose election was the next day. As the news sunk in, McDaniel realized she was too emotional to go inside. She decided to drive away.

SEVEN:
"A NASTY TITLE"

Trump and a handful of advisers gathered in Mar-a-Lago's library bar to watch Biden's State of the Union address. Unlike the club's open-air patio, which often had a boisterous and party-like atmosphere, the bar—a small mahogany-paneled room just off the lobby area—was quieter and more private. Trump used the space for many of his most important meetings. When VIPs made their pilgrimages to Mar-a-Lago, many of them would find themselves sitting with Trump at one of the circular tables that dotted the room, like supplicants kissing the ring of Don Corleone on his daughter's wedding day.

Things were looking up for Trump, in ways big and small. First, Haley had finally dropped out of the race the day before. Haley's stubborn refusal to withdraw had infuriated Trump. After New Hampshire, Trump had complained in a phone call to a Republican senator that the longer the primary went on, the more campaign cash he would have to blow, and therefore the more likely it was he would lose to Biden. Second, Trump had his plane back in commission. A few weeks earlier, a mechanic had accidentally deployed Trump Force One's inflatable slide while it was parked in Nashville, sending it into the repair shop. Trump was livid when he found out what the hapless mechanic had done.

"He's fucking fired," Trump steamed to aides. "Get him fired now. Have someone walk him off the property."

Now, Trump was at last the presumptive nominee, and the matchup between him and Biden was set. Biden's nationally televised speech that evening represented the start of the general election. It also provided a glimpse into how Biden planned to dissuade voters from supporting Trump—by casting him as a dark, apocalyptic figure who would end the American democratic experiment and use the Oval Office to exact revenge on his political enemies. Biden's address felt like a political rally, and he used the address to savage Trump, whom he did not refer to by name, only as "my predecessor."

"My lifetime has taught me to embrace freedom and democracy. A future based on the core values that have defined America. Honesty. Decency. Dignity. Equality," Biden said. "Now some other people my age see a different story. An American story of resentment, revenge, and retribution. That's not me."[1]

Trump thought Biden performed decently well. The eighty-one-year-old president was facing mounting questions about his advanced age and mental acuity, and Democratic Party chieftains were grumbling it might be time for him to make way for a younger candidate. The president had been looking increasingly frail as his term progressed, and there had been no shortage of elderly lapses and mishaps. But Biden made it through the sixty-seven-minute speech without any big verbal fumbles, and the mainstream media reviews were mostly favorable, with many describing the speech as "fiery," if not a little over-caffeinated.

Trump had taken to privately calling Biden "retarded" and had started to believe the president wouldn't end up running for reelection. Trump wasn't worried about most of the prospective Biden replacements. He dismissed Illinois Governor JB Pritzker as a "fat slob." Vice President Kamala Harris was an "idiot" and a "radical"—although he liked that Harris and her husband, Douglas Emhoff, had been nice to Melania when she attended the funeral of former First Lady Rosalynn Carter, who had died in November the previous year.

One person he had been worried about was California Governor Gavin Newsom. Always fixated on visuals, Trump thought the handsome, hair-gelled governor was "slick" and the future of the Democratic Party. (He was also annoyed that for some reason Sean Hannity kept having him on his show.) But in November, Newsom and DeSantis held a mano-a-mano debate on Fox News, and Trump thought Newsom had bombed. "Ron's an idiot, he doesn't have what it takes. But I thought Newsom would be better," Trump said at the time.

In any case, Biden's speech had, for the time being, extinguished chatter that he would step aside.

As Biden spoke, Trump micromanaged his team's response, dictating to those assembled in the library's makeshift war room Truth Social posts he wanted published in real-time. When Biden brought up revenge, Trump turned to those in the room.

"Listen, everybody," Trump said. "There will be no retribution, there will be no revenge. Wink-wink."

Trump had made the joke before, many times. "There will be no revenge," he had said on the plane one day, his voice dripping with sarcasm. "I will not allow revenge to be part of my White House."

Trump, though, had left little doubt. He wanted to exact revenge on the people who, in his view, had stymied his 2020 reelection campaign and were trying to block him this time. After backing her primary challenger Harriet Hageman back in the midterms, Trump's attacks on Liz Cheney grew increasingly hard-edged. He would say she should "go to jail along with the rest" of the House select committee members that investigated the January 6 attack.[2] He'd also told an interviewer he was open to using the FBI and Department of Justice to go after his detractors, since, he claimed, they had been weaponized against him. "What they've done is they've released the genie out of the box," Trump said.[3]

Trump also went after donors, posting online that anyone who had contributed to Haley would be "permanently barred from the MAGA camp."[4] A-list Republicans who'd waited until late in the primary to endorse Trump were struck from his VP shortlist. Trump could not believe that Sarah Huckabee Sanders, his White House press secretary who was now Arkansas governor, had held off on endorsing him until November, one full year after he announced his candidacy. When she did announce her support, Sanders had wanted Trump to come to *her* turf in Arkansas for the public reveal. Team Trump told her people no. She would have to come to Florida.

Sanders would never be anything more than a staffer in his eyes, Trump complained to allies at Mar-a-Lago the week after he locked up the nomination. And he wouldn't forget what she'd done. "Things will never be the same," he told one aide.

Trump was also continuing his strategy of attempting to oust Republican lawmakers who had defied him. A few weeks

after the State of the Union, Trump endorsed a primary opponent to Dan Newhouse, a Washington State congressman who
had backed his impeachment. He also took to Truth Social to
call for a challenger to Florida congresswoman Laurel Lee, who
had endorsed DeSantis, to "PLEASE STEP FORWARD!"[5] If Trump's
goal was to bend Lee to his will, it worked. Soon after, Lee
attended a high-dollar Trump campaign fundraiser to pay her
respects to Trump.

Publicly, Trump was embracing inflammatory rhetoric sur-
rounding everything from the escalating migrant crisis at the
border to his criminal trials to what would happen if he was
defeated in November. He was painting the election in existential terms, focusing in particular on what he described as the
dire threat of illegal immigrants flooding into the country. Then,
during a rally in Ohio on March 16, Trump said if he lost the
election, it would be a "bloodbath for the country."[6]

The line came during a riff about Trump's plans to impose
tariffs on foreign-made cars, and how a failure to do so would
devastate the US automobile industry. But it played directly into
Biden's playbook. The president was portraying Trump as a pro-
ponent of political violence, and he didn't give a damn about the
context in which the comment was made. It was ammunition.
Two days later, Biden's campaign released an ad interspersing
Trump's "bloodbath" declaration with a clip of him equivocat-
ing when asked about the deadly 2017 white supremacist rally in
Charlottesville. They also included footage of Trump refusing to
disavow violent extremist groups during the 2020 election, and
spotlighted Trump's vow that, if elected, he would pardon the
rioters imprisoned after January 6.

Trump labeled those rioters "hostages," victims of the same
justice system that was chasing him. He often started his rallies

with a recording of "Justice for All" by the J6 Prison Choir, a mash-up of January 6 defendants singing the Star Spangled Banner with Trump reciting the Pledge of Allegiance. Trump aides had ensured that an audio-only version of the song was played. A video version, complete with images of the Capitol being attacked, had been played during a March 2023 event. The lieutenants were infuriated and thought it made Trump look like he partook in the riot. *How the fuck did that video get on the screen?* one of them wondered. The event, it just so happened, had been held in Waco, Texas, which thirty years earlier was the site of a deadly standoff between federal agents and a religious cult—an incident that became a rallying cry for antigovernment extremists.

Trump took pride in the song, and after it reached the top of the digital song sales chart, he showed off a plaque celebrating the hit. Trump didn't just sympathize with the imprisoned rioters; he identified with them. He was convinced that they, too, were being treated unfairly by an unjust legal system. He believed they deserved vengeance, and he wanted to be their voice.

Some Trump allies were growing concerned about the electoral implications of Trump's focus on January 6 and retribution, not to mention his incendiary language. None of it, they worried, would play well with the moderate suburbanites who would hold an outsized role in deciding the election. Lindsey Graham thought Trump had gone to a dark place and believed he should focus on laying out his policy agenda for a second term rather than talking about revenge. During a December interview with Sean Hannity, Trump had been asked whether he would promise to "never abuse power as retribution against anybody." "Except for day one" Trump had responded.[7] According to a Quinnipiac University poll taken after, a majority of voters—53 percent—said they were "concerned" about the "day one" comment.[8]

Graham took his concerns public, telling ABC News later in December he was "worried about 2024," and Trump should focus on outlining what he planned to do in a second term—on immigration among other things—rather than exacting retribution.

"If President Trump puts the vision out," Graham said, "he will win. If he looks back, I think he will lose."[9]

That same month, Trump said at a rally that undocumented immigrants crossing the southern border were "poisoning the blood" of the country.[10] The Biden campaign pounced, saying Trump was "parrot[ing] Adolf Hitler."

There was evidence Trump's strongman-like rhetoric was seeping into the electorate. A mid-December Harvard CAPS/Harris poll found 56 percent of voters thought Trump would act like a dictator in a second term.[11] While campaigning in New Hampshire, aides told Trump his "poisoning the blood" comments were drawing extensive media coverage and some in the press were calling it Hitleresque. Trump pushed back. It's all manufactured outrage, he protested. If it's not this, it will be something else. Plus, he was skeptical Hitler had ever used such a line.

Trump's rhetoric only intensified. In January, Trump attended a Washington court hearing in which his lawyers argued he should be granted immunity from Jack Smith's 2020 election interference case because, as a sitting president at the time, he was engaging in official duties. Speaking to reporters at the Waldorf Astoria hotel after, Trump said there would be "bedlam" if he lost the election because of his criminal indictments. As he was leaving, a reporter asked Trump if he would tell his supporters to not engage in violence. Trump, already on his way out the door, didn't answer.

It blew up. "Trump warns of 'bedlam,' declines to rule out violence after court hearing," blared the *Washington Post*.[12] The

Biden team struck. "President Biden has always been absolutely clear when it comes to this. Political violence has no place whatsoever in America," White House press secretary Karine Jean-Pierre said from the briefing room.[13]

▬

On January 10, Trump was due to hold a town hall with Fox News in Iowa. On the flight there, he chatted with Vince Haley, a White House speechwriter who was now running Trump's policy operation. Those titles understated Haley's influence. The fifty-seven-year-old Haley, a University of Virginia–educated attorney who had a degree in European Union law and spent a few years studying abroad in France and Belgium, was an intellectual force behind the campaign and had a deep understanding of Trump's populist movement. He flew under the radar but had played a major role in helping Trump craft some of his trademark rally lines, including the one about the US becoming a "nation in decline."

Haley was on alert. He had been warning fellow aides on daily conference calls that Democrats were trying to paint Trump as a bloodthirsty strongman. After Trump's appearance at the Waldorf Astoria, it only made sense the Fox moderators would press him.

"Sir, they're going to ask you about violence. They want to get you on violence," Haley told Trump, bringing up the *Washington Post* story. "If you give any equivocation, they'll make it out that you give your supporters a license for violence."

Trump indicated he understood.

The town hall was to be moderated by Bret Baier and Martha MacCallum, prominent anchors who had experience interviewing

Trump. Before taking the stage for a series of questions from the duo and audience members, Trump and his team huddled in a holding room. The lieutenants were still peeved at Fox, whose coverage they continued to find antagonistic, and did not want the former president to do the prime time event. But Trump had a good relationship with Baier—they were golf buddies—and wanted to do a sit-down. That didn't do much to reassure his team. Baier and MacCallum, they knew, had reputations as being tough questioners. They'd almost certainly try to pin him down and ask him things he didn't want to talk about. More concerning was that Trump didn't take prep for the telecast seriously. He'd basically be winging it.

The team was gathered in a small, crowded holding room. About thirty minutes before the town hall was due to start, a senior aide started getting text messages from a person on the inside at Fox. *Holy shit*, the team thought. They were screenshots of all the questions Trump would be asked and the planned follow-ups, down to the exact wording. *Jackpot.* This was like a student getting a peek at the test before the exam started.

The test, it turned out, wouldn't be an easy one. The moderators planned to ask Trump if he would divest from his businesses if he won, and whether the party was taking a risk nominating him given his indictments. As Haley predicted, they would press Trump to disavow political violence and ask him to explain his prediction of "bedlam." There would also be a question about if a Trump White House would be focused on retribution.

Trump was pissed. These questions felt like attacks designed to put him on the defensive. With the questions in hand, Trump huddled with his team and workshopped answers. He knew he wanted to come up with something new on retribution. Trump was annoyed he was getting blasted for his "day one" comment.

Total bullshit, he thought. Everyone was taking it out of context. But he also agreed with his team that the whole thing was becoming a distraction.

A little after 9 p.m. Eastern Time, Trump was called onstage and took a seat opposite Baier and MacCallum. When, thirty-seven minutes in, Baier asked him about revenge, Trump had a ready response.

"I'm not going to have time for retribution," Trump said coolly. "We're going to make this country so successful again, I'm not going to have time for retribution. And remember this, our ultimate retribution is success."

Trump was happy with the line, but it did nothing to change Biden's approach. During the weeks after the State of the Union, the president accelerated his efforts to turn Trump's fixation on revenge into a political weapon. During a campaign event in New York on March 29, Biden hit Trump on everything from his forecast of a "bloodbath" to his promise to pardon the January 6 rioters.

"His focus is on anger and hate, revenge and retribution," Biden said. "Some of the oldest ideas of humankind."[14]

—

Trump was playing defense on another potentially election-deciding issue: abortion.

Biden was savaging Trump for appointing the three conservative Supreme Court justices who tipped the scales to overturn *Roe v. Wade*, the 1973 decision constitutionally protecting abortion rights. Democrats had already made big gains off the decision in the midterms, held just over four months after it was handed down. Now, they were leaning in big. Following the State of the Union, Kamala Harris traveled to Arizona and Nevada as part of a "Fight for Reproductive Freedoms" tour. Biden said at a campaign event that there was "one reason" why *Roe* had been overturned: "Donald Trump."

Trump had reason to be concerned. A late March poll by Fox News showed 59 percent of voters thought abortion should be legal, and 68 percent supported the legalization of the abortion pill mifepristone.[15] Another survey, from NPR/PBS NewsHour/ Marist, revealed 84 percent of voters believed women who got abortions should not be penalized.[16] A third poll, taken a month earlier, from the health policy organization KFF, found voters trusted Biden more than Trump on reproductive policy by a 38 percent to 29 percent margin.[17]

Conservatives had spent nearly four decades fighting to overturn *Roe*. Trump, who had said in the 1990s that he was "very pro-choice," was late to the game and during his first campaign pledged to appoint Supreme Court judges who would follow through on taking down *Roe*. Once in office, he followed through, appointing conservative justices Neil Gorsuch, Brett Kavanaugh, and Amy Coney Barrett, giving conservatives a six to three advantage over liberals on the court. Now that *Roe* had been dismantled, the move wasn't all that popular. Trump had been worried since the moment the Supreme Court announced its decision.

That day, June 24, 2022, Trump had been meeting with Wiles and LaCivita at his Bedminster, New Jersey, club. The group had much to discuss. The midterms were just over four months away, and Trump would be launching his comeback campaign in the not-too-distant future.

LaCivita's iPhone pinged with a news alert. He read it and said: "Congratulations sir. You did what Ronald Reagan couldn't do."

Trump blanched. "Oh, no. They overturned *Roe v. Wade*?"

"Yes sir," LaCivita said.

"I'm going to get blamed for this, aren't I?" Trump asked.

Trump's reaction underscored something fundamental about his approach to politics. At his core—and like the transactional New York political boss he fashioned himself as—Trump cared most about winning. In his first campaign, he embraced the pro-life cause to fire up his base. But now, he told people, the anti-abortion hardliners in his party couldn't win. In the wake of the *Dobbs* decision overturning *Roe*, he would bring it up constantly. There was Pennsylvania governor candidate Doug Mastriano, who said women who violated the six-week abortion ban he proposed should be charged with murder. There was Michigan governor hopeful Tudor Dixon, who opposed abortion for victims of rape and incest. *What was with these people?* "She's going to lose," Trump said of Dixon. And she did. So did Mastriano, and a bunch of other Republican midterm contenders. *You can oppose abortion all you want*, Trump thought. *But if you can't win, what's the point?*

Back during his 2023 speech at the Conservative Political Action Conference, the former president had been planning on mentioning his pro-life credentials, but then took it out. It would be politically dangerous to do so, he believed.

Now, Trump recognized he would need to come out with a definitive position on abortion. For more than two decades, he had waffled on the issue and essentially gotten away with it. No more. Abortion had risen to the center of American politics and he was under immense pressure to blunt Biden's attacks.

Trump would have to walk a seemingly impossible line. Among his supporters were religious conservatives whose marriage of convenience with Trump, a trash-talking Manhattan tabloid fixture, had helped propel Trump to the Oval Office. For them, and for his own ego, he wanted to take credit for the momentous decision. At the same time, he would need to appeal to the more moderate and independent-minded voters who were registering their displeasure with the undoing of *Roe*, including at the voting booth. They were repulsed by the idea of expanding restrictions to abortion access.

In the wake of the *Dobbs* decision, Republican governors clamped down. Ron DeSantis signed legislation outlawing abortions six weeks following conception, and Nebraska Governor Jim Pillen signed a twelve-week ban. But conservatives also wanted federal laws that would expand restrictions nationwide.

Within the upper echelons of the campaign, an early consensus emerged: Trump should just kick it back to the states. To the lieutenants, it was a pretty easy call. For starters, Trump had publicly embraced that position before—after *Roe* was overturned, Trump said the decision "belonged" to the states—and now supporting a national ban would make him look like a typical flip-flopper. Not great for a guy who branded himself as the anti-politician. Second, a number of pro-Trump states had already passed anti-abortion laws since *Dobbs*. Trump would be stepping on them if he backed federal restrictions that differed. Also not great. And then there was the polling. John McLaughlin had been polling Republican primary voters for the past year on abortion, and the results were clear: People wanted to send the issue back to the states.

Trump's top aides told him that was the way to go. Backing a national ban, they said, would be poison.

Wiles and her team felt they were making real progress. But they soon confronted an age-old problem. Outside allies were always trying to influence Trump, and that was very much the case during his first two campaigns and in his White House administration. Now, on the abortion issue, Kellyanne Conway and Lindsey Graham came knocking.

Conway had been the campaign manager for Trump's 2016 campaign and a senior adviser while he'd been in the White House. Kellyanne—or KAC, as she was known throughout Trumpworld—wasn't on the campaign per se, but she still had Trump's ear. Conway owned a prominent polling firm and was a master messenger and a powerful fundraiser with a grassroots following. When Republicans sent out digital fundraising appeals signed by Kellyanne, it was *cha-ching!* And Trump still had a fondness for his former aide. She had a juicy contract with the RNC, with his approval.

When it came to abortion, Kellyanne parted ways with the Wiles- and LaCivita-led apparatus. Conway argued that Trump should embrace a fifteen-week national ban, with exceptions for rape, incest, and the life of mother. In August 2023, Conway had coauthored a *Washington Post* op-ed with Marjorie Dannenfelser, the president of the anti-abortion Susan B. Anthony Pro-Life America, that argued many Republicans had "panicked" after the *Dobbs* decision and "chose to bury their heads in the sand" rather than defining their position and putting Democrats on defense. Republicans, the piece argued, were simply using the "states' rights" line as "an excuse to tape their mouths shut."[18]

Conway was privately encouraging Trump to get on the fifteen-week train and presented him with polling data to make her case. So, too, was Graham, one of the former president's closest Senate allies and informal policy advisers. Graham saw fifteen weeks as a reasonable compromise. He had sponsored similar legislation back in September 2022, calling it "responsible" and "in line" with laws adopted by a number of European countries.[19] The bill went nowhere—Graham's Senate Republican colleagues were pissed he'd introduced a federal ban so close to the midterms and swatted it down—but the South Carolinian stuck with the proposal.[20] He thought it was a winner.

While Trump weighed his options, an urgent matter presented itself. On February 16, the Alabama Supreme Court ruled frozen embryos were children and said destruction of them—accidental or otherwise—could lead to criminal liability. The decision sparked outrage, both in the state and around the country, as people worried that providers would no longer be able to provide them with in vitro fertilization, commonly referred to as IVF.

Republican Alabama Senator Katie Britt looked on with worry. The forty-two-year-old mother of two who was married to a former NFL player and had an All-American Girl sensibility was an avatar for the suburban mom demographic the GOP wanted back. In the days after the decision, Britt's phone lit up with messages from constituents—many of them Republicans—who were freaking out. When she stopped by a restaurant or her son's soccer game, it was more of the same. Britt knew the ruling was a political disaster in the making for her party and it needed to be handled.

The following week, she dialed up Trump. The former president was on his plane with aides when he took the call.

"Mr. President, I'm not sure if you're tracking this, but this is going to be a major issue politically," she told him.

Trump told Britt he understood. After hanging up, Trump turned to his advisers. We need to do something here, he said. They agreed. The group began workshopping a statement for social media, and Trump called Britt back. He went over the wording with her and did some live editing—"I'd rather say this . . . I'd rather say that"—and after about forty minutes, they were done.

The final version left no doubt where Trump stood.

"Like the OVERWHELMING MAJORITY of Americans, including the VAST MAJORITY of Republicans, Conservatives, Christians, and Pro-Life Americans, I strongly support the availability of IVF for couples who are trying to have a precious baby," he posted to Truth Social.[21]

Abortion was also beginning to permeate Trump's nascent vice presidential search. In late February, Trump met at Mar-a-Lago with South Dakota Governor Kristi Noem. The fifty-two-year-old, gun-toting Noem was an obvious contender for the post. She was female, camera-friendly, and a conservative darling. Corey Lewandowski, who was a political aide to Noem after advising Trump's campaign, came to the meeting armed with polling data highlighting the governor's popularity in Midwestern swing states. Trump liked all that, but he also recalled his final meeting with Ronna McDaniel earlier that month, where she had warned him he needed to parse where the VP wannabes were on abortion. Noem, McDaniel had pointed out, hailed from a state with some of the toughest laws, and that could be a problem. Trump thought it was way too extreme that women who were raped, who were victims of incest, or whose lives were endangered by the pregnancy should be forced to have the baby. Not to mention it was a political loser.

Trump pressed Noem.

"Where are you on exceptions?" he asked.

"We don't have exceptions in my state," she said. "But I inherited that. I didn't pass it myself."

Trump came away impressed by Noem but remained concerned about how her state's laws could be used against her by Democrats.

Trump knew the clock was ticking on formulating his position. He had done his research, picking the brain of Ben Carson, a former surgeon who had served in Trump's cabinet, hearing out Conway and Graham, and learning about fetuses and when thumb-sucking starts in the womb. He'd pondered the fifteen-week idea, but kept coming back to the states-based approach. It just seemed to make the most sense politically.

During a flight to Michigan on April 2, Trump huddled with his lieutenants. There was a slide deck they wanted him to review. A few days earlier, Vince Haley had circulated an email to senior staff outlining his argument for why a national ban was political suicide—a move designed to prod along a final decision. Soon after, the presentation took shape.

"How a Nationalized Abortion Policy Will Cost Trump the Election," it was headlined.

"Who made this? Who made this deck?" Trump asked. "Kind of a nasty title."

"We made it, sir," said James Blair, a political adviser who had moved over to the campaign after serving on the pro-Trump MAGA Inc. super PAC. "For your eyes only, sir."

"Okay, my eyes only. Walk me through it."

The deck outlined how if Trump adopted a fifteen-week policy, he would be jeopardizing his prospects in several battleground states. The plan, it said, would effectively increase abortion restrictions in Pennsylvania, Michigan, Wisconsin, and possibly a Nebraska congressional district that awarded a single Electoral College vote. If Biden won each of those, it would be tough to stop him from being reelected.

That clinched it. Trump would be going the states route. He'd made a political decision, one that in his mind gave him the best shot at winning.

"All right, let's go," Trump said. "We've got to get this thing down. We're gonna put this behind us, and we gotta lay out our position."

The plan was to put out a video. Trump sketched out a draft script, then asked Vince Haley to dress it up. Haley drafted about four pages and showed it to the boss. There was a bunch of "We love babies" verbiage in there that Trump didn't like, too much faith stuff. Trump was more comfortable with the concrete than the abstract, more prone to the blunt than the subtle.

With the statement settled, Trump's aides notched a big win, but they knew nothing was set in stone until it was. Upon landing in Michigan, Trump told reporters he would make an announcement the following week on abortion. That meant there would be plenty of time for the fifteen-weekers to lobby Trump.

The lieutenants wanted to shorten the time frame and arranged for Trump to cut the video three days later. In the end, Trump used the four-minute recording to reiterate his support for IVF, accuse Democrats of supporting the post-birth "execution" of babies, and highlight his backing for exceptions. "Now it is up to the states to do the right thing," he said.

Trump's position had been thought through, calibrated, and poll-tested. But it had also opened a rift with Graham. The two were close—but odd—friends. Graham had initially been a Trump critic but over time became a golfing buddy and counseled the former president on any number of things. Trump treated Graham like a little brother and gave him the occasional noogie. Sometimes, he would call Graham onstage at rallies, fully knowing the Beltway creature would get booed by the MAGA fanatics.

Graham had talked to Trump a ton about abortion. But the former president didn't want to give him a heads-up before the video went out. Trump thought Graham was a leaker and would spill it to the press. So Graham found out about it when everyone else did. Graham issued a statement saying he "respectfully disagree[d] with President Trump's statement that abortion is a states' rights issue" and he would continue pushing for a fifteen-week ban.[22]

Trump blew his fuse. *Total bullshit. Why did Lindsey pop off like this?* The boss went on Truth Social and hammered out several scorching posts, including one in which he said he "blame[d]" himself "for Lindsey Graham" because he had endorsed him for reelection.[23] For good measure, Trump put in an ask to an aide.

"Go tell Lindsey we're not friends anymore."

EIGHT:
"FUCK THIS,
WE'RE GOING TO FIGHT"

APRIL 2024

"E. Jean Carroll says I fucked her, Stormy Daniels says I fucked her. But I never fucked them," Trump bellowed to an aide. "Everyone's fucking everybody, but I never fucked any of these people."

That was Trump's refrain throughout the spring, as he dealt with a stinging loss in the Carroll civil case and girded for the Stormy Daniels criminal trial. Publicly and privately, Trump never gave an inch. Nothing had happened with either woman. Period. It was all a sham. A witch hunt. Deny. Deny. Deny.

For all Trump's claims of innocence, the law was bearing down on him. Yes, things were looking good for Trump politically. Polls showed him holding small but consistent leads over Biden in a number of battleground states. But on the legal front, Trump had reason to be worried. The two trials presented existential threats to the former president—one to his financial livelihood, the other to his personal freedom.

Carroll, the New York writer who'd accused Trump of sexually assaulting her in a Bergdorf Goodman changing room back in the 1990s, was draining Trump's bank account. In late January,

Trump was found liable for defaming Carroll and was ordered to fork over $83 million in civil damages. It was the second time Trump had lost to Carroll. In a separate case she brought a year earlier, Trump had been ordered to pay $5 million. *Total BS*, Trump thought. He'd always insisted she was a psycho and said her claims never made sense. "She's not even my physical type," he would say. If he wanted to hook up with Carroll, he cracked to a group of lawmakers, why would he do it in a Fifth Avenue department store? He owned plenty of apartment buildings in the area that he could have taken her to. Trump Tower, after all, was right across the street.

"Fuck this, we're going to fight it," Trump told Boris Epshteyn after getting the news of the $83 million judgment. Trump insisted he was liquid enough to pay, but his financial straits were about to get worse. Later that month, a New York judge fined Trump $355 million in yet another civil case, ruling the Trump Organization had misled borrowers by issuing false financial statements that inflated its assets. The judge threw in close to $100 million in prejudgment interest for good measure. It was a massive blow for Trump, undermining his decades-long image as a Gotham real estate titan and boardroom killer.

In the three other criminal indictments Trump was facing, his delay, delay, delay strategy was working. It was increasingly doubtful any of them would start before the election. The classified documents case in Florida was bogged down in pretrial motions. The start of the January 6 case was delayed after the Supreme Court took up Trump's assertion that as president he had immunity from prosecution. In the Georgia election interference case, Trump's lawyers had moved to get Fulton County District Attorney Fani Willis booted, arguing that her romantic relationship with special prosecutor Nathan Wade constituted a conflict of interest. The ensuing hearings bogged down the case.

Trump's biggest legal migraine, it was clear, was the Stormy Daniels trial. He would essentially be sidelined from the campaign trail while he sat in a dingy Manhattan courtroom. The accompanying media circus would eclipse the campaign. *How could it not?* While the case wasn't about sex per se—Trump was not on trial for allegedly having an affair with Daniels, but for concealing a $130,000 payment to her ahead of the 2016 election to keep her quiet about their alleged July 2006 liaison—there would be no lack of salaciousness. Daniels would be a star witness for the prosecution. So, too, would be Michael Cohen, Trump's bombastic fixer-turned-adversary, who was accusing his former boss of green-lighting the hush money scheme. God knows what they'd dish out on the stand.

The case threatened something central to Trump: his aura of force, power, and control. Whether Trump would remain a free man was out of his hands and in the hands of a judge and jury. It would be humbling.

Trump's inner circle had noticed something different about the boss as of late: He was kind of . . . chill. By Trump's standards, anyway. After presiding over a chaotic White House, he appreciated the calm that Susie Wiles had brought to the campaign and the lack of leaking and backstabbing. He was less imperious toward his staff and more interested in taking in their feedback. He wasn't firing everyone. He was more fatalistic and willing to accept outcomes, even if he didn't like them. He seemed to exhibit a genuine intellectual curiosity about American history. He'd recently consumed a Civil War podcast and was particularly interested in an episode about Gettysburg ("You really need to listen to this," he told Wiles) and was now on a Ronald Reagan kick. He was eight years older than when he first came down the escalator, had been president for four years, and was now on his third campaign. He recognized the things that hadn't worked for him previously and was open to changing them.

But when it came to the courtroom . . . forget about it.

Trump saw court as a battlefield, and he wanted lawyers who did whatever it took to demolish the opposing army. "Where's my Roy Cohn?" Trump would famously ask, referring to the ruthless attorney and fixer who worked for him in the 1970s and 1980s. Now, as the Stormy Daniels trial kicked off, Trump was pressing attorney Todd Blanche to fight, fight, fight. Trump had been calling for Judge Juan Merchan to be recused because his daughter, who Trump once called a "Rabid Trump Hater" on Truth Social, had worked for a Democratic consulting firm. Merchan slapped him with a gag order in response, which was only the latest such warning from the judge. Trump didn't care. He wanted Blanche to join in the assault. He needed him to object more, to savage Cohen—who in 2018 had pleaded guilty to lying to Congress about plans to build a Trump Tower in Moscow—for being a liar. Go harder, Trump prodded Blanche. Lean into it.

The former president wasn't confident about his prospects of winning the case. This, after all, was New York City, and Manhattanites were more likely to spend the weekend at a hipster coffee shop than going to a Trump rally. Jury selection wrapped up on April 18. There would be seven men and five women on the jury, most of them white-collar workers. Trump believed there was nothing to suggest they would give him a fair shake.

Trump still didn't like that he'd been indicted, but he was gradually coming to believe that going to jail wouldn't actually be so bad. Trump saw himself as a martyr, and he believed going to jail would be seen as the ultimate act of defiance. His supporters would rally behind him. Trump believed he could win the presidency if he was behind bars or not.

"I'm willing to do it," Trump would tell aides. "There's nothing that they can do to me that isn't worth it for the country."

A prison joke was in the offing. "You wouldn't want to become some prisoner's girlfriend," one of the lieutenants cracked. Trump was not amused.

If anything, the former president saw the case as a PR battle, one that fit neatly into his argument that he and his supporters were being persecuted by a deep state justice system controlled by the Democratic Party. After an emotionally disturbed man lit himself on fire outside the courthouse, Trump pressed his political team to tell reporters the guy was a supporter who was protesting Trump's plight. That's not true, they told him. Well, do it anyway, Trump insisted. Now, he needed Blanche to step it up.

"You need to put up a fight," Trump said.

Blanche, a former prosecutor for the Southern District of New York, had left his job at the posh New York City firm Cadwalader, Wickersham & Taft to represent Trump. He saw it as his job to fight for his client, but, like the big-law, white-shoe guy he was, he knew there were boundaries he couldn't cross.

The lead prosecutor was a killer. Joshua Steinglass had successfully prosecuted a case against members of the Proud Boys, the extremist group that was involved in the January 6 attack, back in 2019, and three years later won a tax fraud case against the Trump Organization. Now he was in the courtroom, with his big, booming voice and air of authority.

"You guys are going to lose this trial," Trump barked at his lawyers one meeting in mid-April. "You guys are good, but the other guy's really good."

The judge was eviscerating Blanche, turning him into absolute mincemeat. On April 23, the second day of the trial, Merchan ripped Blanche over whether Trump had violated his gag order, and told the lawyer he was "losing all credibility with this court."[1] In Trumpworld, you were either an alpha or a beta. And Blanche was looking like a beta.

Why do I pay these people? Trump thought.

"You've got to be way stronger up there," Trump told Blanche one day.

—

The courtroom was now the campaign trail.

Blanche told the campaign team that Trump needed allies in the room. "It's important that he turns around and is able to see somebody," he said.

It wasn't hard to see why. Every day, the courtroom's benches were filled with prominent media personalities—many of them antagonists of the former president. There was conservative lawyer George Conway, an outspoken Trump basher and the ex-husband of Kellyanne Conway. There was Andrew Weissmann, a former prosecutor who had remade himself into an MSNBC legal analyst after serving on the team led by Robert Mueller to investigate Russia's interference in the 2016 election. Liberal cable news anchor Lawrence O'Donnell made an appearance. Legendary actor and Trump critic Robert De Niro showed up outside the courthouse one day, but got shouted down by the former president's supporters. Trump approved, telling reporters the Oscar-winning actor "got MAGA-d."

To Trump, they were all enemies and haters, people who wanted him locked up. It was one more kick in the groin, one more indignity. He hated sitting there while everyone—the prosecution, the judge, the George Conways—pummeled him. Instead of being in Palm Beach, where his friends lived and where Mar-a-Lago was about to close for the summer, Trump was spending his time in a ratty courtroom in liberal New York. The germophobic ex-president was hostage to the grimy conditions of the fifteenth floor of 100 Centre Street. He couldn't believe the courtroom was in such bad shape. He noted the exposed wiring, the mold, how outdated everything looked. The toilets were stained, and when he opened the bathroom door, he sometimes used a tissue as a protective glove. Other times, he asked his valet Walt Nauta to open the door for him. And he wouldn't stop talking about how goddamn cold it was in there.

"Fuck. Convict me and send me to Rikers already," he joked. "At least they probably have the heat turned on."

Trump's campaign team used a vacant adjacent courtroom as a makeshift operations center. It had two closed circuit TVs that carried a live feed of the trial. There was an L-shaped table with a printer on it, allowing the ever-present Natalie Harp to print things out for the boss. Tables were stacked with copies of the *New York Post*, evidence, and whatever happened to be the lunch choice of the day. Often, it was pizza. They were big orders, enough to feed Trump, the Secret Service detail, and the support staff, with pepperoni and cheese among the usual toppings. After carb loading and spiking their blood sugar during the lunch

break, lower-level aides sometimes fell asleep, their snores rever-
berating off the mahogany walls.

The operations center included a small private room for
Trump, a space that had two bathrooms and a mahogany table
piled with many of Trump's favorite snacks: Starburst candy,
KIND Bars, Oreos, Nutter Butter cookies, water, and Diet Coke.

But most of Trump's time was spent in the courtroom, where
he would sit at the defendant's table four days per week. He found
it numbing. One day, the prosecution played a recording of
Trump discussing the hush money plan with Cohen and
reporters spotted Trump dozing off. While he publicly denied
it—"Contrary to the FAKE NEWS MEDIA, I don't fall asleep during
the Crooked D.A.'s Witch Hunt," he wrote on Truth Social—
privately it was a different story.[2]

"Yeah, that happened," he told aides when they asked him
about it.

Trump groused that too few of his supporters were congre-
gating around the courthouse. He wanted to see the MAGA loyalists out in force, not just some fine-arts-majoring, soy-latte-
sipping Upper West Side Pilates enthusiasts who thought he was
the devil. During a motorcade ride to the courthouse in early
April, Trump complained about the intense security around the
perimeter. If not for that, Trump said, there would be "thousands of people" there.

Trump's aides hatched a plan. Each day, some of them would
join him at the courthouse. Susie Wiles, Chris LaCivita, Jason
Miller, and Steven Cheung would play a part, as would Boris
Epshteyn, Margo Martin, Walt Nauta, and others. It was the
least they could do for the boss.

As the trial got further along, something happened. His
allies started showing up. First it was just one or two, then a few

more, and then it was an avalanche. House members, senators, and former rivals like Vivek Ramaswamy. Buddies like Steve Witkoff showed up, as did JD Vance and North Dakota Governor Doug Burgum, both of whom Trump was considering for his vice presidential pick—and who saw an opportunity to curry favor with him.

Others were there to bend the knee. As the trial reached its fifth week in mid-May, Virginia Congressman Bob Good and South Carolina Congressman Ralph Norman trekked to Manhattan. They had crossed Trump during the primary, with Good endorsing Ron DeSantis and Norman backing Nikki Haley. Now they were there to prove their fealty.

At one point, Trump walked over to Norman while they were in the operations center and asked, "How did your gal do?"

Good chuckled.

"What are you laughing at?" Trump shot back at Good. "How did your guy do?"

Hoots and hollers went up from those in the room.

"You guys are all coming back into the fold," Trump said. "They all do, Mr. President," one Trump ally responded.

———

Some were staying away from the courthouse. Among them: Melania Trump.

Who could blame her? When Stormy Daniels took the stand, prosecutors were bound to ask her about her tryst with Trump, which took place a year and a half after his wedding to Melania and just several months after she had their son, Barron. Melania hadn't said much about the case to her husband's aides in the run-up to the trial, but they didn't have to ask. They knew she wasn't likely to be there. She had been hurt by her husband before. During the final days of the 2016 race, she had been upset about the *Access Hollywood* tape, in which Trump said that "when you're a star . . . you can do anything," including "grab 'em by the pussy." In the wake of that incident, Trump told an ally he was less concerned about the media firestorm than about Melania.

Melania's absence aligned with the low-profile approach the former first lady was taking in the campaign. She had done a few things publicly. She'd attended a fundraiser hosted by billionaire investor John Paulson, headlined an event for the Log Cabin Republicans, a conservative pro-LGBT group, and had voted with Trump ahead of the Florida primary on March 19. But mostly, she had been off the trail. The lieutenants had given Melania a wish list, but she was always choosy about what she would do. She had been focused on caring for her mother, who passed away in January, and on seeing Barron off to New York University in the fall.

Privately, though, Melania was a political force. When Trump returned to his quarters in the evening, she gave him strong opinions that he listened to. Some were stylistic. The ever stoic Slovenian American didn't like when Trump danced at his rallies and thought it looked unpresidential. Some of it was tactical. The former president had yet to post on X since being unbanned by Elon Musk in November and considered sending out his first post at the same moment DeSantis was launching his campaign via an event on the site hosted by its new owner. It would step all over Ron, Trump believed. But Melania put a stop to the idea. If you do that, she said, you'll make it look like you're getting back on the platform just because of Ron. When Wiles talked to Trump on the phone in the evenings, Melania was often right there with him. To her, they felt like three-way calls.

Trump's daughter Ivanka and her husband, Jared Kushner, otherwise known as "Javanka," were also steering clear. After playing a central role in the White House, the couple had decided they were now onto other things. Ivanka had even skipped Trump's campaign launch. Kushner's biggest contribution to the campaign came the previous fall, when he arranged for Trump to do an interview with Univision, a Spanish-language TV network. Trump's aides were glad for Trump to do it. They increasingly believed there was an opportunity to win over Latino voters, many of whom were working class and upset with the way the economy was going.

Politically, Javanka was basically out of the picture. They told people they were focusing on building their $24 million Miami mansion, spending time with their kids after four chaotic years in the White House, and, well, making money. Jared had launched a private equity firm that by the end of 2021 had raised $3 billion—some of it from Saudi Arabia, whose crown prince, Mohammed bin Salman, had developed a close working relationship with Kushner during the Trump White House years. Whatever their reasons, the couple's absence came as a relief to some in the campaign, who believed they had done a disservice to Trump in 2020. Trump didn't have much of an issue with it, either. He privately blamed his son-in-law for many of his missteps in the White House, particularly the First Step Act, a Kushner-backed criminal justice bill that Trump now regretted signing.

"It was Jared's thing, and Jared's a Democrat," Trump would say.

Two Trump family members were a near-constant at the courthouse: Don Jr. and Eric. Don, in particular, had emerged as a lover of the political game and a savvy inside player. He'd been hitting the campaign trail, was raising money, and, under the radar, was helping Senate Republicans with some key races. He'd become close with the men who were increasingly loud supporters of Trump or of his worldview—people like JD Vance and Tucker Carlson. Like Eric, Don Jr. was an outspoken defender of his father, but when it came to the trial, he realized his father didn't stand a chance.

"It's Manhattan," he said privately. "They're going to fuck him."

———

Back in Florida, Tony Fabrizio, Trump's chief pollster and senior strategist, was gauging the trial's political fallout.

Unlike so many others in Trump's orbit, Fabrizio had a reputation as a truth-teller—someone who gave the boss his unvarnished opinion, regardless of whether he wanted to hear it or not. (There were plenty of times Trump *did not* want to hear it. He'd screamed at Fabrizio more than once over the years.)

Fabrizio had spent much of 2020 warning that Trump's perceived mishandling of the coronavirus pandemic was damaging his reelection prospects. Fabrizio had come to recognize COVID-19's impact early. In February 2020, a few weeks before Trump's administration declared a national emergency, Fabrizio had met in Israel with Prime Minister Benjamin Netanyahu, a client of his. At the time, Trump appeared to be in solid political shape, but Netanyahu warned Fabrizio the public health crisis could upend the president's quest for a second term. Pretty soon, Fabrizio realized Netanyahu was right.

Now, Fabrizio wanted to know if the hush money trial could derail Trump. He guessed in the short term it would cost Trump marginally in the polls, but enough to give Biden the lead in a few key states. In April, a few days before the trial opened, he quietly began working on a polling project to survey voter opinions on the case. Each Sunday, Tuesday, and Thursday, he would poll eight hundred people across seven battleground states.

The behind-the-scenes project was a recognition of the fact that while of course the trial would have legal consequences for Trump, it would also have political repercussions. While twelve jurors were deciding whether Trump had orchestrated a hush money payment to a porn actress, it was voters who would be deciding the outcome of the election in just around six months. Would they want a convicted felon in the White House? Or would they not care?

To Fabrizio, the results of his work were surprising. At least so far, the trial was having a negligible impact on the contest, he found. Most voters following the trial had already made up their mind about who they supported. And a majority of undecided voters said the case was politically motivated, perhaps an indication that Trump's attacks on the justice system were working. An acquittal or conviction, Fabrizio's numbers suggested, would do little to alter where the race stood.

The case was still wreaking havoc on Trump's campaign plans. With court in session four days per week, Trump was spending lots of time in New York, time not spent in swing states that would decide the election, like Michigan, Pennsylvania, and Wisconsin. For the duration of the trial, Biden mostly had the battlegrounds to himself.

Team Wiles got creative. They packed Trump's schedule with fundraising lunches and dinners. He met with foreign dignitaries who'd been pining to get face time with the former and potentially future president, including former Japanese Prime

Minister Taro Aso and Polish President Andrzej Duda. They also planned what the lieutenants liked to call "street theater"— impromptu stops Trump would make in the city that would draw loads of media attention.

Transporting a former and potentially future president around one of the busiest cities in the world wasn't simple. At one point, the lieutenants considered having Trump go to Columbia University, which was being roiled by protests following Hamas's deadly October 7, 2023, attack and Israel's military response in Gaza. The idea was to have Trump show solidarity with Jewish students, which would coincide with a broader GOP effort to yoke the anti-Israel protesters to the Democratic Party. The Secret Service scotched the idea, deeming it unsafe. At another point, the campaign considered holding a special graduation ceremony for Columbia's Jewish students. But it would be a massive organizational enterprise, and the Trump team ended up passing.

Trump hated the improvisational stops his aides put on his schedule, but he went along with it anyway. His advisers loved the visuals. After leaving court on April 16, Trump visited a Harlem bodega, where two years earlier a clerk had been arrested after stabbing to death a customer who had attacked him. Trump used the stop to slam Manhattan DA Alvin Bragg as being soft on crime, decry rising lawlessness in blue cities, and throw in a jab at rising prices under Biden.

It was not what Trump wanted to be doing after spending eight hours in a depressing courtroom. But he relished the opportunity to go after Bragg, who had indicted him thirty-four times in the Stormy Daniels case. And it gave Trump—ever the showman—a massive platform, drawing scores of journalists and supporters. "It went well," he said after it was over.

—

By mid-May, the trial was winding down. Over five weeks, the prosecution argued that Trump had falsified business records with an eye toward influencing the election. To make its case that Trump was guilty on all thirty-four counts—one for each alleged falsified record—it produced reams of documents and trotted out twenty witnesses to establish Trump was part of a conspiracy aimed at concealing payments to Daniels to ensure word of their affair didn't become public.

The defense, led by Blanche, tried to argue Trump wasn't involved in the business transactions—though evidence included checks signed by him—and that trying to influence an election was simply what political candidates did. But mainly the team focused on tearing down witnesses.

Merchan took a hard line on Trump, slapping him with ten gag order violations and fining him $1,000 each time. At one point, the judge threatened to jail Trump if he didn't stop posting online about the case.

"The last thing I want to do is to put you in jail," Merchan said on May 6. "You are the former president of the United States, and possibly the next president, as well."[3]

After that, Trump didn't violate the gag order again.

Trump said just before the start that he planned to testify but did not end up going through with it. As the trial drew to a close he kept telling his inner circle he had no chance of being acquitted. Why get up there and get whacked by Steinglass?

"Anything I did in the past, they can bring everything up, and you know what, I've had a great past—but anything," Trump said in a May 22 radio interview.[4]

The case went to the jury on May 29. Blanche said the longer the deliberations went on, the more likely it was there would be a hung jury. That's exactly what the Trump team wanted. An acquittal, they knew, was unlikely. But if there was a hung jury, Bragg would have to decide whether to retry the case, which would be tough given the short window until the election.

The jury went home for the day without a verdict, then came in again the following morning. For the Trump team, it was now a waiting game. Copies of the *New York Post* were stacked on tables. The front page blared "NOTHING TO BRAGG ABOUT," and Trump couldn't get enough of it. He had an assistant get a bunch of copies. The team had pizza from Pie Guy for lunch. Trump was in a good mood, shooting the breeze in his makeshift office with a group that included Blanche, Harp, and Eric. Every hour that went by and closer to 4:30, when the jury was set to be excused, the better it was. Blanche told Epshteyn he might make it to the New York Rangers Stanley Cup playoff game at Madison Square Garden that night. Epshteyn said he might ask his buddy, former Goldman Sachs executive Gary Cohn, to hook him up with a ticket.

The clock struck four, and it looked like deliberations would restart the following day, a Friday. If they could make it to the weekend, Trump's lieutenants believed, they had a shot. Then, all of a sudden, Merchan called everyone into the courtroom. We have a verdict, he said. There were gasps in the audience. *We're fucked*, one member of Trump's entourage thought.

Thirty minutes later, the jury was brought into the room, and their judgment was read.

Count 1: Guilty.

Count 2: Guilty.

Count 3: Guilty.

Count 4: . . .

All thirty-four counts were read out, Trump guilty on each. To his supporters in the room, it felt like they read off 134 counts. His inner circle knew he would be convicted, but hearing it was still shocking.

Trump didn't say much when he left the courtroom. For the first time in history, a former president had been convicted of a felony. After huddling with his team briefly, Trump addressed reporters outside the courtroom. He knew what he wanted to say and didn't need much input.

"We will fight until the end," he said, "and we will win because our country has gone to hell."

Merchan set Trump's sentencing hearing for July 11—two weeks after his debate with Joe Biden.

NINE:
"I DON'T WANT TO KNOCK HIM OUT OF THIS"

JUNE 2024

onald Trump knew he had screwed up his first debate against Joe Biden in 2020. He didn't want to blow it again.

The then-president had been borderline manic during that showdown. Trump—who tested positive for the coronavirus a few days after the debate—repeatedly interrupted Biden, spoke over moderator Chris Wallace, and blew past the time constraints both campaigns had agreed upon. Biden had scored the soundbite of the night when he told Trump: "Will you shut up, man?" Trump performed better in the second debate a month later, but the damage had been done.

With his first debate of the 2024 campaign just weeks away, Trump was thinking back to his missteps four years earlier. He recognized he needed to rein it in this time. Barron, now a teenager, told him he flapped his gums too much last time and needed to let Biden do more of the talking. Trump listened to his son, who was expressing some interest in politics and a willingness to be more public, after being shielded from the cameras during the White House years. When the Stormy Daniels trial was on, Barron had told his father that if the judge didn't let him out of court to attend his high school graduation, Barron would skip the ceremony and go to the trial instead.

"Everyone says I didn't do well in the first debate and I kept interrupting," Trump told his team. "I know how I want to approach it."

The admission provided a window into Trump's mindset. For all his public bombast about the 2020 election, he understood he'd made missteps that cost him the race. Now, he was determined to correct them. A debate redux with Biden—sure to attract tens of millions of viewers—would be a big opportunity. Trump was hungry for it. The former president thought Biden was clearly less sharp than he was four years ago. "Anytime, anywhere, anyplace" was Trump's mantra when it came to scheduling the debate. Biden, however, wouldn't commit. "It depends on his behavior," the president said.

Biden changed his tune in late April, telling radio show host Howard Stern he would be "happy" to debate Trump. Susie Wiles was in a car outside Rockefeller Center in New York when she got the news. This was a surprise. A month earlier, Wiles met Jen O'Malley Dillon, Biden's campaign chair, at the Gridiron Dinner, a stuffy white tie event in Washington where guys wore tails. The low-profile Wiles hated the DC circuit—"I don't want to go to the White House Correspondents' Dinner," she said after getting an invite to the media's prom night party—and had left the Gridiron early. But she'd gotten O'Malley Dillon's phone number, which would now come in handy.

Wiles reached out to O'Malley Dillon and asked for clarification to see if it was true the president was down for a showdown. O'Malley Dillon said that was the case. They agreed to stay in touch.

With his "anytime, anywhere, anyplace" promise, Trump had little leverage in the debate negotiations. He'd basically have to take whatever was presented to him. That came in mid-May, when Chris LaCivita got a call from Christie Johnson, a senior producer for the not-so-Trump-friendly CNN.

"I have a debate proposal for you," Johnson said.

About two hours later, LaCivita, Wiles, and Fabrizio hopped on a conference call with Johnson and Mark Preston, another CNN bigwig. Johnson and Preston went over their proposal. The moderators would be Jake Tapper and Dana Bash. There would be no studio audience (something Trump thrived on but organizers considered a distraction). There would be time limits for responses, and mics would be cut when it was reached (which would make it tougher for Trump to interrupt). The Trump aides had some objections. First, they claimed Tapper was too much of a Trump critic. They were also suspicious about what questions would be asked. LaCivita said Biden would be queried about the issue Trump wanted to talk about (immigration) while Trump would be pressed on the issue he didn't want to talk about (January 6).

"I've seen this fucking play before," LaCivita said.

Well, this is what we think is most fair, the duo from CNN said.

The Trumpers weren't thrilled, but they didn't have much latitude to push back and agreed to the terms. Trump was set for a June 27 face-off with Biden, to take place on CNN's turf in Atlanta. It would be the earliest presidential debate in modern history.

The Trump crew decided they would wage a concerted effort to work the refs. About a week after the call, LaCivita, Wiles, and spokesperson Danielle Alvarez met with CNN executives in New York. LaCivita, always eager to play bad cop, lit them up.

Your coverage sucks, he told them. Your ratings suck. We know we had no leverage in negotiating the terms of the debate, but we don't appreciate how you rammed it down our throat. Tapper couldn't be fair, LaCivita told the CNN executives. (Trump publicly played along with his team's anti-CNN offensive, using interviews and rallies to call Tapper "Fake Tapper," a nickname an aide had suggested to him during a flight on Trump Force One. Privately, though, he predicted Tapper would be fair.) The CNN higher-ups pushed back, arguing their crew was objective and professional. The Trump team left the meeting feeling like they'd accomplished their objective: pressuring CNN to not favor Biden in the debate.

Unlike 2020, when he had a few slapdash sessions in the White House with former New York City Mayor Rudy Giuliani and former New Jersey Governor Chris Christie, Trump took prep seriously this time. Jason Miller and Stephen Miller (not related) led up the effort, which started in earnest in early June. Both were key figures. Jason Miller was a dedicated loyalist, having advised Trump in his 2016 and 2020 campaigns, and even back in 2012, when Trump flirted with running for president. After Trump won the presidency, Jason Miller had initially been tapped to serve as White House communications director, though he withdrew after it emerged he had had an extramarital affair with a fellow Trump campaign staffer that resulted in a son.

But Trump always kept the strategist in the fold. The former president saw Jason Miller as a good-luck charm, because he worked for him when he won in 2016, and Trump trusted him to accurately communicate his MAGA message. Trump also appreciated that Miller—at least some of the time, anyway—was willing to give him unvarnished advice. The fortysomething Washington State native had a long history working for insurgent candidates and had an intuitive feel for the antiestablishment campaign Trump was running.

Stephen Miller, meanwhile, was a major intellectual force behind Trump's hardline stance on immigration. During Trump's White House years, the thirty-eight-year-old senior policy adviser was the architect of Trump's travel ban on Muslim-majority countries and its policy of separating the children of migrants crossing into the country. After Trump left office, Stephen Miller launched a legal organization conceived as a conservative counterpart to the American Civil Liberties Union. Should Trump win, it was all but certain Miller would be a senior figure in his administration and play a major role in shaping his policy agenda.

The Millers set up practice meetings, which Wiles dubbed "policy time," centered on subjects like immigration, the economy, and abortion. Trump, who put his phone away and refused to take breaks, drilled the practice questions over and over. While the Giuliani and Christie sessions were filled with bickering and squawking, these were focused. Still, there was an air of informality. Trump opted against doing a mock debate against a Biden impersonator—something he had done prior to his 2020 debate debacle—and instead chose to have aides lob him questions.

The campaign brought in a host of former Trump officials to help guide the discussions as policy experts, like Tom Homan, former acting director of Immigration and Customs Enforcement, former economic adviser Kevin Hassett, and former US trade representative Robert Lighthizer. Tennessee Senator Bill Hagerty, a foreign affairs hand who'd served as Trump's ambassador to Japan, was involved. So, too, was Missouri Senator Eric Schmitt, a former state attorney general.

When Matt Gaetz got the text from Jason Miller, he boarded the first flight to Palm Beach. Trump had been pissed at Gaetz lately—Trump had endorsed a candidate in a Virginia congressional primary, and Gaetz was supporting a rival candidate, a big no-no in Trump's book—but the congressman was a star when it came to debates. He was great at recommending what retorts Trump could use and how Trump could pivot to a more favorable subject when asked about something he didn't want to talk about. He understood Trump, knowing you had to challenge him without offending him.

Beyond that, the Wiles team tried to keep the circle tight to ward off the possibility of leaks. They didn't want Biden knowing their guy was doing real prep this time around. Cheung even did some misdirection with the press, telling reporters Trump was doing some practice here and there, but nothing serious.

As the debate neared, Trump prepared for what could be the stickiest topic of all: the Capitol riot. Early on the morning of June 23, John McLaughlin sent a few members of the campaign leadership a memo outlining some possible answers Trump could give when questions of democracy came up. McLaughlin suggested Trump say he'd urged supporters to protest "peacefully." If he were asked if he accepted the results of the 2020 election, Trump should dodge by saying "I'm here to talk about this election." And if asked if he would accept the 2024 election outcome, he could give another non-answer: "If it's a free and fair election."

There was also a likelihood Trump would have to address Project 2025, a nearly nine hundred-page book of policy proposals drafted by the conservative Heritage Foundation. Its recommendations included banning pornography, doing away with the Department of Education, and promoting capital punishment, among other things. Democrats had seized on Project 2025 as a means of casting a second Trump presidency as extreme. That former Trump White House officials, like John McEntee and Russ Vought, contributed to the plan, only bolstered their case.

Trump kept insisting he had nothing to do with the enterprise. The problem for him was that the Democrats were gaining traction. The Trump campaign's polling showed voters were expressing familiarity with the proposals. Wiles met privately with Heritage Foundation President Kevin Roberts, and the Wiles-LaCivita tag team released memos assailing the initiative. The campaign's message: Knock it off or we'll come after you.

The debate would present other major challenges. Lieutenants worried Trump would overcorrect. Yes, they believed, Trump should generally avoid interrupting, but that didn't mean he should let up on Biden. Some worried he'd take Biden's bait and end up talking about the trial rather than inflation and immigration, the issues Trump was making the focus of his campaign and where Biden was most vulnerable. There was uniform agreement that moderators wouldn't give Trump a fair shake.

Trump had another worry. Questions about Biden's mental fitness had not abated. In mid-June, a clip circulated of former President Barack Obama guiding the elderly president offstage at a Los Angeles fundraiser. What if he clobbered Biden and forced him out of the race? The White House line was Biden was staying in. But the Democratic National Convention was still two months away, meaning Democrats had time to get a new nominee.

"I've got to be careful how hard I hit him," Trump said during a prep session. "I don't want to knock him out of this."

The assembled team didn't think Trump should alter his approach. Look, Miller told him, you can't let that stop you. You can't control how Biden does. You've got to play to win.

On the afternoon of June 27, Trump boarded his plane en route to Atlanta with the understanding it was a major moment in the race. A good debate would solidify his front runner status. A less-than-impressive performance would put Biden back in the game. Trump was ready, his advisers believed. He'd spent hours preparing. He'd gone over what questions were likely to be asked. He knew what attacks to use, how to pivot, how to play defense when he was being pressed. To drive it home, his advisers handed him a carefully prepared three-page day-of-the-debate memo outlining their suggested pivots and snappy one-liners. "The question isn't whether Joe Biden can make it the next four months—it's whether Biden can make it the next 4 years," read one.

The debate was a few hours away, and the aides knew that even if they felt they had everything locked up, that meant there was, as always, still plenty of time for someone to feed him bad advice.

When they looked at the flight manifest, the aides realized they had a problem. Trump was in a gregarious mood and had allowed a bunch of people onto the flight. Corey Lewandowski, Trump's fiery former campaign manager, would be onboard. So would Paulette Robinette, an adviser to energy bigwig and Trump donor Harold Hamm. (Robinette, who had no real political experience to speak of, was involved in the debate prep but hadn't contributed much.) And of course there was Natalie Harp, sitting in her regular seat a few feet behind the ex-president. Any one of them could get in Trump's ear—or in Natalie's case, slip him an article she'd just printed out from whatever website she'd stumbled upon—and suggest a line that could change the course of the debate.

The Wiles team came up with a plan. They would form a human shield around Trump, blocking anyone who could be a problem. Gaetz, they decided, would sit directly across from Trump. Jason Miller and Stephen Miller sat across the aisle.

Vince Haley, Steven Cheung, Wiles, and policy adviser Ross Worthington were nearby. At one point, Robinette came up to offer an idea but was shooed away.

After landing, Trump and his team got into the motorcade and made their way to the CNN studio, where they did a walk-through of the set. The former president was in TV producer mode, asking the people from CNN all types of questions. What do you know about the lighting and the locations of the camera? The sound? What's the temperature going to be?

Back in the holding room, Trump sat down to watch pre-debate coverage. It was not the most comfortable setting, sparsely decorated with chairs and a desk. The TV could be tuned only to CNN, and the anchors weren't saying great things about Trump. After about fifteen minutes, Trump got agitated and asked if he could watch Fox. An aide went to find an IT guy to change the channel, but he couldn't figure out how. One aide grew antsy. *What if Trump gets psyched out?*

It was almost 9 p.m. Trump did his own makeup and took a call from the mother of a woman who had been killed by an undocumented immigrant—an "Angel Mom," as Trump referred to them—with whom he had been playing phone tag. Walt Nauta steamed the former president's new custom-made Brooks Brothers suit. Trump had long been a Brioni loyalist, but he was warming to the American brand. He'd recently gifted LaCivita a Brooks Brothers shirt, purchased from the chain's Rockefeller Center store. "Chris, the best shirts in the world," Trump wrote in black Sharpie on a Post-it Note. "Enjoy."

Then it was showtime.

Tapper called Biden onstage, and the president shuffled in. Trump couldn't understand why Biden had agreed to come out first. *During a prizefight, the challenger entered the ring first and the champ went second*, the boxing-obsessed Trump thought. *What was going on?*

Tapper directed the first question to Biden. Seconds in, it was clear something wasn't right with the president. Biden sounded raspy and looked pale and lost. Things would only get worse for the president—and better for Trump—as Biden fumbled phrase after phrase. When asked about the national debt, Biden lost his train of thought and said: "Look . . . If . . . We finally beat Medicare." ("Well, he's right, he did beat Medicare," Trump pounced. "He beat it to death.") Talking about abortion, Biden said "there's a lot of young women being raped by their in-laws, by their spouses, their brothers and sisters." He trailed off unintelligibly when talking about immigration, leading Trump to retort, "I really don't know what he said at the end of that sentence. I don't think he knows what he said, either."

Watching on a big-screen TV backstage, the lieutenants couldn't believe their eyes. A wave of jubilation took over the room. Gaetz asked Fabrizio how much Trump would gain in the polls. Three points, Fabrizio said.

"That would be a landslide," Gaetz said.

Fabrizio smiled.

As LaCivita took in the scene, he had a realization. Like others, he had entertained the possibility Biden would withdraw from the race. But now, he thought, it could actually happen. There was no way the president could survive this.

The media began asking "Will Biden drop out?" before the debate was even over. "OPERATION: REPLACE BIDEN," blared the headline of the Drudge Report, a tabloid-style news site. "DEMS SCRAMBLE WITH 100 DAYS TO GO! DEBATE CATASTROPHE."

When he made it back to his holding room, Trump was greeted with a round of applause.

"Did you like that?" he asked the group. He went around the room and shook everyone's hands and thanked them for their help.

Trump and his team were thrilled. Whether Biden dropped out or not, they felt Trump had succeeded in focusing on his central message: that he'd be able to rescue the working class from rampant immigration and economic hardship. Trump had some undisciplined moments—at one point he got into a back-and-forth with Biden about his golf skills—but he was effective in using the pivots, just as he and his team had practiced. When asked about January 6, he responded not by focusing on the violence of the day, but by saying "on January 6th, we had a great border . . . the lowest taxes ever, we had the lowest regulations ever." When abortion came up he managed to again "pivot" back to immigration. After Biden said women had little recourse to deal with pregnancies if they were raped by a family member, Trump responded: "There have been many young women murdered by the same people he allows to come across our border."

Trump managed to land a number of body shots on Biden without losing his mind. He'd followed Barron's advice: Talk less. The exuberant former president told his team he knew it was over after the first few seconds—"If you go back and watch you can see it on my face"—and said the biggest challenge he had was keeping up the momentum for the full ninety minutes.

Still, he couldn't help but wonder about Biden. He was particularly baffled by Biden's out-of-nowhere line about Medicare, he told his team. For months, Trump had been poking fun at Biden's seemingly diminished mental state. But this, he said, was bewildering.

"What was up with that guy?"

TEN:
THE MOST AMERICAN PHOTO

Donald Trump's motorcade snaked toward a private hangar at the Palm Beach International Airport. Trump Force One was fueled up and ready to go. The former president had a rally to get to.

It had been just over two weeks since the debate. In that time, it was Biden—not Trump—who was sucking up all the media's attention for a change. After his debate debacle, the president was facing pressure from within his party to withdraw from the race and make way for another candidate. Who that candidate was didn't really matter to the Democratic bigwigs who wanted Biden gone. They just needed someone else. Biden was fried, they argued, and just couldn't beat Trump. Biden's poll numbers had continued to slide after the debate, and it turned out that sinking Trump through the courtroom wasn't so easy. Trump's sentencing in the hush money case had been postponed until September. And the Supreme Court had ruled that Trump had immunity from some actions he took as president, likely further dragging out Jack Smith's January 6 case. *Delay. Delay. Delay.*

For all the good news, Trump felt slighted. He'd prepared for the debate and had done well, yet the media was ignoring that and focusing on Biden's catastrophe. The lieutenants tried to soothe him. After pro-Trump talking heads went on cable TV and praised the ex-president for his performance, aides clipped their appearances and made sure the boss saw them.

"No one will ever give me credit," Trump said privately.

Trump was about to seize back the attention he craved. The Republican National Convention was the following week in Milwaukee. Trump was planning to use the event to unveil his vice presidential pick, and the press had spent months guessing about who that might be. North Dakota Governor Doug Burgum? Maybe Florida Senator Marco Rubio? Ohio Senator JD Vance? Trump—always the showman—had been stoking the intrigue for months, and he loved toying with the contenders. "Youngkin's pretty good, isn't he?" Trump had asked Rubio one day, referring to Virginia Governor Glenn Youngkin, another prospect.

In terms of drama, Trump's rally that evening in Butler, Pennsylvania, wasn't expected to offer much. It would be like any other MAGA rally. He'd walk onstage to Lee Greenwood's "God Bless the USA" before launching into a speech decrying Biden's handling of inflation and accusing him of allowing immigrants to flow into the country. Butler wasn't far from the Ohio border, and there had been speculation Trump would announce Vance as his VP nominee at the rally. Networks wanted to send a bunch of people in case Trump did a big reveal. But the campaign waved reporters off. Not happening, the campaign said. We'll see you in Milwaukee.

That didn't mean the trip was unimportant. Trump was planning to spend plenty of time in Pennsylvania, a state that could determine the outcome of the election. Trump needed to maximize votes from places like Butler County, which backed him over Biden by a two-to-one margin in 2020. Butler—heavily white, heavily agricultural, heavily conservative—was Trump Country. As Trump Force One took off from Palm Beach International Airport, thousands of fans were already waiting in Butler's ninety-degree heat for him to arrive, some with umbrellas to give them shade from the summer sun. They had a Saturday evening date with the ex-president on the Butler Farm Show Grounds.

Trump's traveling entourage that evening was smaller than usual. Wiles, Cheung, Dan Scavino, Walt Nauta, Margo Martin, and Ross Worthington were among those who boarded the flight, as did more than a half dozen Secret Service agents. The flight to Butler was a quick one, just a couple of hours. During the flight, Trump talked about his looming VP pick, went over his speech, and watched a feed of the rally's kickoff speakers. Senate candidate David McCormick spoke, as did Army veteran Sean Parnell and several members of Congress.

"I'll say it before and I'll say it again," Congressman Dan Meuser said to cheers. "There's nothing like a Trump rally."

When they deplaned at the Pittsburgh International Airport, Trump got into an SUV for the roughly fifty-mile drive to Butler. His aides scattered into other cars. Trump was due to have an interview with conservative writer Salena Zito before taking the stage, and to take some photos—"clicks" as they were known internally—with supporters. But when Trump got to the rally site, he was running late. Not wanting to keep the rally-goers waiting, the campaign told Zito she would do the interview after Trump finished speaking.

After the clicks, Trump made his way to a white tent positioned about thirty feet to the right of the stage which was functioning as an operations center.

"How many people do you think are out there?" Trump, always looking to measure his crowd size, asked Cheung.

"It's actually a pretty big crowd," the aide said. "I would say around thirty thousand to thirty-five thousand."

"I can see it," Trump said. "Probably closer to forty thousand."

"Okay, I'll tell reporters that," Cheung said. "We're all good."

A little after 6 p.m., Trump took the stage to "God Bless the USA." Scavino and aide Margo Martin left the tent to record some video for social media. Worthington stayed back with the teleprompter operator. Cheung hung back in the tent. Wiles was nearby, positioned next to a production unit.

Trump opened by boasting about his "big, big beautiful crowd." A few minutes into the speech, he began talking about how the influx of illegal immigrants had worsened under Biden. "We have millions and millions of people in our country that shouldn't be here, dangerous people. Criminals, we have criminals. We have drug dealers," Trump said. He pointed to a big screen above the stands showing a graph illustrating the spike.

Then there was the sound of a crackle. Then another. Then another.

Cheung, who'd been catching up on unread emails and text messages, thought it was firecrackers. Then he looked at a monitor. Trump was grabbing his ear, and there was blood.

Wiles screamed.

"Everyone get down!"

LaCivita always thought they would try to kill Trump. Who "they" were wasn't clear. But he believed there were ominous, shadowy forces who wanted to take out the former president. LaCivita didn't bring it up with the boss. *Hell no.* That was the job of the Secret Service. But it was something he thought about. LaCivita wasn't alone. During the White House years, Trumpians buzzed about a "deep state" of federal bureaucrats determined to stop him from pursuing his agenda. Now that he was out of office, people like Tucker Carlson worried "they" would assassinate him.

"Are you worried they're going to try to kill you?" Carlson asked Trump point blank in an August 2023 interview on his podcast. "Why wouldn't they try to kill you, honestly?"

It wasn't just the deep state in the minds of the Trumpers. There were also the Iranians. Trump lieutenants, his security encourage, and the former president himself were well aware that Iranian leaders wanted to kill Trump in retaliation for his January 2020 assassination of Iranian military officer Qasem Soleimani. The threat had lingered since Trump left the White House.

There were plenty of reasons for concern for Trump's safety. After Trump left the White House and was ensconced at Mar-a-Lago, aides found his security apparatus lacking. The club was like a fishbowl, crawling with all kinds of visitors from God knows where. People who went to Mar-a-Lago specifically to meet with Trump got wanded by the Secret Service. But others often got in unchecked. And given that Trump many times spent the dinner hour at his open-air patio, someone could simply walk up to him with a gun. After Ye and Nick Fuentes were able to make it through the gates, the looseness of the club's security protocols burst into public view.

As Trump's campaign kicked into gear, the security failures continued—and they weren't limited to Mar-a-Lago. When Trump visited a Washington courthouse on August 3, 2023, for his arraignment in the Capitol riot case, Secret Service and the US Marshals had neglected to shut off the public's access to the elevator Trump was using, leaving him exposed to whoever was in the building. Trump's elevator stopped at each floor, and after the door opened onlookers gawked.

"Holy shit! It's fucking Trump!" one person said.

Total freakshow, an aide with Trump in the elevator thought.

Things weren't better on the five-mile ride back to Reagan National Airport, when police didn't clear the roads for Trump's motorcade. As the black SUVs barreled out of the city and onto the George Washington Memorial Parkway, it was clear there was a problem. Rush-hour drivers had clogged the rain-soaked roads and were weaving in and out of the same lanes as Trump's vehicle. At one point, an accident was averted when a car cut in front of a van transporting the press pool, causing the van's driver to slam the brakes. *Trump could get rammed*, thought one member of Trump's entourage.

Trump had a smaller security detail than when he was in the White House, as was typical for ex-presidents. But Trump was embracing a post-presidential life that was far more public than Barack Obama or George W. Bush before him. The Secret Service was feeling the strain. Later in August, Trump campaigned at the Iowa State Fair. For the Secret Service, it was a nightmare. They had initially planned to have Trump walk down the fair's main street. But they realized it would be clogged with people, many of whom would be only lightly screened by the fair's magnetometers. Iowa was an open-carry state, and who knew what someone might have in their bag. A knife? A gun? A bomb? The campaign eventually settled on a plan where Trump would make three appearances in different locations, each of which would be in a confined space where attendees would be extensively searched. The Iowa trip caused a freak-out within the Secret Service, which stretched to meet the demands.

The Secret Service saw danger whenever Trump threw himself into chaotic environments. During a return visit to Iowa the next month, Trump had visited a frat house, where he checked out a barbecue pit and tossed footballs to the college bros, some of whom were catcalling one of Trump's assistants. The day before, agents had visited the house for a walk-through and discovered dozens of guns inside. You're going to have to lock those away, the agents told the kids. You can't have them around when Trump comes.

After visiting the frat house, Trump was to watch a college football game in a private suite. Rather than taking a more protected route to get to his box, Trump decided to wade through a throng of screaming fans. It was a crazy scene. Students in front of him, behind him, and on the balcony above were screaming at him, flashing him thumbs-up, and chanting "USA! USA!" Trump fed off it and wasn't going to let anyone get in his way. A back-and-forth with his detail ensued.

"I'm going over here," Trump told one of his agents.

"No, sir, we're going here," the agent told Trump, trying in vain to divert him.

"No, I'm going here," Trump said.

Trump, though, loved his Secret Service guys. He'd sometimes invite them to sit with him in the front of the plane to watch combat sports and have the flight attendant serve them dinner and sodas. Sean Curran, Trump's detail lead, had the respect of the Trump team. Curran was a tough, serious dude who didn't seem to smile much—an "OG," in the words of one Trump aide. Trump considered Curran a friend. The two spent countless hours together, from the golf course to the motorcade. Within Trump's inner circle, there were rumors Curran could be in line for a staff job in a future Trump White House.

"We love Sean," Wiles would say.

As the campaign wore on, tensions between the Trump lieu-tenants—and members of his detail—and the Secret Service leadership in Washington began to bubble. The Trump cam-paign and Curran wanted more assets; the threat level surround-ing Trump, they believed, was increasing. But the agency, which had been struggling with staffing shortages, denied some of the requests. As the Republican convention neared, the Trumpians were asking for the perimeter around the site to be expanded, so protesters couldn't get so close to attendees. Secret Service lead-ership in Washington insisted the plan they already had was fine.

LaCivita was at the Trade Hotel in Milwaukee on the evening of July 13, helping to get ready for the convention. It had been a busy few days, and there was still a lot of work to do. LaCivita had just finished editing videos and had Trump's rally playing in the background, though he wasn't fully paying attention. At one point, he got a call from his daughter, Victoria, who was also working on the campaign.

"Dad," she said, "something has happened to the president."

———

The bullets came flying from Trump's right. He pressed his hand to his ear, then looked down at it, like he had been stung by a bee. Trump turned his head to the right at the last moment; had he not, it was likely the bullet would have pierced his skull and almost certainly killed him. As Trump ducked behind the podium, Secret Service agents piled on top of him. Curran came in from Trump's left, throwing himself onto the former president to shield him.

It was chaos. Rally-goers behind Trump—some of whom just moments before were holding placards reading "Joe Biden: You're Fired!"—cowered. The agents were talking to one another, trying to figure out what was next.

"What are we doing? What are we doing?"

"Hold, hold. When you're ready, on you. Move! Move!"

"Hawkeye's here," said one, as a helmeted officer with a submachine gun patrolled the front of the stage.

About forty seconds after the first shot was fired, one of them could be heard saying: "Shooter's down."

"Are we good to move?"

"We're clear! We're clear!"

The agents began lifting Trump up, forming a circle around him.

"Let me get my shoes," Trump said.

Trump's shoes had slipped off during the maelstrom. The former president had as of late been wearing shoes made by the Swiss manufacturer Bally. While the shoes were designed to be tied on, Trump had turned them into slip-ons.

Trump appeared to search for them, and then stood up, looking as if he were in shock. Then, as his agents tried to maneuver him off the stage, he peered out between them at the crowd. He pumped his fist three times and said, "Fight, fight, fight." The audience erupted.

The moment embodied the heart of Trump's comeback campaign and underscored the spirit of his appeal to his diehard fans. For the last twenty months, Trump had cast himself as the fighter who was clawing his way back to power from the forces that, in the minds of him and his supporters, had unjustly taken it away from him. To his backers, Trump was the fighter who was looking to dismantle the system that had failed them.

The detail guided Trump offstage, his typically immaculately sprayed gold hair out of place and his bloodied MAGA hat in hand. Descending the stairs, he wrapped his arms around an agent to his right. The loyal Curran was on his left. Once they got to the bottom, it took the agents another twenty seconds to get Trump into his SUV. Before getting in, he raised his arm once more.

Trump's motorcade set off to Butler Memorial Hospital, eight miles away. The lieutenants had sprinted to the SUVs, but Cheung couldn't find his car. Wiles rolled her window down.

"Just get in my car," she said.

Cheung got in the passenger's seat. Wiles, in the back seat with Scavino, got a call from LaCivita.

"How bad is it?" he asked.

"I just don't know," she said.

After pulling up to the hospital, Wiles, Cheung, Scavino, and Nauta headed for the emergency room. The building was going into lockdown. Secret Service agents had their long guns out; nurses were wheeling patients out of units so they could create a secure wing for Trump. Hospital workers then stretchered the former president through the emergency room doors. Trump's bloody hat, suit jacket, and white collared shirt were off; he was only in an undershirt and suit pants. His shoes, in the end, had been left onstage; they would be retrieved by a production worker and brought to the hospital later in the evening.

"This is going to make some news," Trump told his team.

After doctors took Trump into a room, the Secret Service examined the lieutenants to ensure they weren't wounded. So many texts and calls were coming through, their phones were melting down. Members of the media were already asking if they could land the first interview with Trump. Others were asking what hospital they were at so they could send reporters, cameramen, and photographers to stake it out. Misinformation was flying. One news outlet had reached out to Cheung saying they were going to report that Trump had passed away at the hospital. Cheung, deciding he needed to say something publicly before things got out of hand, hammered out a statement on his phone saying Trump was "fine." After showing it to Wiles and Scavino, he hit Send.

The doctors wheeled Trump out of his room to get a CT scan for a possible concussion. The test came back clean, and Trump wanted the records.

"Can you give me a copy of these?" Trump asked a nurse. "Because I want to make sure I can show reporters that my cognitive function is 100 percent. You can't say the same about Joe Biden."

"We can put it on a CD for you," the nurse said.

"OK," he said. "We'll release that at a later date."

Biden was about to give televised remarks about the shooting. Trump was back in his hospital room, and there was no TV. Cheung pulled up a feed from CNN on his phone and they watched. After the president was done, Trump asked to see some of the pictures that had been taken during the attack. One, from the *New York Times*'s Doug Mills, showed a bullet whizzing by Trump's head. Another, by the Associated Press's Evan Vucci, depicted a bloodied Trump defiantly raising his fist, with the American flag behind him.

"Wow, that's iconic," Trump said. "That's the most American picture I've ever seen."

Before being discharged, Trump was given back his bloodied clothes. ("This is going into the museum," he said.) The Secret Service had a call to make: Where would Trump go next? Investigators were still in the early stages of figuring out what had happened. By this point, law enforcement had IDed a shooter: Thomas Matthew Crooks, a twenty-year-old man from Bethel Park, Pennsylvania. It wasn't yet clear if he was part of a larger plot or what the threat level was. The question now was how to get Trump home safely.

Curran offered three options. First was Bedminster, Trump's New Jersey golf club. But it was summer, and the club was full of people. Mar-a-Lago was another option. But that would be a longer flight, and being in the air for an extended period of time could put him at risk in the event there was a broader conspiracy and someone was looking to shoot the easily identifiable Trump Force One down. Then there was Milwaukee, where Trump was already scheduled to arrive later on Sunday for the start of the convention. While there were plenty of law enforcement assets in the city, officials didn't think it would be sufficiently secured until the following morning. The Secret Service settled on flying back to Bedminster; they would kick out the club's guests that evening before Trump arrived.

Trump and his crew set off for the hour-long drive to the Pittsburgh airport. When they got there, Secret Service officials said they needed time to sweep the plane and make sure someone hadn't shot at it or there wasn't a bomb planted onboard. So Trump, Wiles, Cheung, and Scavino huddled in a conference room at a private terminal and watched Fox News. After an hour, they got on the plane for the flight to Newark. Pizza was served.

By the time Trump pulled up at his cottage in Bedminster, it was after midnight. Jared and Ivanka were waiting for him. After stepping out of his SUV, he gave his daughter a long hug.

Trump had survived an assassination attempt by a mere fraction of an inch. His convention was a day away. And he had thirty-six hours to make one of his biggest decisions yet: Who he would pick for VP.

ELEVEN:
A "NEVER TRUMP" GUY

"What do you think about Maria?"

Maria Bartiromo, an anchor at Fox Business who had embraced the nickname "Money Honey," was a Trump favorite. She'd done numerous softball interviews with him over the years, including his first on-air sit-down following the 2020 election, for which she had given his team a heads-up on her questions ahead of time. She had defended his actions as president and then promoted his false voter fraud conspiracy theories.

Now, Trump was eyeing her as a last-minute contender in his VP search.

Trump was most focused on three men—Doug Burgum, Marco Rubio, and JD Vance—and his team was ready for each of them. It had produced introductory videos for each that could be rolled out when the pick was unveiled. But now he was dead serious about Bartiromo and was making the case for her during the flight to Butler. She was great with the big-donor Wall Street types and she knew how to do TV, Trump told his team. When he asked them what they thought of the idea, they didn't hold back. There was no time to vet Bartiromo, as they had spent months doing with other candidates. Plus, just because Bartiromo could read a script and ask questions didn't mean she could handle the back-and-forth with the media in a presidential campaign.

Wiles put an end to the conversation.

"No, you cannot choose Maria," Wiles said. "She's great, but it's just too late in the process."

Trump's eleventh-hour flirtation with Money Honey revealed just how uncertain he was about whom to select. (Bartiromo wasn't the only Fox personality Trump had floated. Days earlier, he had raised the prospect of picking Fox News anchor Harris Faulkner.) For all Trump's bluster and projection of strength, he could be profoundly indecisive. During the 2016 veepstakes, Trump had wavered over choosing between Chris Christie, Newt Gingrich, and Mike Pence. Now, it was happening all over again. After months of researching, vetting, and interviewing candidates, the convention was nearly here, and Trump still hadn't made up his mind.

Trump recognized the significance of his decision and the role it would play in shaping the future of the Republican Party. The ex-president was limited by the constitution to serving only one more term, and the race to succeed him would start immediately after the election. Whoever he picked would have a head start and his imprimatur of support. Trump was being pulled by opposing wings of the party. On the one side was the GOP establishment pushing Trump to choose a traditional conservative. On the other was a populist-minded, shatter-the-glass insurgency that was looking for Trump to choose one of their own.

———

When he first surveyed the field, Trump had plenty of people to choose from. There were MAGA superstars like Kristi Noem,

Elise Stefanik, and JD Vance. There were the young up-and-comers, like Vivek Ramaswamy and Katie Britt. There were the guys who could help him make inroads with minority voters, like Tim Scott and Florida Congressman Byron Donalds, both of whom were Black, and Rubio, who was Hispanic. He could choose one of the foreign policy hands (Arkansas Senator Tom Cotton or Tennessee Senator Bill Hagerty), the guy who could help him pick off a Democratic state (Virginia Governor Glenn Youngkin), the businessman outsider (Burgum), or the establishment favorite (Nikki Haley).

None of them was perfect, and perfect is what Trump was looking for. Wiles, who was leading the VP search, would joke he wanted a "unicorn"—an "Asian woman who ran a Fortune 500 company with Polish parents."

Youngkin was too tall. Ramaswamy too thirsty. Trump's base hated Haley, who they regarded as a Never Trumper and a neocon (a Trump aide warned if he picked her, Tucker Carlson could launch a third-party campaign against him). South Dakota Senator John Thune had urged Trump to pick Britt, but she had flopped in her nationally televised Republican rebuttal to Biden's State of the Union address. At another point, Trump had gotten a phone call from Steve Wynn, who hyped another Republican senator.

"Mr. President, I want you to take a look at Tom Cotton," Wynn said.

What do you think of JD Vance? Trump asked.

"He's fine, but Tom Cotton has great charisma," Wynn said.

Cotton was an accomplished guy—military veteran, Harvard educated, and an Armed Services Committee member. He was a contender for a cabinet position in a Trump White House. But he wasn't exactly electric, most Republicans would agree.

"Wow. Steve is even more blind than I thought he was if he thinks Tom Cotton has charisma," Trump said after hanging up. (Wynn suffered from retinitis pigmentosa, an incurable eye disease.)

Noem made a lot of sense on the surface: attractive, female and staunchly loyal to Trump. To many in the former president's orbit, she bore similarities to Sarah Palin, the bomb-throwing Tea Partier who was John McCain's running mate in 2008. Noem clearly wanted the job. During a September 2023 rally Trump in South Dakota, Noem allies had constructed a Trump-Noem electronic billboard.

Yet there was a problem. Within Trumpworld, people had long gossiped that Noem had been having a prolonged extramarital affair with Corey Lewandowski. They were together all the time, and Lewandowski followed the governor around like a puppy dog. Trump advisers had seen Lewandowski, who was also married, slap her on the butt. Trump himself was aware of the scuttlebutt. Trump referred to Noem as Lewandowski's "girlfriend," and when the subject came up, he would raise an eyebrow mischievously. (Trump thought Lewandowski, who had also once been rumored to have been involved with Hope Hicks, the former aide in the Trump White House, had game when it came to courting women. Lewandowski, Trump said, knew how to bat out of his league.)

Trump's aides knew if Noem was picked, her relationship with Lewandowski would become one hell of a distraction. It had already become tabloid fodder. On September 15, 2023, the *New York Post* and the *Daily Mail* published separate stories about the alleged involvement, the latter of which included numerous pictures of the two together.[1] Noem would consistently deny any involvement with Lewandowski, and a spokesperson told me "the allegation of an affair is completely false." Then Noem self-immolated. In April, she published a book in which she wrote of shooting her fourteen-month-old dog, Cricket, whom she called "dangerous" and "untrainable" and said she "hated." The revelation set off a firestorm, and Noem was making things worse by defending it. Trump didn't have a dog—in fact, his dislike of canines was well known—but he understood that the idea of bragging about killing a puppy was bonkers.

"That's not good at all," Trump told Don Jr., an avid hunter. "Even you wouldn't kill a dog, and you kill everything."

With Noem et al. out, Trump was narrowing his list.

Doug Burgum had flamed out in the primary. The former software company executive had spent $14 million of his own money but got nowhere in the polls and dropped out before the Iowa caucuses. But Trump saw a lot to like in the North Dakota governor. He thought Burgum had "the look," considered the wealthy sixty-eight-year-old an equal, and perceived the governor as someone who could be a loyal number two.

That became abundantly clear shortly after the New Year, when Burgum, his wife Kathryn, and top political adviser Chip Englander went to Mar-a-Lago to meet with Trump. ("This beautiful couple!" Trump said upon greeting them.) Burgum, who'd withdrawn about a month earlier, offered the former president an unconditional endorsement. Let me know how I can help, he said. I don't need anything in return. The Trump team liked it. Let's announce it in Iowa, as part of our closing message before the caucuses, they said.

Burgum did everything the Trump team asked: TV interviews, rallies, fundraising. Trump took notice. After Burgum campaigned for Trump in the Nevada caucuses in February, Trump invited him onstage for his victory party in Las Vegas. Later in the spring, Trump invited the couple to attend Easter brunch at Mar-a-Lago. Englander joined the Trump campaign as a strategist.

Burgum got his first indication he was in the VP mix on May 17, when he was campaigning for Trump in Minnesota. Wiles—always holding her cards close—cryptically asked the governor if he wanted to participate in a vetting process. Sure, he said. Okay, lawyers will be reaching out, Wiles said.

Then there was Marco Rubio. While the senator wasn't exactly close with Trump, he was seen within the campaign as a powerful communicator who could help Trump expand his reach. But Rubio had a big complication: his residency. Like Trump, Rubio lived in Florida, and there were questions about whether it was constitutional for two candidates on the same ticket to hail from the same state. The campaign had asked several lawyers to look into the issue, and they all came back with the same answer: It's fine; you're on safe ground to pick Rubio. Still, there was a nagging uneasiness that wouldn't go away. If Trump picked Rubio, some in the Trump orbit feared, then Democrats could go to court.

And then there was Vance. The tale of the Trump-Vance bromance was a long and winding one. A venture capitalist who had written *Hillbilly Elegy,* a bestselling memoir about growing up in hardscrabble Appalachia, Vance had been a cable news favorite during the 2016 campaign. TV bookers saw him as someone who could explain the Trump phenomenon. The thing was, he wasn't a Trump supporter himself—not at all. At the time, Vance called himself a "Never Trump guy" and compared Trump to Adolf Hitler.

Then, like so many other Trump critics within the GOP, Vance transformed.

In the spring of 2021, Vance went to Mar-a-Lago to meet the former president. Vance was about to launch a Senate campaign, and he needed to make nice. Trump was always amenable to former detractors who wanted to kiss the ring. Look, Vance told him, we're both populists, we agree on things. Vance didn't stop there. He became friends with Don Jr., was a regular on Tucker Carlson's show, and became tight with MAGA stars like Charlie Kirk. The courtship appeared to be working. Trump warmed to Vance and endorsed him, vaulting him to victory in his Senate race. Vance soon became a go-to on Trump's phone tree. Trump, Vance believed, was like a regular dude who had thoughts about everything—from the party's midterm disaster to the McDonald's McRib sandwich.

But it was Trump's blue-collar instincts, his ability to connect with everyday people, that impressed Vance the most. When the senator joined Trump in rural, sparsely populated East Palestine, Ohio, in the wake of a disastrous train derailment in early 2023, he couldn't believe the response. It was a cold, rainy day, but Trump fans were lined up like their favorite rock star was coming to town. When he and Trump visited a restaurant, people cheered and screamed. Trump was chatting people up, signing hats, and feeding off the energy. *Holy shit, this is awesome*, Vance thought. He'd been around a lot of politicians, but he'd never seen anyone with Trump's touch. Afterward, Vance and Don Jr. told Wiles they believed Trump should do additional retail appearances. The impromptu stops would ultimately become a centerpiece of Trump's campaign.

Trump was just as taken. The then-thirty-nine-year-old Vance was great on TV, Trump believed. He could boil down complicated things and hold his own on unfriendly outlets, and he was a relentless defender of the former president. Vance, unlike scores of Capitol Hill Republicans, didn't nag Trump for favors. Plus, Vance was looking good, Trump noted. He'd been grooming his beard, wearing tailored suits, and losing weight. No more chubby cheeks. (He'd shed the pounds the old-fashioned way, no less: by running, not by using the blockbuster weight-loss drug Ozempic, which Trump had jokingly suggested some of his advisers should use.)

"Look at him; he's a handsome son of a bitch," Trump said.

By mid-2023, rumors were starting to circulate: Vance could be on a Trump ticket. "Look, dude. It's going to come down to three people, and you're going to be one of those three people," Fabrizio, who had also done work for Vance, told the senator.

Vance didn't like it. He still wasn't convinced he was a serious contender, and he didn't want a bunch of stories being published about something that likely wouldn't happen. VP chatter, he thought, wasn't helpful. He called his top political lieutenant, Andy Surabian, who doubled as an adviser to Don Jr. Shut it down, Vance told him. They did the best they could. Then toward the end of the year, Vance's name started appearing in the press's list of potential candidates. When Vance visited Mar-a-Lago, Trump alluded to it.

"Everybody is talking about you. So hot right now," Trump said.

By late January 2024, Vance and his team decided he'd make a go for it. Why not? It was a win-win. If he got picked, great. If he didn't, he'd raise his profile and position himself for a presidential bid down the road. Plus, Vance was feeling good about his prospects—in fact, he thought, he might even be the favorite. He and his team drew up a plan. First, Vance would hit the media circuit and talk up Trump wherever he could—conservative media, liberal media, wherever. He'd also hit the fundraising circuit. Vance, who'd been a mentee of PayPal co-founder Peter Thiel, had deep connections with tech donors. Over the coming months, Vance would launch an aggressive effort to get Silicon Valley bigwigs onboard. Surabian, meanwhile, began a Vance-for-VP shadow campaign and worked to build support for the senator in Trumpworld.

Trump's finalists couldn't be any more different. Vance was a hard-charging populist and isolationist who threw himself into culture wars. Burgum, like Rubio, was more buttoned-down, open to intervention overseas, a conservative in the traditional mold. To the Republican establishment pooh-bahs, that made Burgum a favorite—and a vehicle to stop the Vance renegade freight train.

Burgum's number one fan happened to be the person at the top of the GOP media hierarchy: Rupert Murdoch. After leaning in for DeSantis during the primary, Murdochland was back on the Trump train. While Rupert may not have been the biggest Trump guy, his outlets needed him for business. Trump, meanwhile, wanted Murdoch's acceptance.

That spring, leaders from the Murdoch family–controlled *New York Post*, including editor-in-chief Keith Poole, visited the former president at Trump Tower to smooth things over. Yes sir, we'll do whatever you want, they told him. We're back with you. Trump rubbed it in. You guys have done a 180 since I kicked

DeSantis's ass, he said. Yes sir, now that you're the nominee we're behind you. Before they left, Trump signed some hats for them and handed them some merch.

Going forward, things looked a lot better for Trump in the *Post*, a paper the former Manhattanite cared about. The Trump team worked closely with the tabloid, feeding it stories and suggesting captions to photos and ideas for the cover of the paper, known as the "wood." Just like that, Trump and Murdoch were talking again.

And it was through Trump that Murdoch connected with Burgum. The governor was in New York with Trump for the hush money trial when the former president's phone rang. Trump picked up.

"Hey, Rupert, I'm with Doug," Trump said, before handing the phone over to the governor.

A relationship was born, and in the weeks that followed the Murdoch empire went all-in for the governor. In late June, the editorial page of the *Wall Street Journal*, also owned by the Murdoch family, called Burgum Trump's "best" VP prospect, while savaging Vance as a "political opportunist" for opposing US funding for Ukraine. A few weeks later, the *New York Post* ran an editorial "implor[ing]" Trump to pick Burgum.

The ninety-three-year-old Murdoch, who had just been married for the fifth time, was a man on a mission. In early July, he and Burgum met at the Allen & Company conference, an annual power-vest-filled masters-of-the-universe gathering in Sun Valley, Idaho. Murdoch's theory was that you just had to keep calling Trump. Murdoch was calling so often that once, while talking to Burgum, Trump said: "I have to go, it's Rupert." After wrapping up with Murdoch, Trump buzzed Burgum back. But then Trump said he had to drop off. Why? Well, Rupert was calling again.

—

Thiel had warned Vance earlier in the year that the establishment would mount an effort to stop him, and now it was happening. But Vance had his own backers, people like Don Jr., Tucker Carlson, and Elon Musk. They had one thing in common: They were flamethrowing insurgents who wanted to rid the Republican Party of the establishment.

Musk, the world's richest person, had been a Trump critic during the 2016 campaign. But he had gradually warmed to Trump, as evidenced by his behavior on his platform X, and the two now spoke regularly. Word was circulating through Republican circles that Musk could use his $200 billion-plus fortune to help Trump. He also liked Vance, who, like him, railed against liberal "wokeism." Trump was in New York for a court case one day when he got a call from Musk. The billionaire put on a hard sell.

"You know, Elon really wants JD," Trump told his aides after hanging up.

With time for Trump to make his pick nearing, things got ugly. Silicon Valley venture capitalist David Sacks, a Musk friend who'd also been prodding Trump to pick Vance, took to X to attack Burgum for his support for funding Ukraine. The Burgum forces were also mobilizing. Republican megadonor Ken Griffin, who had deep ties to the party establishment, took a hammer to Vance during a dinner with Trump.

On June 27, presidential debate night, the VP contenders gathered in Atlanta. Everyone was nice to one another, but there

was an undercurrent of cattiness. After attending a fundraiser at
the lavish home of former Senator Kelly Loeffler—complete with
an indoor basketball court that had a glass ceiling and chande-
liers—the group got into a bus together headed for a debate
watch gathering at Georgia Tech. After arriving, aides to the various VP hopefuls noticed Rubio had accidentally tucked his shirt
into his underwear, which was riding above his suit pants. Quiet
snickering ensued.

As the veepstakes neared an end, the pro-Vancers plunged
the knife. Don Jr. handed his dad a Breitbart News article detailing how the Bush dynasty's Karl Rove had called Burgum the
best pick. It was a message Don knew his father would be recep-
tive to. The former president loathed Rove, who he believed did
the bidding for Never Trumpers.

On top of that, Trump had been annoyed when Burgum
indicated to him he wouldn't be interested in a job other than
VP, and he thought Rubio interrupted him too much when they
talked. On the morning of July 13, Vance flew to Mar-a-Lago on
Steve Witkoff's G6 Gulfstream for his de facto job interview.
When it was over Trump stopped short of telling the senator he
was the pick. I like talking to you a lot more than the others,
Trump told him. "I think we're going to be working together
very closely."

Trump appeared close to making his choice, but with his
indecisiveness, nothing was set in stone. Trump was was sitting
alongside Lindsey Graham on the July 14 flight to Milwaukee for
the convention, and the senator was pushing for him to pick
someone other than Vance. He's good on paper, Lindsey said,
but what has he really done? Graham tried to get Lara Trump
onboard, telling her that if Rubio got picked, DeSantis might
appoint her to Rubio's open Senate seat.

It was yet another example of the built-in chaos of Trump-world. While Wiles and LaCivita had established systems that made Trump's campaign far more operational than it was in 2016 and 2020, all it took was for one person to get in Trump's ear to upend their well-laid plans.

The lieutenants steamed. They were exasperated with the process and wanted it over. Wiles had been careful not to take sides in the VP search, but the last thing she wanted was this dragging out any longer. She needed to get people to push back, and pronto. After conveying to the Vance team what had happened on the flight, they rallied the cavalry.

Carlson called once Trump landed in Milwaukee. You gotta go with JD, he said. Trump also got calls from Sacks and Musk. If you pick a mainstream number two, Musk said, it will give the deep state establishment more incentive to try to kill you.

Trump still wasn't certain, and Team Burgum hadn't given up. Another big gun stepped in for the governor: Amazon founder and *Washington Post* owner Jeff Bezos. During a call with Trump, Bezos praised the former president for how he dealt with his assassination attempt and told him Burgum would be a great choice. It was a remarkable moment: Trump and Bezos had feuded for nearly a decade. Now, a few days after Burgum first told Trump that Bezos wanted to speak to him (Burgum also gave Bezos's contact details to Trump's team so they would recognize the number when he called), one of the world's richest men and the former and possibly future president were talking.

The next morning, Trump told Wiles and LaCivita he was mulling things over. The Vance camp again mobilized and got other bold-faced names to call Trump, including Matt Gaetz.

Finally, early that afternoon, Trump made up his mind. It was Vance. The insurgency had won out, dealing a blow to the

Murdoch-led establishment forces that had waged a no-holds-barred effort to stop Vance. The defeated Murdoch would soon be arriving in Milwaukee, where he'd be staying at the same hotel as Carlson, his former Fox News employee who had helped Vance seal the deal.

With delegates about to make their way to the floor of the Fiserv Forum to formally nominate the ticket, time was up. Wiles buzzed Rubio and Burgum to give them the bad news. Trump phoned Vance, but Vance missed the call. After getting word from Wiles that Trump was trying to reach him, Vance rang Trump.

"You missed a very important phone call," Trump joked to Vance. "I'm picking Marco now."

——

Trump walked into Milwaukee like King Kong. He had just survived an assassination attempt, the GOP was rallying around him, and polls were showing him solidly ahead of Biden. The convention would be a four-day party for the seemingly unstoppable former president and would cast him as a figure of brute strength. Trump had invited famed wrestler Hulk Hogan and UFC CEO and president Dana White for prime time speaking slots. Convention-goers were preparing to turn Trump's "Fight, Fight, Fight" declaration into a rallying cry. And Trump's speechwriting team had tossed his planned convention speech and were drafting a new one highlighting his tale of survival.

To make things even sweeter, on the first day of the convention a federal judge had dismissed Jack Smith's classified documents case, ruling that Smith's appointment was unconstitutional. Trump was on quite a roll.

Underscoring Trump's dominance, vanquished Republican rivals like Ron DeSantis and Nikki Haley trekked to Milwaukee to deliver speeches proclaiming their support for Trump. When DeSantis passed by a pair of Trump aides backstage the night of his appearance, the defeated governor averted his eyes. *Punk*, the lieutenants laughed after he had passed.

But there was angst beneath the surface. The Trump team wanted answers about what had happened in Butler, and they found the security in Milwaukee to be inadequate. The day after the shooting, they had asked the Secret Service to put magnetometers at the entrance of the Trade Hotel, where much of Trump's family was staying. The Secret Service declined, saying their blueprint for the week would suffice. Wiles reached out to the White House, which also declined the request.

Tensions flared again when Wiles met with Secret Service Director Kimberly Cheatle, who was also in Milwaukee. Cheatle told Wiles she wanted to put Curran on leave. Curran had been worried the Secret Service's leadership wanted to throw him under the bus, and that's exactly what seemed to be happening. Trump still had confidence in Curran. While he recognized there had been a security failure, he didn't blame Curran for it. Curran was accompanying Trump to the convention, and later in the month he would be going off with his family to their cottage in Nags Head, North Carolina, for a long-ago planned vacation.

Wiles told Cheatle to back off. If you don't, she added, we'll go public.

—

As the convention went on, Trump aides picked up intel from reporters that Biden was about to withdraw. Senior Democrats were making it clear to Biden he had no chance and should allow someone else to step up. Biden dug in, but the pressure was becoming overwhelming, and he was starting to listen. Trump was on a glide path to defeating the damaged president. If he got out, what would Trump's prospects be then? A new opponent, like Kamala Harris or Gretchen Whitmer or Gavin Newsom, would upend the race.

Trump's lieutenants decided he should project an air of unity in his convention speech, an approach they believed would work regardless of who his opponent would be. Trump could use his nationally televised address to capitalize on the goodwill after Butler and attract voters who might not otherwise support him. Over the course of the week, Trump and his team drew up an eleven-page draft speech in which Trump would promise to heal "the discord and division in our society" and would say he was "running to be president for all of America." Shortly before he was to deliver the speech on Thursday evening, excerpts were delivered to major TV outlets so they could preview them on-air.

But when Trump took the stage, his speech was very different from what his team had in mind. Trump, who was wearing a bandage on his right ear, went wildly off-script, delivering a ninety-minute diatribe in which he went after "crazy Nancy Pelosi," talked about the fictional serial killer Hannibal Lecter, and called Democratic Senator Jacky Rosen of Nevada a "total lightweight." While the draft included no mentions of Biden, Trump veered and ripped the president.

Republicans couldn't believe it. What a missed opportunity.

The lieutenants shrugged their shoulders. There was never a guarantee that Trump wouldn't improvise. It was what it was. At the very least, he had used the top of the speech to talk rivetingly about the shooting, which was what people would remember.

As Trump left Milwaukee, it was hard not to feel good about his prospects. With less than four months until the election, you'd much rather be in his position than Biden's.

Trump spent the next few days at Mar-a-Lago. It had been a dizzying week. With the convention, the VP pick, and the shooting behind him, things might now settle down.

Then, on Sunday, everything changed.

TWELVE:
TOUR OF SELF-DESTRUCTION

AUGUST 10, 2024

Trump's plane lurched toward Aspen, Colorado. The ski-resort-dotted town in the Rockies was notoriously dangerous to fly into, with the wind bouncing off the mountains creating choppy air. Today was especially bad. The chartered aircraft—which, unbeknownst to the Trump team, had once been used by the late financier and convicted sex offender Jeffrey Epstein—was pitching uncontrollably, its nose jerking up and down and sideways. The flight was only around an hour long, but it felt like an eternity. *I'm going to die*, one of the lieutenants thought.

The ex-president was usually oblivious to turbulence, but not this time. "You may want to put on your seat belt," he said.

Trump was in a horrific mood. The election was three months away, and he was spending precious time in non-battleground states kissing rich guys' asses. He'd been plenty aggressive about hitting up donors throughout the campaign, but today he had two events on the schedule—one in Jackson, Wyoming, and one in Aspen—and he just didn't feel like it. There was something else gnawing at him. When Trump turned on the TV, he saw tons of Democratic ads, but none for him. Why was he spending all this time fundraising if donor dollars were supposed to fund commercials? What the hell was going on?

Even before that treacherous descent into Aspen, it had been a rough three weeks. Following weeks of pressure, Biden dropped out of the race on July 21 and endorsed Vice President Kamala Harris as his successor. Harris was running a sharp, well-orchestrated campaign and, unlike the elderly Biden, was able to complete a sentence. She wasn't talking up policy so much or detailing what she'd do as president, but that didn't matter. She was running on *vibes*. Harris was holding mega-rallies—taking a page out of the Trump playbook—where she walked out to Beyoncé's hit single "Freedom" and vowed to run with "joy." Pop culture superstars were lining up behind the vice president, like musician Charli XCX, who had gone viral with a tweet calling Harris "brat," a reference to the singer's inescapable summer album. Harris was throwing a party, and Trump had replaced Biden as the dreary old man.

Trump had been jolted. The attack in Butler was only the start. During a conversation with a former aide the day after, Trump said he knew that if the bullet had been a hair closer, his head "would have exploded like a watermelon on live TV."

"I almost died," Trump said. "It was the scariest moment of my life. I've never experienced anything like it."

Since then it had been a whirlwind: the Vance selection, the Milwaukee coronation, followed by the sudden Biden-Harris switcheroo. He was disoriented. He had been on the cusp of returning to the Oval Office, and then, just like that, the race was upended. Within days of her anointment, Harris had caught up with Trump in the same polls that once showed him ahead. Trump wouldn't stop talking about how unfair it all was.

"Can you believe these people?" he would say.

Trump was certain the elites who had always stood in his way were trying to stop him again. First they lined up behind DeSantis. Then, they tried to throw him in the slammer. Now, they had conspired to whack Biden.

In truth, the ever-suspicious Trump had always been wary of prognosticating his victory. During an April dinner with former British Prime Minister David Cameron, Cameron had asked Susie Wiles what she thought Trump's chances were.

"I'm not going to handicap it," she said. "But it's ours to lose, and they're very good."

Trump interjected. "You're so confident," he said, half-jokingly. "You don't know."

Sometimes, the former president would tell the story of a golfer playing for the club championship who had a six-shot lead by the time he hit the thirteenth hole. Then, his wife walked up to watch him play and the guy got distracted. He ended up bogeying the final five holes and lost by a stroke. You never know.

Trump's queasiness was partly due to what transpired in 2020. Trump thought he was going to win that year, egged on by campaign honchos who gave him rosy talk and told him what they thought he wanted to hear. Wiles thought it was malpractice. Running Trump's Florida operation at the time, Wiles would get on Thursday morning conference calls where campaign leaders went through data and presented an overly optimistic case. Wiles wasn't part of the senior national leadership, but she knew it didn't add up. She recalled getting a call from one of the campaign's top Georgia staffers.

"I don't know what to do," the staffer said. "They honestly believe they're going to walk away with Georgia by a four-hundred-thousand-vote margin."

"It's just garbage," Wiles replied.

Sure enough, Trump would end up losing Georgia by nearly twelve thousand votes.

Biden's exit only confirmed Trump's fear that victory would be taken from him. The lieutenants tried to reassure him he was still in solid shape, and Harris's honeymoon would be short-lived. It did little to mollify the pissed-off Trump. To his closest allies, it was clear something was going on with him psychologically, like a switch had been flipped. He would regularly talk about how close he came to dying. One person who was regularly in touch with Trump was convinced he was suffering from post-traumatic stress disorder. Whatever the case, his stress was pouring out and manifesting itself in anger. Trump had for the last year and a half run a disciplined campaign and was—relatively speaking—on message. Now, he was raging.

Soon his private angst spilled out into public. On July 31, Trump was due in Chicago for an interview at the annual gathering of the National Association of Black Journalists. He was ripshit about it.

"Who the fuck put this on my schedule?" Trump asked aides soon after boarding the plane. (Truth was, Trump's aides had told him about the event and he'd okayed it.)

Trump had reason to be concerned. This would be no Sean Hannity interview. He'd be getting tough questions about issues that mattered to Black voters amid his campaign's broader effort to peel Black men in particular away from Democrats. Accusations of racism had dogged Trump since his years in New York real estate and only grew during his campaigns and when he was in the White House. NABJ's decision to platform Trump had prompted a revolt among its members, with the event's co-chair resigning in protest.

"It's going to be a disaster," Trump vented as the plane hurtled toward the Windy City. "This is a complete setup."

Talk turned to who would be moderating the panel. One journalist would be Rachel Scott, a reporter for ABC News who was well regarded among Trump advisers, but Trump had other ideas. "ABC has fucking George Slopadopoulos," he said, using his derisive nickname for the network's Sunday morning show anchor, George Stephanopoulos, a frequent target of his attacks.

"He's feeding her questions."

The next moderator would be Fox News's Harris Faulkner, whom he was fine with, and the third would be Kadia Goba of Semafor, a newly launched digital outlet.

"Sema-what?" Trump said. It's a startup news site, one of the lieutenants explained.

"Why am I talking to someone from a startup news company?" Trump asked. "I've never even heard of them." (Trump had apparently forgotten he had given an interview to Goba at Mar-a-Lago in June.)

Once he arrived at the Hilton Chicago, Trump went into a holding room and had a drink of water. From there, he and his team walked to an area about thirty feet from the stage, where the former president waited to be called out for the interview. And waited. And waited.

"What the fuck is going on?" Trump said after twenty minutes.

A technician approached to say there was an audio issue. After it was fixed, Scott took the stage and told the audience Trump's appearance would be fact-checked in real-time on social media—something the Trump team insisted they hadn't agreed to. Trump was already pissed at the delay, which put him dangerously close to running late for his next event in Harrisburg, Pennsylvania, a key battleground state. Now he was furious.

When Scott finally brought Trump onstage, he was met with near total silence from the crowd. Things went downhill—fast.

"I want to start by addressing the elephant in the room, sir," Scott said. Scott ran through Trump's history with Black people—noting his propagation of the "birther" lie that Barack Obama was not born in the US, making him ineligible for the presidency, his attacks on Black journalists, and his dinner with Nick Fuentes. When Scott was done, she asked, "Why should Black voters trust you?"

Trump unleashed. "For you to start out a question-and-answer period, especially when you're thirty-five minutes late, because you couldn't get your equipment to work, in such a hostile manner I think it a disgrace," he said. Here was Trump as so many Americans remembered him, furious at the situation he found himself in, targeting a journalist personally.

Things did not get better from there. When Scott asked Trump if he thought Harris was "only on the ticket because she is a Black woman," Trump went down a dark hole.

"She was always of Indian heritage. She was only promoting Indian heritage. I didn't know she was Black until a number of years ago when she happened to turn Black and now she wants to be known as Black," Trump said to gasps in the room.

The interview ended awkwardly after about thirty-five minutes, with a smattering of boos. Trump aides knew they had a problem. Once they got back to the motorcade, Trump's team furiously dialed up Black supporters and urged them to praise Trump on X—messages that could then be printed out and shown to the boss. But it did little to stop the firestorm. "Trump attacks Harris's Black identity," blared the headline in the *Washington Post*. Harris pounced. "The American people deserve better," she said.

Trump was steaming. "Who thought this was a good idea?" he said. "Why am I in Chicago? Why did I go to this thing?"

▬

Trump's tour of self-destruction made its next stop three days later. On August 3, Trump boarded his plane en route to Atlanta, hoping to build support in a state that could decide the election. Trump had a complicated relationship with the Republican governor. He had given Brian Kemp a pivotal endorsement during the 2018 midterm election, but their alliance ruptured two years later, when Trump lashed out at him for refusing to overturn Georgia's election result. As part of his midterm retribution campaign, Trump endorsed Kemp's primary challenger in 2022, but the popular governor fended him off.

Now, Trump needed Kemp's help. Polls were showing the race in Georgia neck-and-neck, and Kemp was a political force who laid claim to a formidable voter turnout machine that could propel Trump to victory in the all-important Peach State. Trump, however, wasn't focused on that. Instead, he was fixated on Kemp's wife, Marty, who had said earlier in the year she would write in her husband's name rather than vote for Trump. Trump was also under the impression Kemp wasn't doing enough to combat what he perceived as voter fraud.

On the flight, Trump told the team he planned to use the rally to go after Kemp. He had always thought Kemp owed his position to him and didn't understand why the governor couldn't just be on the team. He also knew it was a good way to get attention.

"You know if I do this, it's going to make news?" Trump said.

LaCivita gently pushed back, reminding Trump his target was Kamala Harris, not Brian Kemp. But you're the boss, LaCivita said.

Wiles tried to get Trump to stand down, as did Cheung. "You don't want to do anything to jeopardize what's going on behind the scenes, because you have to win Georgia, right?" Cheung said, referring to the efforts Kemp's political operation was undertaking to help Trump in the state. "Without winning Georgia, it's pretty hard to get to 270 electoral votes."

Trump appeared to relent. "Eh, I agree," he said. "Maybe I'll just give him a jab here and there."

When Trump took the stage at the Georgia State University Convocation Center later that day, all that went out the window, and he spent ten minutes straight savaging Kemp and his wife. Trump called Kemp "a bad guy," "a very average governor," and foisted upon him a new nickname: "Little Brian." He also tore into Marty Kemp, calling both her and Kemp "disloyal."

Republicans were shocked. Trump had needlessly provoked Kemp, who could make or break his prospects of winning Georgia— and potentially the presidency. The governor fired back, writing on X: "My focus is on winning this November . . . not engaging in petty personal insults, attacking fellow Republicans, or dwelling on the past. You should do the same, Mr. President, and leave my family out of it."

Trump's verbal assault emanated from a familiar figure: Natalie Harp. Ahead of the rally, the Human Printer had handed over articles about Kemp that set the former president off. To Trump's aides, it was more evidence Harp was an agent of chaos. Many of the bad decisions Trump made were tied to her, staffers believed. Alas, there was nothing anyone could do to stop it.

Harp was still unfireable and operated as if she answered to no one in the campaign hierarchy except Trump. She was still bombarding him with text messages and handwritten letters expressing her unyielding loyalty to him.

Harp wasn't the only one causing headaches. Another figure had emerged on the scene who would jolt the campaign machine to its core.

Corey Lewandowski was a Trumpworld lifer. He was Trump's first campaign manager, helping him steamroll through the 2016 primaries. After being fired during that race he became a pro-Trump talking head on cable news. When Trump won, Lewandowski cashed in, opening a consulting firm and publishing a book titled *Let Trump Be Trump*.

Lewandowski had a reputation as a sharp-elbowed, take-no-prisoners alpha male. Those who crossed him would, not so coincidentally, soon thereafter find themselves the subject of unflattering stories in the press. At one point, things got so heated he got into a physical altercation outside the Oval Office with John Kelly, then Trump's chief of staff.[1]

There was something else about Lewandowski: He had a history of allegedly bad behavior toward women. In 2016, he was charged with battery after being accused of jerking the arm of a reporter. (Authorities later dropped the charges.) The following year, a pro-Trump singer filed a police report in which she accused Lewandowski of slapping her butt at the Trump International Hotel in DC. In 2021, a Trump donor pressed charges against Lewandowski, alleging that he made unwanted sexual advances toward her, including touching her butt, bragging about his sexual prowess, and throwing a drink at her. Lewand-owski would later cut a plea deal in the case, in which he agreed to undergo eight hours of impulse control training, serve fifty hours of community service, and pay a $1,000 fine. After the story broke, a Trump spokesperson said Lewandowski had been cut off from the ex-president's orbit.

But after Biden dropped out of the race and was replaced with Harris, Trump made a proposal to his team. "Corey's around. Let's find something for him to do. Let's just get him on the team."

The former president's decision underscored something fundamental about Trumpworld: Those who demonstrated their fealty to him always had a place. Trump had a soft spot for Lewandowski. He liked his aggressiveness, his machismo, his willingness to do *anything* to defend him. Trump loved nothing more than to see people on TV backing him up, and his idea was to bring Lewandowski into the fold as an on-air gabber.

The reaction from Trump's inner circle was unambiguous: not good. He'll shiv us and leave the blade in while we bleed out.

LaCivita understood the concerns about Lewandowski but was willing to accommodate him. He told the team there were things Lewandowski could be helpful with. In fact, he had long thought it was only a matter of time before Trump brought Lewandowski into the campaign. If it was merely as a surrogate, it would cause relatively few headaches. Wiles disagreed but at times deferred to LaCivita. He did the same with her. That was how their relationship worked.

Among those trying to talk the campaign out of it was Paul Manafort, Trump's 2016 campaign chair, who feuded bitterly with Lewandowski—a fight that ultimately led to Lewandowski being pushed out of the campaign. Manafort's message to the Trump team: You'll regret this.

The Wiles crew was already jittery. On August 2, the day before Trump nuked Kemp, Kellyanne Conway had visited Trump at Bedminster. The meeting immediately set off alarms among Trump aides, who believed she was trashing Trump's campaign leadership. When an aide heard about the Conway-Trump tête-à-tête, he alerted Wiles. She was confused. This meeting wasn't on the schedule, Wiles said. *What is Kellyanne doing?* Conway denied she badmouthed the team, but the meeting set off shockwaves. Trump had a long history of summertime campaign shake-ups, and when things were going in the wrong direction, he tended to bring in new blood.

Despite their fears that Lewandowski was the new threat, the Trumpians acquiesced. On August 15, Wiles and LaCivita issued a joint statement announcing that he was back onboard as a senior adviser.

It didn't take long for things to go sideways. Lewandowski wasn't content to flap his gums in a Fox News studio. He was telling people he was the new sheriff in town and was asking for details on how much aides were making. He was calling the campaign's operatives in swing states, demanding to know what their strategies were. At one point, he sat in the lobby of the campaign's West Palm Beach headquarters and kept track of when people were arriving for work. At another, he told Wiles he was taking charge of the budget. She pushed back.

Lewandowski's issues with women were also rearing their head. Aides noticed that shortly after coming aboard, he paraded Kristi Noem through headquarters. To staffers, it felt like he was showing off his woman, and they were uncomfortable witnessing it. (For them, Lewandowski's romantic escapades were the subject of endless bewilderment. At the Republican National Convention a few weeks earlier, he was spotted separately with his wife and Noem. Lewandowski would tell people his wife and Noem were staying in different rooms on the same floor of the same hotel.) The biggest flare-up came when an aide reported to human resources that Lewandowski had been inappropriate toward a female member of the staff. When HR approached the woman about the supposed incident, she said nothing untoward had happened. (It wasn't the first time the campaign faced a disciplinary issue. While in the office one day, a staffer named Derek Silver brought his gun to the office. Soon after, he was let go.)

Despite the woman's denial, it was enough for LaCivita to intervene. Look, he told Lewandowski, I don't know if any of this is true. But people are talking about it, and you need to be aware of it.

It didn't happen, Lewandowski said.

Okay, LaCivita said. Just letting you know.

Trump was desperate to win, but, by late August, the race appeared to be slipping from him. A CBS News poll showed Harris with a three-point national lead over him—a flip from a month earlier, when CBS had Trump with a three-point edge over Biden. Easily the biggest vulnerability for Trump was abortion, an issue Harris was making a centerpiece of her campaign.

Trump was facing a massive gender gap, with women supporting Harris by a twelve-point margin in the CBS poll. Trump worried abortion would cost him the election.

On the morning of August 23, he took to Truth Social to declare: "My Administration will be great for women and their reproductive rights."

WTF? the Trumpers thought. The boss had given no heads-up he planned to put the post out. Abortion was the last thing he should be talking about. Pro–reproductive rights voters wouldn't give him their votes, and by aligning himself with them he was antagonizing abortion opponents. But Trump doubled down. The following week, Trump was asked whether he supported a Florida ballot measure that would allow abortions to take place up to twenty-four weeks post-conception. While he did not indicate explicitly how he planned to vote, he said women should have longer than six weeks, the state's current limit, for getting a procedure.

Abortion foes were on the verge of rebelling. Lila Rose, an outspoken anti-abortion activist, ripped Trump for "trying to sound like a Democrat." The lieutenants told Trump in no uncertain terms: If you piss off them off too much, you'll lose the election.

Then Trump changed course. On August 30, Trump was asked again about the ballot measure. The lieutenants hoped Trump would give an evasive answer that would avoid antagonizing the pro- or anti-abortion forces. But Trump said outright he would oppose it. It was a mess. Trump was being derided in the press as a flip-flopper. Worse, he was furious at what he'd done, believing that by expressing his opposition he was imperiling his prospects.

He got a call from Tony Perkins, a prominent evangelical leader, thanking him for coming out against the Florida measure—which only served to piss Trump off more. "If that nut is calling me and thanking me, I definitely fucked up," he said.

Trump had no one to blame but himself. His fear of losing had resulted in him acting impulsively. He'd hurt himself and he knew it.

As Trump was spiraling, Harris was seizing the moment. There she was in Philadelphia, portraying herself as the tough prosecutor against the convicted felon Trump. At rallies around the country, she cast herself as the fresh face in politics, vowing to enormous crowds "We will not go back." Harris had chosen Minnesota Governor Tim Walz for her vice presidential pick, and he was getting endless attention for calling Trump and Vance "weird."

All the while, Trump's lieutenants were fielding calls from top Republicans wondering what the hell was going on with the campaign. Vance had spoken with his old mentor Peter Thiel, who expressed concern that something was very wrong. Don't worry, Vance told the billionaire. The race has tightened, but we're still ahead.

Trump had never met Harris before, but he knew he didn't like her. He called her a "retard" and talked obsessively about how she shouldn't be in the race. The two would finally meet on September 10, at a debate hosted by ABC News. Trump loathed the network, and his feelings hardened after watching a contentious interview it aired on August 25 with Senator Tom Cotton, a steadfast ally and potential cabinet member. Anchor Jonathan Karl pressed Cotton on Trump's dropping poll numbers, on his statement that he would be "great for women and their reproductive rights," and on how a number of Republicans had spoken out against Trump at the Democratic National Convention held just days earlier. After it was over, Trump called Cotton to vent about the network.

To Trump, it was proof that—especially after his exchange with Rachel Scott in Chicago—ABC would try to embarrass him at the debate.

"You know what, they're going to try that with me," Trump told his team.

The day after the Cotton interview aired, Trump drafted a Truth Social post in which he would announce his withdrawal from the debate and propose holding it on another network. Once again, the lieutenants scrambled. Such a move, they and others like Vance knew, could further damage Trump's prospects, making it seem he was afraid to take on the ascendant vice president. Dealing with the abortion contortions had exhausted the team, and now they were trying to stop Trump from doing something else he would later regret. They bought time, telling him the announcement would dominate the news and overshadow the endorsement he was getting that day from Tulsi Gabbard, a former Democratic Congresswoman and Iraq War veteran who had broken with her party and become a MAGA favorite. Trump saw their point and stood down.

The Trump-Harris showdown was on.

—

Trump had prepped religiously ahead of his June square-off with Biden, but this time he was mad and struggling to pay attention. Trump couldn't stop talking about how unjust the switcheroo was and how he shouldn't have to debate Harris in the first place. She was an idiot, he thought. He still couldn't wrap his head around the whole thing.

"I shouldn't be debating," Trump said. "I beat Biden. They shouldn't be able to swap him out. It's unconstitutional."

Trump was mailing it in. During one prep session in Las Vegas, he rolled in an hour late and then said he didn't want to practice because he had to live-post reactions to Harris's speech at the Democratic National Convention on Truth Social. Trump blew off another practice session at Bedminster, showing up late and saying he wasn't interested. Trump's team had established "contrast points" to use against Harris, but he wasn't absorbing them.

Matt Gaetz, who once again had been brought in to help Trump get ready, saw things going south. This is going to be a train wreck, he told a member of the Trump team.

On the evening of September 10, Trump walked into the National Constitution Center in Philadelphia for his first matchup against Harris. Trump's entourage that evening was sizable, including mainstays like Wiles and LaCivita. There was also Trump attorney Alina Habba, who was increasingly seeking the spotlight and casting herself as an on-air surrogate. Habba, who'd represented Trump in some of his most high-profile civil cases, had drawn the attention of Barstool Sports, the male-oriented pop culture and sports website. One article prominently displayed a picture of her in a bathing suit and said she looked "amazing in a bikini." "Habba Habba," read another. Habba later told people she liked Barstool's coverage of her.

Staff called Trump and Harris to take their places a little after 9 p.m. Harris crossed the stage to shake Trump's hand and introduce herself. Then they took their positions at their podiums.

The lieutenants had warned Trump that Harris would try to bait him, and bait him she did. He fell for it every time. Asked about the Biden administration's policy record, Harris instead goaded Trump into defending his rally crowd sizes. Another bad moment came when he conceded he didn't have a plan to replace Obamacare, saying he only had "concepts of a plan."

Trump spent the debate on the back foot. But the most shocking moment came during a discussion on border security. Immigration was central to Trump's pitch to voters, and a perceived weakness for Harris, who the Trump camp had taken to calling a "border czar" responsible for the spike in crossings that had appeared under the Biden administration. Trump was promising an across-the-board crackdown on immigration, saying he would "carry out the largest domestic deportation operation in American history" and implement an ideological screening process for those looking to enter the country, among other things.

Moderator David Muir pressed Trump on why he had pushed congressional Republicans to kill a border security bill earlier in the year that had garnered rare bipartisan support. Rather than answering the question, Trump turned to a growing online rumor that Haitian immigrants in Springfield, Ohio, were killing residents' pets.

"In Springfield, they're eating the dogs. The people that came in. They're eating the cats. They're eating—they're eating the pets of the people that live there," Trump said.

Trump had thrust an unproven rumor from the dregs of the internet to the national stage. The former president had first read about it on the Federalist, a conservative website, which had published a call a resident had made to a sheriff's department over the issue. Vance had been hearing about the rumors from his Ohio constituents months earlier and, after they went viral, posted on X about it. It was a sensational story saying that Haitian immigrants legally living and working at a small town in Ohio were hunting residents' pets. There was just one problem: Local officials were saying it wasn't true.

Muir jumped in to note that Springfield's city manager had said there had been "no credible reports of specific claims of pets being harmed, injured, or abused by individuals within the immigrant community." It turned into a back-and-forth, with Trump insisting he'd seen people on TV talking about how their dogs were "taken and used for food" and Muir responding, "I'm not taking this from television. I'm taking it from the city manager."

It was a baffling moment. Polls consistently indicated immigration was a point of vulnerability for Harris, with the public believing the White House was doing a poor job of managing the border crisis. Trump had plenty of anecdotes and statistics he could have used to make the case against the vice president. By invoking such a far-fetched—and false—rumor, he gave Harris an opening to cast him as conspiratorial and dangerous.

"Talk about extreme," she said.

Backstage, aides knew things weren't going well. And they were infuriated Muir had fact-checked Trump. They angrily confronted a producer, insisting there had been no agreement the network would engage in fact-checking. LaCivita proposed storming the stage during a commercial break to admonish Muir, but decided against it.

In the days that followed, there was broad agreement in the political punditry that Trump had gotten smoked. The Drudge Report deemed it "The Night Trump Lost It All." Donors were suddenly not returning the campaign's calls. Even some of Trump's closest allies were getting skittish. Mike DeWine, Ohio's Republican governor, who had been born in Springfield, wrote an op-ed saying he was "saddened" by how Trump, Vance "and others continue to repeat claims that lack evidence and disparage the legal migrants living in Springfield."[2]

Trump was determined to campaign in Springfield, and a group of Ohio Republican congressmen—including Max Miller, a former Trump White House aide who had won his seat with Trump's backing—was pleading with Trump and his campaign not to go, arguing it would be a political disaster. Miller, whom

Trump had appointed to serve on the United States Holocaust Memorial Council, was privately infuriated. He was uncomfortable with where the campaign was heading, having privately lobbied Trump against picking Vance for VP. During a private discussion with a fellow Jewish Republican, he likened the attacks on Haitians to the "target[ing]" of Jews.

The lieutenants agreed among themselves a Springfield trip couldn't happen, and they eventually got it killed. As a compromise, they told Trump he would instead campaign in a pair of communities in Wisconsin and Colorado he had also cast as war zones overrun with illegal immigrants. Trump was sated.

While his campaign stewed, Trump was insistent he'd done well in his showdown with Harris. During the flight back from Philadelphia, he vented while watching Fox News, complaining that Bret Baier and Martha MacCallum were wrongly insinuating Harris was the victor.

"They're giving the wrong analysis," he said. "I won that debate."

THIRTEEN:
"SOMETHING'S UP"

SEPTEMBER 15, 2024

Steve Witkoff pulled into the Trump International Golf Club for breakfast with Trump.

It was a warm Sunday in West Palm Beach, with temperatures expected to soar into the nineties. Weather was one of the things that attracted wealthy retirees to the area. That, and golf. Lots and lots of golf. While golf wasn't on Trump's official schedule that day, Witkoff made sure to pack his equipment in the car that morning in case the ex-president called an audible. Witkoff knew how important golf was to Trump. It was how the former president blew off steam, and the two had played countless times during their decades-long friendship. If it was the weekend, there was a good chance Trump and Witkoff would be on the greens of the Trump International, about fifteen minutes down the road from Mar-a-Lago. Steve was well accustomed to making the trip from Miami to tee off with his friend.

Sitting with Trump at the club's grill, Witkoff dug into his plate of bacon and eggs. It was his second breakfast of the day. He had just come from City Diner, a retro-themed restaurant in West Palm Beach, where he'd been with Sean Hannity and had

ordered the same meal. It was a double-bacon-and-eggs kind of
day. After they polished off their platters, Trump indicated that,
sure enough, he wanted to hit the links.

"Do you want to play?" Trump asked.

"One hundred percent," Witkoff said. "I'm getting tired of
losing to you, Mr. President. But I'll give it another go."

Trump had met Witkoff in the mid-1980s, when Witkoff was
working as a New York real estate lawyer. Witkoff would soon
become a bigshot developer himself. As their friendship grew,
they went to Yankees games, had dinners, and, of course, golfed.
Witkoff testified on Trump's behalf in an early 2000s arbitration
dispute over ownership of the General Motors Building in Manhattan, went to Trump's wedding to Melania in 2005, and got to
know Trump's children.

Trump valued Witkoff's loyalty. While other friends had
ditched him after the January 6 Capitol riot, Witkoff didn't. Not
one time did he ask Trump about his actions that day. And unlike
others in Trump's orbit, Witkoff did not want anything from the
former president. He wasn't in search of fame like other Trumpworld figures. During the Republican National Convention, Witkoff delivered a speech in which he called Trump a "true and dear
friend for many, many years in good times and bad times."

While Witkoff did not have an official role in the campaign,
he was a central behind-the-scenes figure. Witkoff sat in on
Trump's debate prep sessions and helped arrange for Teamsters
President Sean O'Brien, his friend, to speak at the convention—a
coup for the former president, who was making a play for working-class voters. It was Witkoff who brokered a sit-down between
Trump and Ron DeSantis after DeSantis dropped out. More
recently, Witkoff had gone to Kiawah Island, South Carolina, to
huddle with Nikki Haley, Trump's former primary rival, in

hopes of achieving a rapprochement. After Trump assailed Brian Kemp, Witkoff flew to Georgia to smooth things over with the governor. Kemp was still flummoxed by Trump's verbal assault, but Witkoff helped bring him along. Soon after, the governor appeared on Sean Hannity's program, proclaiming: "We need to send Donald Trump back to the White House."

Witkoff had become a regular part of Trump's entourage, flying on Trump Force One, sitting in court with the former president, and attending his campaign events. Witkoff would talk of feeling a sense of "obligation" to be there for his friend. Witkoff almost traveled with Trump to Butler, Pennsylvania, for the fateful rally, but ended up spending that day with his mother on Long Island, where he'd rented a house for the weekend. Witkoff would never forget that day. He was grilling steaks outside when someone yelled that Trump had been shot. Witkoff scrambled to find out what happened, sending texts to everyone from Sean Curran to Walt Nauta. He got Melania on the phone soon after and was able to reach Trump later that night, when the former president was on the way back to Bedminster from the hospital.

"I'm not taking calls from anybody, but I'm taking a call from you, Steve," Trump said.

After breakfast, Trump and Witkoff made their way to the first tee. Trump had bought the club in 1999, making it the first of eighteen golf properties he would own. The course spread out across more than two hundred acres and boasted waterfalls, lush palm trees, and immaculately cut greens. It had drawn a number of A-listers over the years, including Tiger Woods, whom Trump played a round with while president-elect in December 2016. Like many golf clubs in the area, Trump's had an air of exclusivity. In 2021, the *Washington Examiner* reported its initiation fee was $350,000.

Trump was the bigger golf obsessive of the two. Golf was everything for Trump, but Steve had other ways of unwinding, like taking long walks or playing gin. Still, they were competitive when they hit the links—they would talk smack, and Witkoff would liken Trump and himself to "two children whose parents told them they can go out and play stickball because they did their homework." That was the case today. By the time they reached the fifth hole, Trump had a one-shot lead over his good friend.

Then there was a crackling sound.

Gunshots.

It was happening again.

—

While Trump and Witkoff were rounding the course, Ryan Wesley Routh was lying in wait. Routh had been camped out in shrubbery across from the sixth hole for the past twelve hours. With him was a SKS semi-automatic 7.62x39mm caliber rifle, with a scope attached and eleven rounds of ammunition. The gun's serial number had been scratched off. He had attached a GoPro camera to a chain-link fence separating him from the course. Inside the black Nissan Xterra he had parked nearby were a passport, two license plates, and six cell phones, one of which contained instructions on how to get to Mexico from West Palm Beach. Routh also had a list of dates tracking Trump's recent and upcoming appearances.[1]

From Routh's vantage point, he would have a clear shot at Trump once he got to the sixth hole. It was not hard to get inside the shrubbery, which had gaps that made it easy for someone to burrow through. With the exception of a few "WARNING! NO

TRESPASSING" signs the Palm Beach County Sheriff's Office had put up, there wasn't much of anything keeping anyone away. Anyone could walk down Summit Boulevard, cross a strip of grass separating the sidewalk from the brush, and take up residence next to the chain-link fence.

Routh had become an outspoken advocate for Ukraine after Russia launched its full-scale invasion in February 2022, claiming to news organizations soon after that he had recruited soldiers for the besieged Ukrainians and had himself fought for the country. "I AM WILLING TO FLY TO KRAKOW AND GO TO THE BORDER OF UKRAINE TO VOLUNTEER AND FIGHT AND DIE," he posted on his X account. He also had developed a hatred for Trump, who spent years cozying up to Vladimir Putin and wavered when it came to support for Ukraine. In 2023, Routh authored a book in which he criticized himself for his past support of the former president and told Iran it was "free to assassinate Trump as well as me for that error in judgment."

As Trump and Witkoff were battling it out on the fifth around 1:30 p.m., a Secret Service agent began patrolling the sixth hole. The agent noticed something—the barrel of a rifle was poking through the fence. Before Routh could take a shot, the officer pulled out their weapon and fired. Routh fled.

Secret Service agents immediately jumped on Trump and led him to the back of a golf cart. As the vehicle sped off toward the clubhouse, Trump looked back at Witkoff and two other friends who were playing with him to make sure they were okay. Witkoff, who had been ten yards away from Trump when the shots rang out, had immediately thought it was a full-on assassination attempt. The real estate developer had plenty of experience with guns, and he knew the sound he heard sure as hell wasn't fireworks. Agents began converging on the sixth hole, and snipers were setting up tripods and pointing them toward where the gunfire had erupted from.

After a few minutes, Trump's guests headed back to the clubhouse's locker room to join the former president. It was locked down. Dozens of Secret Service agents and Palm Beach County sheriff's officers—some wielding machine guns—were packed into the room. Trump called Melania and JD Vance. The ex-president—always eager to play the role of host—asked the chef to cook hot dogs for everyone and hugged his golf partners and asked if they were okay.

"I was one up, Steve. I think that counts as a win," Trump said lightheartedly.

"We didn't finish nine holes," Witkoff said. "You can't count that as a win."

Trump, as was typical, was wondering how the news was playing in the press. He called Steven Cheung to ask about the coverage of the shooting. Cheung didn't know what he was referring to.

"The assassination attempt," Trump said

"There was another assassination attempt?" Cheung asked.

Yep, Trump said. "I was about to putt for birdie, and I couldn't even finish that hole."

Trump had a meeting with House Speaker Mike Johnson and decided to keep it on the books. Routh had been caught after a short manhunt, and before Trump could leave, security personnel did another sweep of the golf course to ensure there wasn't a second shooter. After getting the all-clear, Trump got in his motorcade and jetted back to Mar-a-Lago.

Trump and Johnson had become close allies. After two of Johnson's teenage kids almost drowned at a beach in South Florida in November 2023, just weeks after he had been elected speaker,

Trump had called repeatedly, which had touched Johnson and solidified their relationship.[2] Now Trump was calling for Republicans to shut down the government because he didn't like a spending package making its way through Congress, and Johnson wanted Trump to cool it. The speaker came armed with polling showing a shutdown would cost Republicans dearly in down-ballot races.

After the day's turn of events, though, there wouldn't be much appetite to talk about government spending. Most of the meeting was taken up talking about the shooting.

After Trump left Mar-a-Lago, Witkoff began the seventy-mile trek home to Miami. It had been a long day. Witkoff's girlfriend had on occasion told him to be careful while out with Trump. There were a lot of people who wanted to harm him. But Witkoff and Trump had played golf dozens of times this year alone, and from a security standpoint, it had been uneventful.

No longer.

The Trump team was on edge even before the foiled attack. After Butler, Trump's beloved Mar-a-Lago turned into a fortress. Cameras had been installed. A guard tower had been erected, with snipers standing guard. The street in front of the club had been closed, which had infuriated the locals. The residents of nearby Billionaire's Row on South Ocean Boulevard didn't move there so they would have to deal with inconveniences. Trump was getting complaints from Mar-a-Lago members that the street closure was making it hard to get in. Hell, he didn't like it much, either.

The near-disaster at Trump International kicked things into a totally different gear. Armed security patrolled the campaign's

West Palm Beach headquarters, its entry points guarded by marked police cars. Men wielding machine guns now occupied the back rows of Trump's plane. Trump's motorcade had gotten bigger, and it was escorted by a gunboat when it drove along the Hudson River in New York City late one evening. As Trump's caravan wound through the streets of Chicago, rifle-wielding SWAT guys decked out in Kevlar vests and battle gear stood guard. When Trump's plane flew into Washington, DC, it was accompanied by a pair of helicopters, one on each side.

"Hey, look at that," Trump said as he glanced out the window.

There were more scares. Three days after the incident on the golf course, Trump held a rally on Long Island. On the way there, some nut had gone up to Trump's motorcade and punched a car window before being swarmed by NYPD officers. Then, after Trump wrapped up, the Secret Service warned Chris LaCivita they had picked up intel someone might be looking to shoot up the motorcade on the way back to the airport.

"Don't fucking hang out the window and take photos because you're a fucking target," LaCivita darkly joked to Dan Scavino, Trump's social media guru. Wiles reclined her seat back.

During a trip to Pennsylvania the following week, Secret Service agents noticed a drone was following the motorcade. Officers in one of the cars opened up the moonroof and shot it with an electromagnetic gun, disabling it. Drones had become a big worry.

As for Trump's high-profile on-air supporters, they were starting to wonder if *they* were safe at their own homes. They didn't have the benefit of Secret Service protection. Could they be targeted? LaCivita was at his home in Virginia's Northern

Neck the day of the second assassination attempt getting a security assessment of his home. LaCivita had been getting suspicious packages and threatening phone calls from crazies.

"I was so glad you called," he told one of the callers. "Your mother left her panties at my place. I was hoping you'd come by to pick them up, you piece of shit." (LaCivita's wife didn't like how he handled the calls, and he soon stopped treating the callers the way he would telemarketers.)

Security concerns had thrown a massive wrench into Trump's life. Golf? That was over for now. Trump's favorite weekend activity and principal form of relaxation was deemed too dangerous. Then there was his campaign. Trump relished doing big, flashy events. Now he was forced to do smaller gatherings, many of them inside, with fewer attendees. To do an outdoor rally, Trump would need to be encased in bulletproof glass, but there were limited amounts of the equipment available, and it was heavy and required coordination to transport. Trump got particularly annoyed when the campaign had to cancel events, which happened when they couldn't corral enough Secret Service agents. Wiles was beginning to press the White House for military resources, arguing that the Secret Service was short-staffed and unable to meet the campaign's needs for the final stretch. The White House told Wiles Trump would get everything he needed, but the Trump team felt it wasn't getting enough.

To say the Secret Service was under intense pressure would be an understatement. Part of the blame lay with Trump, who, despite the shootings, remained intent on throwing himself into chaotic environments. On September 28—less than two weeks after the incident at the golf club—Trump attended the marquee Georgia-Alabama college football game. The University of

Alabama's Bryant-Denny Stadium seated one hundred thousand people, and any of them could be a threat. When Trump entered the stadium, it was pure madness. Trump tossed boxes of chicken tenders to fans who were screaming "USA! USA!" At one point, chaos ensued when Katie Britt left the box to get her children. When she returned, the Secret Service pushed back, telling her it was too crowded. She forced her way through anyway.

———

Trump's bitter relationship with America's law enforcement agencies didn't help as his campaign faced threat after threat. He had for years been convinced they were out to get him, from Robert Mueller's investigation to the federal cases against him.

Just before the July convention, Republican National Committee officials were informed by Microsoft that a hacker with ties to the Chinese government had infiltrated the Republican National Committee's email system. Party officials believed the Chinese wanted to find out if the party's platform would express support for Taiwan.

For around three months, the hackers had access to the party's internal discussions.

LaCivita told a small group of senior party officials about the breach in order to prevent it from leaking, worried that publicity would encourage further hacks. Who he didn't tell was the FBI; he thought the campaign could not trust them.

That would be simply the start of the hacking threats the campaign would face.

The morning of July 22, a person using an AOL email address and identifying themselves as "Robert" messaged me promising to provide internal "communications" from the Trump campaign.

Two days later, Robert wrote in broken English that he had "recently gained new accesses and interesting stuff are coming! Stay tuned..."

A few days later, Robert sent a 271-page vetting report the campaign had done on Vance as part of its VP search, and a partial copy of Marco Rubio's vetting file. "If you are interested in JD, dive into the JD Research Dossier. There are many stories and tweets in it!" Robert wrote. "I think this information is worth a good *Politico* piece with your narration. Let me know your thoughts."

In his email, Robert said he also had a "variety of documents from DJT's legal and court documents to internal campaign discussions" but declined to say how he'd obtained them. "I suggest you don't be curious about where I got them from. Any answer to this question, will compromise me and also legally restricts you from publishing them," he wrote.

Politico decided not to publish the documents. The fact the hack occurred, it reasoned, was more newsworthy than the public statements the hack contained.[3]

After *Politico* did not bite, Robert said he would pitch the documents to other outlets. They, too, declined to publish.

On August 10, the Trump campaign confirmed it had been hacked. The FBI immediately launched an investigation, and the Justice Department later announced that it had charged three Iranian men for the intrusion. The Iranians had breached Wiles's computer as well as the computer of Roger Stone. It was an ironic turn of events. Stone—who had long fashioned himself as a dirty trickster—had been caught up in special counsel Robert Mueller's investigation into Russia's hacking of Hillary Clinton's 2016 campaign. When Wiles found out her system had been breached, she was stunned.

The hacking concerns spread from there. LaCivita heard from law enforcement the Iranians were trying to bust into his iPhone. The FBI called Steven Cheung to tell him his device was under intense assault by multiple foreign adversaries. Trump attorney Lindsey Halligan was also targeted. The lieutenants were under siege.

It wasn't just hacking. In July, a Pakistani man who had recently visited Iran was arrested for trying to hire a hitman to kill prominent American officials, including Trump.

Then, after the foiled attack in West Palm Beach, Trump received his gravest warning yet about Iran. Federal officials told him in a briefing that Iran had operatives in the US who had access to surface-to-air missiles. It was stunning. If true, Trump's plane—with its distinctive trump lettering on the side—was an easy target. His security team knew they needed a plan.

They put it into action during a trip soon after the briefing. The Secret Service informed Trump's lieutenants they would be using two separate planes. Trump would fly in Witkoff's jet, while many aides would be using Trump Force One—essentially turning it into a decoy. Trump had frequently made use of Witkoff's Gulfstream G6. The day of the debate with Harris, Witkoff flew his plane thirty minutes to Palm Beach so Trump would have a way to get to Philadelphia in the event Trump Force One broke down. (It got there fine.) But this was totally different. Under the plan, Trump would drive to the airport in one motorcade along one route, and the bulk of his team would use another motorcade along a different route. Wiles would ride with the boss, and LaCivita with the others. Many aides did not find out about the dummy flight scheme until they got on Trump Force One—and realized, after the doors shut, Trump's seat was empty.

"The boss ain't riding with us today," LaCivita informed the aides, many of whom were younger. "We had to put him into another plane. This is nothing but a sort of test for how things may happen in the future."

LaCivita tried to assure them they weren't being used as bait, but some of them didn't buy it. If Iran had agents with weapons that could shoot down the plane, why were they being put onboard? They'd be collateral damage. Natalie Harp was perhaps the most upset about being put in the ghost plane. Afterward she sent Trump a text message complaining she was more important than the other staff members and should have been with him. During the flight, she had wandered into the ex-president's empty bedroom. Staffers were shocked: It was an area of Trump Force One they didn't dare venture into.

The flight was a surreal experience, with gallows humor galore. This was some serious shit, those onboard realized.

Publicly, Trump was defiant. "Fight, fight, fight" had become his campaign mantra.

Privately, he was expressing nervousness about the staging of events and their security. For a long time, he'd boasted at rallies about killing Suleimani. Now, he wasn't talking about it as much. There were also political concerns. What if voters got "assassination fatigue"? Trump asked. Would they want to go through four years of their president being under threat?

Trump wasn't buying into the conspiracy theories floating around some corners of the internet that the deep state had been behind the attempts—people were particularly starting to wonder why investigators were getting nowhere with Crooks, and how the kid had evaded security and managed to get such a clear shot at Trump—but he was starting to ask questions.

"Something's up," Trump said.

■

The Trump team was also dealing with a threat from within.

Since Lewandowski had joined the campaign in mid-August, he'd caused nothing but heartburn. Trump had brought him on to throw bombs on TV and to focus on his home state of New Hampshire. But that wasn't enough for Lewandowski. He was looking to hire staffers and disempower others, pitted departments against one another, and would call junior-level aides into his office and scream at them over seemingly trivial matters. He was attempting to take over spending decisions and launched an audit into how much the campaign's leaders were making, and was claiming to people that he'd been empowered by Trump. If Lewandowski's goal was to intimidate, it was working.

For the Wiles-LaCivita team, it was painful to watch. For the first time since Trump started running for president in 2015, he had a functional, low-drama operation. With a few exceptions, people got along. There wasn't much turnover, and there weren't many leaks. Now, with Lewandowski in the mix, tales of infighting were filtering out of Mar-a-Lago into the press. LaCivita—who initially thought if he welcomed Corey with open arms, he'd be able to control him and make him a constructive member of the team—accepted the blame.

"Boy was I wrong," he told people.

Some of the lieutenants were putting the blame on Trump. Trump liked Lewandowski because he was a fighter, but that blinded him to a cold, hard reality: Not many people really wanted Corey around.

Things finally came to a head in mid-September. During a meeting at the Mar-a-Lago library, LaCivita and Wiles outlined to Trump all the ways Lewandowski had been causing problems and told the boss he faced a choice: It's either us or him.

"Look, we can't run a campaign when somebody is on the inside trying to take it apart," LaCivita said.

It was a turning point. Trump may have liked Lewandowski, but he couldn't lose Wiles and LaCivita, who had been steering the campaign for the past two years, guiding it through the storm of four criminal indictments, the Biden-Harris switcheroo, and two assassination attempts.

While he had accommodated—and even encouraged—chaos during his past campaigns and in his White House, Trump had less appetite for it now. During a flight later in the day, the former president sat down with Wiles, LaCivita, and Lewandowski to settle things once and for all. Wiles and LaCivita are in charge, Trump said. End of discussion. I don't want any fighting. We're one team.

Trump had never shown this degree of loyalty to his team before. When things got rocky during his previous campaigns, Trump dumped his campaign managers during the summer months. Not this time. He was particularly protective of Wiles, who had been with him since the immediate aftermath of January 6 and had rebuilt his political operation from scratch. A few months earlier, Trump had caught word of former Marvel Entertainment executive Ike Perlmutter, one of his closest friends who also happened to know DeSantis, had been talking smack about Wiles. When Trump spotted Perlmutter at Mar-a-Lago, he told him to back off.

Trump's feelings about Wiles further deepened after he won the endorsement of Robert F. Kennedy Jr., scion of the most famous Democratic family in history. Kennedy was running as an independent, having been ostracized by the Democratic Party for his promotion of conspiracy theories and vaccine skepticism, and Trump had long feared he would cut into his vote totals.

Kennedy first spoke to Trump late on the evening of July 13, just hours after the Butler shooting. The call was engineered by Tucker Carlson, a Kennedy ally who shared his distrust of the medical establishment and wanted nothing more than to see the two men join forces. Two days later, Carlson organized a follow-up meeting in Milwaukee. Kennedy mistakenly thought the purpose of the meeting was for Trump to offer him the vice presidency, though he wasn't certain. Regardless, he was about ready to get behind Trump. His candidacy had flamed out, and he was considering announcing his support during the Republican National Convention that week.

At the meeting, he presented a contract to Trump spelling out his terms for an endorsement: If I get behind you, I get a job in your administration. Trump liked the idea of getting Kennedy onboard. This was a Kennedy heir, and to Trump, a baby boomer, that meant something. But he bristled at the notion of signing a contract. No one pushed around Trump. *Ever.* The talks were dead.

Carlson remained determined. He spent a lot of time with Kennedy during the convention in Milwaukee that week, at one point attending an Alcoholics Anonymous meeting with him. Both men spoke openly about their past struggles with addiction, and RFK Jr. was a regular AA-goer.

In early August, Omeed Malik, an investor in Carlson's newly launched media company and a donor to both Trump and Kennedy, co-hosted a fundraiser for the former president in the Hamptons. There, he pulled Trump aside. "If you want Bobby's endorsement, I can make it happen," Malik said. "He just wants some input in your White House."

Both sides agreed to restart conversations, with Wiles taking the lead from Trump's team. The talks culminated in a secret three-and-a-half-hour meeting at Mar-a-Lago on August 12, with Trump, Kennedy, Malik, Wiles, Don Jr., and Amaryllis Fox Kennedy, Robert F. Kennedy Jr.'s daughter-in-law and campaign manager, in attendance.[4] They hammered out the broad strokes of an agreement. Malik had one thing left to do—get Kennedy's family onboard. Malik was particularly focused on his wife, Hollywood actress Cheryl Hines. Hines, who starred in *Curb Your Enthusiasm*, was no fan of Trump. In a family Zoom call, Malik described to her his own past as a Democrat and how he became a Trump backer, and she got onboard. The deal was done.

On August 23, Kennedy announced he was dropping out of the race and endorsing Trump during a joint event in Phoenix. There was some awkwardness—the Trump team had carefully choreographed the rally, but Kennedy missed his cue and joined Trump onstage earlier than he was supposed to. But overall, Trump—who at one point had been so concerned about Kennedy he told his team to "gut" the son of Camelot—was thrilled. The endorsement drowned out the positive coverage Harris was getting from the Democratic National Convention, which had wrapped up a day prior. And, more crucially, it had given Trump a jolt at an otherwise rough moment in his campaign. For the first time since Harris had gotten into the race, Trump had some good news.

"Susie," he said on the way home from Phoenix, "this is all you."

FOURTEEN:
BRAT SUMMER, BRO FALL

OCTOBER 1, 2024

JD Vance and his entourage strode on to the CBS News set in Midtown Manhattan. Studio 45, as it was known, had once broadcast *Inside Edition* and *Inside the NFL*. Tonight, it would be the site of the sole vice presidential debate between Vance and his Democratic counterpart, Tim Walz. The stage was lit with bright LED lights, and adorned with two podiums—in red for Vance, and blue for Walz.

Vice presidential debates, with few exceptions, don't matter. But interest in this one was high. There would be no more presidential debates, and with Harris taking Biden's place, she had less than four months to make her pitch to voters. The public was curious about both men—Vance, a freshman senator and MAGA hero despite years earlier likening Trump to Hitler, and Walz, a former high school social studies teacher, football coach, and self-styled regular dude.

Trump had suffered through a mostly brutal August and September. With a good showing, Vance could staunch the bleeding.

Vance had had a turbulent few months himself. About a week after he was nominated, Democrats began circulating footage from a 2021 TV interview in which Vance ripped Democrats like Kamala Harris and New York Congresswoman Alexandria Ocasio-Cortez as "childless cat ladies" who wanted to make the country "miserable."[1]

It wasn't a one-off. Vance, who'd done a lot of long-form interviews over the years, was an opposition researcher's dream. A lot of past controversial remarks he'd made about women in particular were working their way through the news stream. In 2021, he said that "You have women that think that truly, the liberationist path is to spend ninety hours a week working in a cubicle at McKinsey instead of starting a family and having children."[2] The same year, Vance said if teachers' union leader Randi Weingarten "wants to brainwash and destroy the minds of children, she should have some of her own and leave ours the hell alone."[3]

But the cat lady remarks went viral in a way the others didn't. Pop icon Taylor Swift described herself as a "childless cat lady" in her written endorsement of Harris. Actress Jennifer Aniston weighed in, saying she couldn't "believe this is coming from a potential VP of the United States."[4] Meghan McCain, the daughter of former Republican presidential candidate John McCain, said Vance's comments had "caused real pain" while activating "women across all sides, including my most conservative Trump supporting friends."[5]

Vance was getting pulverized in the press. "JD Vance's 'Cat Ladies' Riff Has Serious Handmaid's Tale Vibes," blared a *New York Times* opinion piece.[6] Liberals weren't the only ones getting in on the action. Some of the negative coverage was fueled by Republicans blowing up reporters' phones with anonymous anti-Vance quotes. There were plenty of people in the party who were against him, from the establishment folks who'd tried to block his nomination to the neocons who hated his noninterventionist foreign policy.

And then there were the Republicans who wanted to run in 2028. Vance, after all, had become the presumptive front runner in the next Republican primary. Here was a golden opportunity to kneecap him. Before long, questions began to circulate about whether Trump had regretted picking Vance and whether he would boot him from the ticket. Trump's GOP allies were bedwetting. Former House Speaker Newt Gingrich, an informal Trump adviser who had long been skeptical of Vance, reached out to the campaign to express his concerns about Cat Lady Gate.

The hits kept coming. Emails Vance had sent to an old friend emerged in which he said he "hate[s] the police." He got heat for saying people who don't have children should pay a higher tax rate than those who do. Then, in July, an X user claimed Vance had written in his *Hillbilly Elegy* memoir that he'd had intercourse with a couch. That, of course, wasn't true; anyone could crack open the book and see for themselves. But the false rumor spread like wildfire and became the stuff of countless memes. Google searches for "JD Vance couch" exploded.[7] Vance was annoyed at the bizarre idea he'd engaged in furniture-fucking. But Vance's rival was jumping on it. "I can't wait to debate the guy . . . that is, if he's willing to get off the couch and show up," Walz said at a rally.

"It's not even in the fucking book," Vance complained to an aide. "What are they talking about?"

Trump was standing by his man. By now, he had developed a relationship with Vance, trusted him, and despite his rocky start continued to think he was a great political athlete. The lieutenants were also all-in. It didn't hurt that Vance had plenty of allies on Trump's team—including Don Jr., his foremost supporter and the guy who played the biggest role in getting him picked. The idea that Trump would throw Vance overboard—it just wouldn't happen. Dining with donors one evening, Trump called the forty-year-old Vance the future of the MAGA movement.

"Don't let them get you down. They're a bunch of scumbags," Trump told Vance. "They give it to me. They're giving it to you. Just fight."

Vance wasn't the type to freak out. If anything, he was a cool-headed political operator. During his 2022 Senate race, he'd surprised Tony Fabrizio, who was polling for Vance's political operation at the time, by asking if he could examine the raw data for a survey he'd conducted. Fabrizio had been polling for decades, and he'd never had a client ask for that. Vance spent much of the night poring over the numbers, then got back to Fabrizio the next day and told him his conclusions were solid. Ever since, he'd been obsessive about reading through polls, understanding the crosstabs, getting into the nitty-gritty of the numbers. While Vance was a political newcomer, he knew the game better than senators who'd been at it a lot longer.

Still, Vance was startled by the incoming fire he was now facing, and he was beginning to worry it would hurt Trump's prospects.

Vance and his political adviser Andy Surabian hatched a plan. Vance had to go on offense. They discussed which podcast he could go on to discuss the cat lady remarks, considering Don Jr.'s show but agreeing it would be a little too testosterone-heavy for the subject at hand. They instead went for Megyn Kelly.

Kelly had a complex history with Trump—she famously tangled with him at a 2015 Republican primary debate, where she confronted him over how he'd insulted women and afterward he set off a firestorm when he said she had "blood coming out of her eyes" and "her wherever." Recently, however, she'd become a pro-Trumper. Vance would address the comments and then reset by casting himself as a policy attack dog and cutting up Harris over her record, especially on immigration, an issue that was the cornerstone of the MAGA movement. Trump's attacks on Harris, they reasoned, focused on her character. That's just what Trump did. The wonkish Vance, meanwhile, would center on her policies. It made sense. Republicans—even his detractors—could agree on one thing: Vance was articulate as hell and could vocalize the tenets of Trumpism even more clearly than Trump could himself.

"If we stay disciplined and we do what we have to do, we'll flip all the narratives about you," Surabian said.

Vance went on Kelly's show on July 26 to argue that his remarks had been taken out of context. "This is not about criticizing people who for various reasons didn't have kids," he said. "This is about criticizing the Democratic Party for becoming anti-family and anti-child."[8]

Over the coming weeks, Vance would embrace the role of attacker-in-chief. He turned his campaign events into press conferences where he'd stick it to Harris and Walz. In one, he said Harris could "go to hell" for the Biden administration's chaotic 2021 troop withdrawal from Afghanistan. He also became a regular on mainstream media outlets and the Sunday show circuit, where he trolled the media. During a September interview on CNN's *State of the Union*, he lashed out at host Dana Bash after she challenged him on his unproven assertion that Haitians were eating pets in his home state of Ohio.

"I want to start with something you said, which I think is, frankly, disgusting and is more appropriate for a Democratic propagandist than it is for an American journalist," Vance said.

During the same interview, Vance appeared to concede that
he had manufactured the cat-eating tale. "If I have to create stories so that the American media actually pays attention to the
suffering of the American people, then that's what I'm going to
do," Vance said.[9]

The press-bashing MAGA supporters loved it. No longer was
Vance on defense. He was a Yale Law–educated senator who'd
struck it rich in venture capital. But deep down, he still thought
of himself as a Middletown, Ohio–born hillbilly who could get
in the muck. Trump's lieutenants were fans of the Vance rehab
tour, among them Wiles, who agreed he needed to fight back
against the cat lady firestorm. Trump couldn't get enough and
was calling Vance to lavish him with praise.

∎

The Vance team started its debate prep about a month ahead of
time. Vance didn't need extensive practice, given he was getting
plenty with his heavy rotation of interviews. He did three question-
and-answer practice rounds—two of them by Zoom—in which a
handful of aides threw questions at him. Then, he had an in-person
mock debate session, in which Monica Crowley, a former Trump
cabinet official and conservative commentator, played the role of
moderator. The role of Tim Walz was played by Minnesota Congressman Tom Emmer, who had served in the same delegation as
Walz. Vance's prep was everything Trump's pre-Harris practice
wasn't: disciplined, buttoned-up, serious. The team modeled what
Walz was likely to say and had a countdown clock so Vance could
practice meeting the agreed-upon time constraints. Vance also
devised plans for what to do if the CBS moderators fact-checked
him, as David Muir and Linsey Davis had done with Trump.

Vance's strategy was to throw Walz off his game and not to come off as a MAGA warrior—as the Harris-Walz team expected—but as a normal guy. Upon taking the stage, he politely shook Walz's hand. As the debate got underway, he pointed out instances where he agreed with the governor and expressed sympathy when Walz said his son had witnessed a shooting. Off the bat, in his answer to the very first question, Vance painted a picture of himself that much of the public had not yet seen, describing his hardscrabble upbringing, his military service, and his mother's struggle with drug addiction. Walz, who furiously scribbled notes throughout the debate, appeared shaky and uncertain throughout. At one point, Walz conceded he was a "knucklehead" for falsely claiming he was in Asia during the 1989 Tiananmen Square protests—a concession that played into Trumpworld's caricature of the governor as a serial exaggerator. At several points, Vance smirked and glanced at the camera while Walz was speaking—a look that went viral online, and earned him comparisons to Jim Halpert's sardonic character in *The Office*.

As Trump's lieutenants saw it, Vance's debate had been a clean kill—so much so, the fear was Trump would start bad-mouthing him because the VP candidate was getting better coverage than he did for his debate debacle against Harris a few weeks prior. Trump, as he had been since picking Vance, was nothing but complimentary. He called Vance shortly after the debate was over. You did good, Trump told him. With a month until Election Day, Vance had given Trump a much-needed boost. And he'd helped himself as well. The press had heralded his performance, and afterward, his aides noticed they were getting fewer inquiries from reporters writing negative stories. Cat ladies had, for now, become a thing of the past.

No one was more vindicated than Don Jr., who had lobbied hard for Vance. For the past few months, he had been dealing with people second-guessing him. Now, those same folks were telling Don he was right. After the debate, he went up to an ally and gave them a fist-bump.

"Told you guys I was right about JD, you motherfucker," the younger Trump said playfully.

Don's dad didn't pay him a lot of compliments, but in this case, he did. Sort of.

"You got this one right, but I was the one who picked him," Trump told his son after the debate.

From the get-go, Don Jr. told people he would never forget those who engaged in what he saw as dirty tricks to stop Vance from getting picked. The day after Trump chose Vance at the convention, Rupert Murdoch, who had lobbied for Burgum, invited Don Jr. to stop by his breakfast table at the Trade Hotel in Milwaukee. The younger Trump obliged. Afterward, Don Jr. had a shit-eating grin on his face. Rupert and his posse were kissing my ass, he told an aide. Now, as Election Day neared, Don Jr. was pledging that the folks who'd come out against Vance wouldn't be involved in the White House transition if Trump won.

Vance's star turn was also vindication for Tucker Carlson. The former Fox News host–turned–conservative podcaster had also pushed for Vance's selection. Tucker saw the veepstakes as a battle between the insurgent-minded Vance and a Republican firmament that was looking to stop Vance at all costs. The day Vance was picked, Carlson approached Surabian and gave him a bear hug. "We won!" Carlson said. He then retreated to his hotel room, where he hammered out a social media post lacing into Lindsey Graham, the establishmentarian South Carolina senator who that day had publicly praised Vance's selection despite having privately tried to torpedo him. Carlson hated the pro-military interventionist posture Graham embraced and wanted to move the party away from it. He also hated that Lindsey was being disingenuous.

"This is disgusting. I can't believe this. I'm going to say something about this," Carlson said, before posting on X that Graham was a "liar."

Don Jr. had forged a close friendship with Carlson and helped bring him fully into Trump's fold. While Carlson had previously expressed reservations about Trump—years earlier, he had said that he "hate[d] him passionately"—he was now an outspoken defender and had given him a crucial endorsement in the GOP primary.

Together, the Don Jr.–Vance–Carlson alliance represented a formidable power center in Republican politics, one that could shape the party for decades to come. The khaki-and-blazer-clad, country-club-frequenting Bush Republican Party was out. A rebellious, hypermasculine, and politically incorrect brand of Trumpian conservatism was in. The trifecta would soon be joined by the richest man on the planet, a Kennedy son and an army of ascendant and like-minded dude podcasters.

Brat Summer had turned into Bro Fall.

Elon Musk's plane touched down in eastern Pennsylvania four days after the vice presidential debate. He was headed to Butler. Trump had been wanting to go back to the town for a rally ever since the July assassination attempt, and he had been getting encouragement from the likes of Fox News host Laura Ingraham. To Trump's team, it was a no-brainer. A celebratory return to Butler would help the scarred city get back on its feet.

"We've got to get back here," Trump had said the night of the shooting.

It wasn't always a sure thing. Butler officials blanched at the idea of approving the campaign's request for a permit to hold the rally, reasoning that the shooting was still too fresh. But Justin Caporale, Trump's deputy campaign manager for operations, had gone to the town and spent three hours meeting with local officials, arguing that the event would be a chance to celebrate the perseverance of the city and memorialize firefighter Corey Comperatore, a rally-goer who had been shot and killed. The board went from being split to giving its unanimous consent.

Trump had the idea to start off his speech at the October 5 rally with the line, "As I was saying," a not-so-veiled reference to the abrupt ending at the rally three months prior. His speech would coincide with the time of the shooting: 6:11 p.m. The former president would pay respects to Comperatore and pushed for a ringing of bells and an opera singer performing "Ave Maria."

The event's headline-grabber, though, would be Elon Musk, whom Trump's team had asked to appear. Shortly after, on the evening of October 3, Musk announced his plans. "I will be there to support!" the mega-billionaire said in response to a Trump post, in which the former president described the event as "HISTORIC!"[10]

The appearance represented a turning point for Musk. While the entrepreneur had long taken an interest in politics, he had never gotten involved in a campaign in such a public manner. With the election exactly one month away, the Tesla CEO would be standing behind a "Trump-Vance" emblazoned podium and exhorting voters to turn out for Trump. Musk had been a past Trump critic—in 2022, he said the ex-president should "sail into the sunset" rather than seek the White House again—but had come around. Musk endorsed Trump on X less than an hour after the Butler assassination attempt, calling him "tough" and likening him to Teddy Roosevelt.[11] And he was telling friends—and his tens of millions of followers on X—he viewed the election as an existential fight that would make or break the country's future.

Upon arriving in Butler, Trump and Musk's teams agreed the former president would call the billionaire onstage and have him say a few words. About thirty-five minutes in, Trump asked Elon to "take over." As Trump made his introduction, Musk, wearing a black "Make America Great Again" hat, excitedly leaped into the air behind him.

When he took the microphone he said, "I'm not just MAGA. I'm Dark MAGA." The crowd went wild.

The rally provided a window into the close relationship that was developing between the two men. Trump had been jazzed about Musk's decision to attend, and the two of them palled around in the production tent before taking the stage. By now, they had become regular phone buddies, and Trump was talking about giving Musk a role in his administration.

Their fond feelings were mutual. Trump was fascinated with Musk—"this is the one with the rockets," he would tell people of the SpaceX founder—and Musk fashioned himself as a Trump-like insurgent who broke China and, despite his fabulous wealth, identified with the working class. After the rally, Trump invited Musk to participate in a tele–town hall for Ohio voters. The tech innovator didn't seem to quite understand what a tele–town hall was—it was a rather old-school way of reaching voters—but he joined in anyway.

Musk soon decided he wanted to hit the trail himself. Sure, he'd done a lot already for Trump. The day before the Butler rally, he'd wired $11 million to a pro-Trump super PAC he was overseeing, bringing his overall investment to nearly $86 million—a massive sum that made him one of the former president's biggest donors. But there was more he could do. Musk would inject his personal brand into the race. Musk had cultivated a rabid following—many of them young men who dug his give-no-fucks, I-like-to-break-shit style—through his purchase and prolific use of X, his Tesla leadership, and his status as the richest person on the planet. The billionaire was on a mission to turn out male voters who had a history of sitting out elections, and he was pushing his super PAC operatives to find ways to get them to vote. Recently, the PAC had run an ad calling Trump an "American Badass"— not something that would necessarily appeal to suburban moms, but *definitely* something that could win over frat boys who spent Saturdays crushing White Claws and watching *College Game- Day*.[12] Musk wanted to understand the psychology of disaffected voters and believed they could turn the election. Trump, Musk was convinced, had a unique appeal to young men, many of whom felt alienated and were struggling economically. There was evidence to back it up. According to an NPR/PBS/Marist survey at the time, Trump had a sixteen-point lead over Harris among male voters. [13]

Musk decided he would set up shop in Pennsylvania, the battleground state where he'd gone to undergraduate school. His first appearance would be the following evening in Pittsburgh, where he'd attend the nationally televised Steelers-Cowboys football game and wear his MAGA hat. He followed that up with a handful of solo events across the state. Musk was fast becoming a MAGA hero. During a two-hour event in Philadelphia, one fan shouted, "I love you, Elon!" while another told him: "You're going to help us win Pennsylvania and the entire race." Another asked him to "buy Disney and fire David Muir." Musk slammed liberal wokeism and threw out some owning-the-libs stink bombs—he said liberal billionaire Mark Cuban and MSNBC host Rachel Maddow looked identical.

He also offered a dark warning: "If Trump doesn't win, I think we're doomed."

■

While Musk was zeroing in on Pennsylvania, another former Trump critic and self-styled disruptor was hopscotching across battleground states for the former president: Robert F. Kennedy Jr.

In Lancaster, Pennsylvania, Kennedy appeared alongside TV star Dr. Phil for a pro-Trump event. In Charlotte, North Carolina, he stood with Tulsi Gabbard—like Kennedy, a former Democrat-turned-Trump backer. On October 29, he was in Madison, Wisconsin. Suddenly, Kennedy was everywhere, on what he called the "Make America Healthy Again" tour, and Trump's fans were eating it up. He was a MAGA superstar.

Trump's supporters couldn't get enough of him. They appreciated his outspokenness against the American health system, and his desire to take a sledgehammer to it. For so long, Kennedy had been treated like an outcast and now found the whole thing surreal and overwhelming. Trump, meanwhile, was impressed.

"Oh my God, look at these crowds!" Trump told Kennedy. "They're cheering so much!"

While Kennedy was crisscrossing the country, Musk was digging deeper into his pockets. By October 15, he'd contributed over $118 million to help elect Trump. The two men were doing something else to bolster Trump: working behind the scenes to get him on the biggest bro podcast of them all.

—

Barron Trump, eighteen and starting a new life as a freshman at NYU, had been shielded by Melania while he was a kid in the White House, but was now becoming increasingly interested in his father's political career. Back in July, Trump singled him out during a rally at his Doral, Florida, golf course and asked him to stand up.

"Welcome to the scene, Barron," Trump said to cheers. "He had such a nice, easy life. Now it's a little bit changed. Anyway, a special guy."

When Trump's advisers came up with the idea of having the former president appear on alternative media platforms, especially podcasts that appealed to young men, it was Barron who would give him key advice.

One day, Alex Bruesewitz, an adviser on the campaign involved in the podcast bro push, called Trump to pitch him an appearance on a show hosted by comedian Theo Von, a popular podcaster.

"Ask Barron," said Trump, who was on the golf course.

By that point, Barron had already gotten Trump to sit down with Adin Ross, a twenty-three-year-old internet personality known for live-streaming video games. Trump and Ross danced, and Ross gifted Trump with a Cybertruck. The interview was a hit, receiving 2.5 million views on YouTube. Trump was just as interested in the number of social media views his podcast appearances got as he was in TV ratings.

After getting Barron's phone number, Bruesewitz got Barron's approval. That's a great idea, Barron said, before suggesting another name: Patrick Bet-David, an entrepreneur who hosted a popular conservative podcast.

Trump did a slew of podcasts that fall. Speaking with Von, he talked about his late brother's battle with alcohol addiction. A clip of the exchange posted on X drew 8 million views. On comedian Andrew Schulz's program, Trump explained "The Weave," his term for his circuitous conversation style, which got 1.6 million views on X. *On Six Feet Under with Mark Calaway,* he dished about professional wrestling—an appearance that got 14 million views. Everyone in a certain sphere of podcast-land seemed to want him. At one point, the Trump camp got outreach from a podcast hosted by Haliey Welch, otherwise known as the "Hawk Tuah Girl." But the talks didn't end up going anywhere because Trump was already overbooked.

There was one host Trump hadn't sat down with: Joe Rogan, the undisputed podcast king.

Rogan's show, featuring interviews that typically ran around three hours, routinely topped the charts. Both Musk and Kennedy had been on *The Joe Rogan Experience* and developed relationships with the podcaster, who similarly fashioned himself as a renegade force independent of the mainstream media.

Despite his prominence, Rogan had never had Trump on. Partly, Rogan was hesitant to look like he was taking sides. He had praised Kennedy when he was in the race—like Kennedy, he had questions about the safety of vaccines and promoted alternative medicinal therapies. That had infuriated Trump. "It will be interesting to see how loudly Joe Rogan gets booed the next time he enters the UFC Ring???" Trump wrote at the time of Rogan, who is also a UFC commentator.[14]

Now, Trump had other reasons. He wanted to do the show, but he thought Rogan should be the one to ask him on.

That fall, Musk and Kennedy began working both sides to make an appearance happen. In early October, Rogan interviewed Calley Means, a health advocate and adviser to Kennedy. When the show was over, Means told Rogan he would like to see Trump on the program and gave him contact information for Trump's people. With the election just one month away, Rogan was hearing from pro-Trump listeners who wanted him to pull the trigger. Musk, meanwhile, made the pitch to Trump. It's the number one podcast, Musk told him. You can't pass this up. Rogan extended a request for an interview in early October, and the two sides agreed on a date: October 25.

That day, Trump's motorcade pulled up to the nondescript building in Austin, Texas, where Rogan produced his show. Trump had spent the ride over prepping for the interview, with particular attention on health-related issues, a focal point for Rogan. From the outside, the podcaster's studio looked like an old industrial shipping facility. Inside, it was a different story, with deer heads mounted on the walls and an embalmed crocodile in the studio. Rogan introduced Trump to his daughter, and the two men took pictures.

The interview lasted two hours and fifty-eight minutes, with topics ranging from UFC to windmills to the question of whether there was life on Mars (Trump thought it was possible). Rogan appeared to sympathize with Trump's ongoing effort to delegitimize the 2020 election results, comparing the mistreatment of election deniers to that of vaccine skeptics like himself. Rogan also had a specific question for Trump: What would he do to ensure that the all-powerful pharmaceutical industry didn't obstruct Kennedy's efforts at reform? A Kennedy ally had encouraged Rogan ahead of time to ask the question, hoping to get Trump on the record. Some in Kennedy's camp remained suspicious of Trump and worried he wouldn't give Kennedy a role. Trump, as was often his practice when put on the spot, did not give a direct answer.

Within three days, the interview had thirty-eight million views on YouTube.[15] For Trump, the timing couldn't have been better. The election was rapidly approaching, and here he was reaching millions of young men with Rogan, a key demographic for the campaign.

After Trump left Rogan's studio, he headed to Michigan for a rally that evening, and then on to Pennsylvania. He was loving this bro approach. The previous week, at a rally in Latrobe, Pennsylvania, birthplace of famed golfer Arnold Palmer, he unleashed on the athlete's vitality. "Arnold Palmer was all man," Trump told the crowd. "And I refuse to say it, but when he took showers with the other pros, they came out there, they said, 'Oh my God, that's unbelievable.'"

Trump's staffers could just laugh and shake their heads. Some voters would like it; some wouldn't. It was what it was. They'd heard him talk about Palmer's anatomy before and figured he'd eventually bring it up publicly. On the plane ride from Latrobe, he brought it up again. It seemed like he was trying to get others to back him up that talking about it was a good idea.

"I wanted to honor my friend Arnie," Trump said. "He was known for having a big schlong."

Trump had long been synonymous with New York City. Tourists would stroll up Fifth Avenue and pass by Trump Tower, the fifty-eight-story skyscraper where he filmed *The Apprentice*. There was his cameo in *Home Alone 2*, where he chatted with Kevin McCallister, the character played by Macaulay Culkin, in the lobby of the Plaza Hotel. Who could forget all those 1990s-era *New York Post* covers documenting Trump's wild dating life?

While Trump had moved his residency from New York to Florida five years earlier, he still cared deeply about the city he called home for decades. Trump and John McLaughlin, his New York–based pollster, had been talking for the last eight years about Trump's desire to compete in the Empire State, despite the fact it hadn't gone for a Republican since 1984. If anything, that made him want to compete in New York even more. Even if Trump couldn't win New York, a better-than-expected showing there could help him take the popular vote, which no Republican had won for two decades.

"Even though I'm not going to win, I want to drive up the vote. I want to win the popular vote," Trump said. "I think we can do it."

Over the course of the campaign, he did a few events in the New York metropolitan area, including one in the Bronx and another on Long Island.

What he really had his eye on, though, was Manhattan's holy grail: Madison Square Garden. Situated in the heart of the Big Apple, the Garden had been home to sports greats like basketball stars Patrick Ewing and Walt Frazier and hockey Hall of Famer Wayne Gretzky. Muhammad Ali had fought Joe Frazier there. Michael Jackson performed there, as had John Lennon and Elvis Presley. Trump frequented the Garden over the years, taking in

Knicks and Rangers games. Trump loved to put on a big show, and there was no better place to put on a big show than Madison Square Garden.

Trump had raised the prospect of doing a blow-out-the-lights MSG rally earlier in the year, and the campaign considered doing it during the hush money trial, but the timing never quite worked. Trump had his own busy schedule, and MSG was often booked. Trump, though, never lost interest. Finally, they nailed down a date: Sunday, October 27, nine days before the election. It would be Trump's big homecoming and the capstone to his presidential campaign.

The lieutenants envisioned a roster of speakers preceding Trump. There were obvious names Trump had in mind, like his sons Don Jr. and Eric, UFC honcho Dana White, and Tucker Carlson. Elon Musk and Robert Kennedy Jr. would be major headliners, further solidifying their star status in Trumpworld. So, too, would, Tulsi Gabbard. There were a lot of other people who wanted in, some of whom were going around Trump's gatekeepers and asking the boss for speaking slots. Pretty soon, random names were showing up on the lineup. Sid Rosenberg, the bombastic New York radio host, got on, as did Cantor Fitzgerald chief executive officer Howard Lutnick, a major Trump donor whose financial firm lost 658 employees in the World Trade Center on 9/11. While Lutnick had an influential role in helping to spearhead Trump's White House transition, he wasn't exactly someone who had sway with Rust Belt voters.

There was someone else: Tony Hinchcliffe, the host of a comedy podcast called *Kill Tony*.

The forty-year-old Hinchcliffe, who was tight with Rogan, was known for a brand of edgy, roast-style comedy that attracted legions of fans but also landed him in hot water. In 2021, he was dropped by his talent agency after mocking an Asian comic using a slur.[16] Hinchcliffe reached out to the Trump campaign back in July to see if the former president would go on his show alongside Shane Gillis, a red-hot bro comedian whose killer Trump impression had gone viral. The podcast taping, ironically, would have been shot at Madison Square Garden. The Trump team liked the idea—getting the former president and Gillis onstage together would surely blow up the internet—but couldn't get the scheduling to work.

As Trump's MSG rally took shape, the campaign's operations department, which was led by Justin Caporale, came up with the idea to bring Hinchcliffe on. On October 16, the campaign formally extended an invitation to the comedian to perform a ten-minute set.

The MSG event was essentially conceived as a second Republican National Convention, complete with a well-lit, sharply designed stage to evoke a feeling of bigness and drama. But the reality was, the organization of the rally was a haphazard mess. While speeches at the RNC were vetted and approved ahead of time, the ones at MSG were not. Speakers were simply going up to the podium and saying whatever they wanted. It was a recipe for disaster. In the aftermath, most senior members of the campaign pointed the finger at Caporale, whose team was responsible for oversight of the event. Caporale had been widely praised for his efforts throughout the campaign, but in this case there was a near-universal belief his team had fallen short.

The first indication Hinchcliffe was going to go off the rails came right before he went on. In a locker room backstage, Hinchcliffe was rehearsing a riff about how political correctness had resulted in a crackdown on free speech. To illustrate the point, he had a joke saying the only people who find the word *cunt* offensive are "cunts."

People spied Alex Bruesewitz, a Trump adviser who helped to orchestrate the bro podcast push, pleading for him to remove it.

"Dude, you absolutely cannot say that," Bruesewitz said.

"Well, it's just a joke," Hinchcliffe said.

"No, it's a terrible idea," Bruesewitz said.

"All right, I agree, I won't say that," Hinchcliffe said. "I don't want to do anything that will hurt the campaign."

But when Hinchcliffe got onstage, he said a bunch of things that did *exactly* that. He took the themes of Trump's campaign and turned the dial to ten, launching into a set focused on anti-immigration humor and deploying racist tropes of seemingly every kind. He talked about how Latinos "love making babies" with "no pulling out." "They come inside, just like they do to our country," he said to the crowd. He went on to joke about a Black person in the audience carving a watermelon, and about Jews being greedy. And then came the joke that landed like a thud, where out of the blue he said there was a "floating island of garbage" in the middle of the ocean. "I think it's called Puerto Rico."

The Trump team immediately knew they had a problem. Hinchcliffe's crass humor threatened to undermine the campaign's elaborate effort to court minority voters, especially Latinos. There were more than 300,000 eligible Puerto Rican voters in swing state Pennsylvania alone, making them a crucial demographic that could tilt a razor-thin election.[17] Trump a week earlier had gone on Univision to make a final pitch for support from Latinos, whom he'd called "special people." Now, that could all be in jeopardy.

The comedian also played directly into Kamala Harris's hands. In the lead up to Trump's event at MSG, Democrats like

Tim Walz and Hillary Clinton had compared it to a notorious Nazi rally held there in 1939. The set only fed that impression and was a gift for Harris, who was ending her campaign by casting Trump as a cold-blooded fascist.

Aides were spread around the bowels of the 19,500-seat stadium, and many of them didn't hear Hinchcliffe's "island of garbage" comments. But all of a sudden their phones were blowing up, and they were trying to get their bearings. Reporters wanted to know if the campaign was standing by what the comedian had said. Florida Representatives Carlos Gimenez and Maria Elvira Salazar, the latter of whom had rankled Trump aides with her stream of unsolicited advice and requests for face time with the former president, were asking campaign officials what was going on. Some Republicans were going public.

"This joke bombed for a reason," Florida Senator Rick Scott, whose home state had the highest population of Puerto Ricans in the country, said on X. "It's not funny and it's not true."

Onstage, things were continuing to devolve. Rosenberg called Hillary Clinton a "sick son of a bitch." Businessman Grant Cardone declared that Harris and "her pimp handlers will destroy our country." David Rem, who referred to himself as a childhood friend of Trump's, called her the "anti-Christ." Carlson used his speech to blast Harris as a "Samoan-Malaysian, low IQ, former California prosecutor."

The Trump team convened a call. Wiles, LaCivita, and Jason Miller argued they needed to put out a statement disavowing Hinchcliffe's remark and distancing Trump from it. But others disagreed, like Cheung and other campaign spokespeople, including Danielle Alvarez, Brian Hughes, and Karoline Leavitt. They thought it would be a mistake to put out a statement, given that it wasn't Trump who made the remarks. Plus, it would only draw more attention to what Hinchcliffe had said.

"I don't think we have anything to apologize for," Alvarez said.

LaCivita disagreed.

"Guys, it's already a big issue," he said. "And every story in America tomorrow is going to be about this."

Wiles, LaCivita, and Miller won out. But there was some question about what to say. While Team LaCivita wanted to slam Hinchcliffe, Alvarez et al. pushed back. After some back-and-forth, they settled on a compromise, which would be a terse, one-line statement: "This joke does not reflect the views of President Trump or the campaign."

The statement did nothing to staunch the bleeding. The next day, a Monday, the Harris campaign released an ad spotlighting the Hinchcliffe joke. Endorsements came in from Latino stars Bad Bunny, Jennifer Lopez, and Ricky Martin, as well as basketball star LeBron James, who posted a video to his tens of millions of followers on X highlighting Hinchcliffe's watermelon remark. Miller wanted to do more to distance Trump from Hinchcliffe but was meeting resistance from other aides, including Alvarez and Hughes, who wanted to let it go. They ultimately decided to have Sean Hannity question Trump about Hinchcliffe during a prearranged interview the following day on Fox News.

"I have no idea who he is," Trump told Hannity. "Somebody said there was a comedian that joked about Puerto Rico or something, and I have no idea who he was. Never saw him, never heard of him, and don't want to hear of him. But I have no idea."[18]

Privately, Trump was infuriated. It was supposed to be his big night.

Melania knew what a big deal the MSG rally was to her husband. She had surprised her husband that night by introducing him onstage—he had no idea she would be there; she even took a separate car.

Melania had largely kept away from the race. Earlier in the year, she told Wiles she was planning on releasing a memoir in October, and that would be her main contribution to the campaign. Unlike Harris's husband, Doug Emhoff (and, before that Joe Biden's wife, First Lady Jill Biden), she would not be hitting the trail or doing speeches. Nor had she spoken at the Republican National Convention, which had come just days after the Butler rally, which she had been watching live when her husband had been nearly killed.

At first, word of the book, titled simply *Melania*, came as a shock. The former first lady would be publishing a personal memoir just weeks before the election. As always, Melania had done things her own way. When it was released on October 8, the lieutenants were thrilled. It was a bestseller, and it put the former and potentially future first couple in a great light. The most newsworthy part of the memoir was that Melania came out of the closet as a defender of abortion rights—a position that, if anything, could help with swing voters.

Now, Trump—and Melania—had been upstaged by a comedian. The former president had spent months cozying up to the bros. There was a clear potential upside, helping endear him to young men who could swing the election for him. But with his rally at the Garden, Trump had gotten burned. By bringing a cast of Smash Mouth dudes into the fold, he had risked turning off minorities, women, and moderate voters.

"I am telling you, even for me, and I voted for Donald Trump last week, it was too bro-tastic. Okay?" Megyn Kelly said on her podcast. "Maybe when you present in front of hundreds—thousands at least in Madison Square Garden, you clean up the bro talk just a little so you don't alienate women in the middle of America who are already on the fence about Republicans."[19]

The question was whether it would impact the outcome of the election, which was now just a week away.

FIFTEEN:
REVENGE

NOVEMBER 2, 2024

Iowa had propelled Trump to the Republican nomination. Now, it could sink him.

Three days before the election, the *Des Moines Register* came out with a stunner of a poll showing Harris leading Trump by three points in the Hawkeye State.[1] It was a nuclear bomb. The blood-red state was seen as a sure thing for Trump, so much so that neither Trump nor Harris bothered to spend a second of their time there. If Trump was losing in Iowa, he'd surely be losing in a raft of other states and would be on the way to a blowout loss. There were plenty of goofy polls released during the election by shady, less-than-reputable outfits. But the *Des Moines Register* survey was overseen by Ann Selzer, one of the most respected pollsters in the game.

Trump was irate.

"What the fuck is this?" he said when he was handed the results.

John McLaughlin was out to dinner that night with his neighbors at the Jersey Shore, when his iPhone started exploding. McLaughlin's clients from around the world were asking if Trump was about to get creamed. McLaughlin scrolled the results. They didn't look right to him, and the methodology seemed fuzzy. McLaughlin went back to his meal.

JD Vance was on his campaign plane when he got word. He was initially concerned, but when the self-taught polling wizard started going through the numbers, it didn't add up to him either.

Tony Fabrizio, the campaign's other pollster, pounded out a memo for the campaign to release to the press. With less than seventy-two hours until voters headed to the polls, the last thing they needed was a bevy of analytical pieces talking about how Trump was about to get clobbered.

A little after 12:30 p.m. the next day, McLaughlin got a call from Susie Wiles. Trump was still pissed. He'd gotten calls that morning from two reporters asking about the poll.

"I need a memo," Wiles told McLaughlin.

McLaughlin had been through this before in his many years of working with Trump. When a "bad" poll came out for Trump, the lieutenants would race to McLaughlin and Fabrizio and ask them to churn out memos documenting the poll's failings.

McLaughlin wrote up a three-page "confidential memo" documenting his issues with the survey and sent it to Wiles. "Despite late biased media sponsored polls, President Trump is in a significantly better position than 2016 and 2020 at this point of time," he concluded.

That evening, McLaughlin texted Wiles to see what the boss made of the memo.

"Perfect and completely changed POTUS demeanor," she wrote back.

Publicly, Trump talked up an inevitable win, but deep down he worried that things could be coming to an end. After all this time, he had remained convinced the 2020 election had been stolen from him and believed voter fraud would occur again. He was prepared to wage another legal battle. The Republican National Committee had been readying for months for a post-election fight. But what would happen if he fell short? His political career, and the movement he created, would go up in flames. His future would be up in the air. Maybe he'd go back to real estate or build more golf courses, he told people.

He was still in legal jeopardy. Trump's sentencing in the New York hush money case was pushed until after the election, and who knew what Judge Juan Merchan had in store for him. Trump's grim mood was manifesting itself outwardly. During a rally in Traverse City, Michigan, two days before the Madison Square Garden imbroglio, he wore a dark overcoat and a black MAGA hat and walked onstage to "Rest in Peace," the theme song used by WWE star the Undertaker. His speech that day was a stream of negativity. He called his adversaries "animals," the Biden White House "idiots," and David Muir a "fake sleazebag."

Trump's stress had been building for weeks, and he was taking it out on the people around him. In early October, Trump lashed out at a finance aide after being told that his campaign had prevented a donor from taking a picture with him. It turned out the aide had done everything right—the donor had refused to pony up the contribution needed for a "click" with the former president. Soon after that, Trump laid into his staff over an economics-focused interview he was to do the following day with Bloomberg editor-in-chief John Micklethwait. Trump demanded to know why it had been put on his schedule. In fact, he had agreed to it himself.

Then there was Madison Square Garden. Trump worried that the party he'd dreamed of at the famed arena had led to his destruction. In the days after, he'd been fielding calls from people who told him he needed to fire his staff. At one point, an executive at News Corp reached out to the campaign with a blunt message: You guys fucked up.

Trump demanded to know who was responsible for booking Hinchcliffe. He suspected it was Justin Caporale, but he was flipping out that he couldn't get a straight answer. At one point, he pigeonholed Wiles.

"Look, Mr. President, at the end of the day, it's Chris and my's responsibility," Wiles said.

"Yes, yes. But it was Justin wasn't it?" Trump said.

Soon, Trump got a reprieve. Two days after MSG, with controversy over Hinchcliffe's Puerto Rico comment still swirling, Biden told listeners on a conference call hosted by a Hispanic advocacy group that "The only garbage I see floating out there is [Trump's] supporters." It felt like the final days of the 2016 campaign all over again, when Hillary Clinton came under intense criticism for calling Trump's supporters a "basket of deplorables." The White House immediately tried to clarify Biden's remarks, saying he was merely calling "the hateful rhetoric" at the MSG rally "garbage." But the damage was done.

Trump was onstage at a rally in Pennsylvania when news of Biden's remarks broke. Taylor Budowich, who had returned to the campaign for its final few months from the super PAC he was running, sensed a golden opportunity. Budowich printed out a copy of Biden's comments and ran it over to a surprised Marco Rubio, whom Trump was about to call onstage to speak. Can you say something about this? Budowich asked.

A few minutes later, Rubio took the mic.

"Well, I wasn't going to say anything, but I have breaking news for you. Mr. President, you may not have heard this. Just moments ago, Joe Biden stated that our supporters are garbage," Rubio said to boos from the audience. "I hope [the Harris campaign] is about to apologize for what Joe Biden just said. We are not garbage. We are patriots who love America. And thank you for running, Mr. President."

"Wow," Trump said as Rubio left the stage. "That's terrible."

Trump wanted to take the whole thing further. On the flight following the rally, he watched a Fox News segment about Trump supporters posing with trash and garbage trucks in the wake of Biden's remarks. He knew what he had to do: pose in a garbage truck himself.

Caporale helped organize the photo op. He approached Trump before he got off the plane with an orange and yellow sanitation worker vest and proposed he wear it. It looks slimming on you, Caporale joked. The former president put the vest on over his white collared shirt, exited the plane, and walked across the tarmac in Green Bay, Wisconsin, to lift himself into a garbage truck that his campaign had gotten hold of.

"How do you like my garbage truck?" Trump asked the reporters gathered around him. "This truck is in honor of Kamala and Joe Biden."

The image went viral. The former *Apprentice* star had long been the master of creating powerful visuals, and he'd done it throughout the race. Most recently, he served meals at a McDonald's takeout window in southeastern Pennsylvania. Trump, a McDonald's fanatic, loved the idea, which Caporale had come up with and then organized with the help of Jim Worthington, a Pennsylvania businessman and Trump supporter.[2] "I've always wanted to work at a McDonald's to see what it's like," Trump told his team.

From his walkouts at UFC fights to his appearances at disaster sites like East Palestine, Ohio, each visual had a strategic purpose, helping him appeal to key demographic groups—be it

Latinos or African Americans, sports-loving young men or blue-collar workers. With the garbage truck stunt, he'd found a way to simultaneously highlight Biden's words and appeal to the working-class voters who formed the crux of Trump's coalition. All told, the McDonald's appearance, the garbage truck photo op, and the Butler return rally drew a combined 4.2 billion views on social media, according to the campaign's figures.

But Trump's nervousness about what had transpired at MSG did not subside. On the afternoon of November 4, the day before the election, Trump chatted backstage at a rally with Rubio and one of the campaign's top spokespeople, Danielle Alvarez. What, Trump wanted to know, would the anti-Hispanic "floating island of garbage" crack mean for him with Latino voters. Rubio assured him it wouldn't matter. Alvarez agreed.

"My culture is not politically correct," Alvarez told the former president. "No one is voting based on what a comedian said."

———

While Trump fretted, his brain trust saw a race that was moving his way. When Fabrizio looked over his numbers on October 30, they were good. Very good. Trump was winning in six of the seven battleground states that would decide the outcome of the election. Michigan was the one state where Trump was trailing Harris, and Fabrizio thought the numbers he had might not be quite right.

And so, Fabrizio saw no reason to overreact to the Madison Square Garden firestorm. No, it wasn't great. But all Trump had to do was stay focused on his central message: That he would fix the problems the Biden administration had created. In Fabrizio's mind, the media had made a big deal about any number of things during the race, and none of them had moved the needle. Hell, Trump had been shot once, almost gotten shot another time, had been indicted four times, had been convicted of paying hush money to a porn actress, and had gotten a new Democratic opponent 107 days out from the election. And yet, his poll numbers had remained, for the most part, stable. Voters had made their minds up about Trump. They either liked him or they didn't. There was no reason to think some ugly jokes from an insult comic would shift the balance of the race.

"Find me a voter that doesn't have an opinion on Donald Trump and I'll tell you they're lying," Fabrizio would say.

Among the most promising signs Fabrizio was seeing: Trump was continuing to make gains with traditionally Democratic constituencies, including Black and Hispanic voters. Trump had been aggressively courting those demographic groups. He would be appearing before Black men at a Philadelphia barbershop and in Allentown, Pennsylvania, a city with a substantial Puerto Rican population (a visit planned before the Madison Square Garden brouhaha). In Pittsburgh, he would be campaigning with Roberto Clemente Jr., the son of the late Pirates star, a visit arranged by Trump aide Tim Murtaugh, whose grandfather Danny Murtaugh was a Pittsburgh Pirates manager.

Trump would also meet with Arab Americans in Dearborn, Michigan. Lebanese businessman Massad Boulos, the father-in-law of Trump's daughter Tiffany, had been working aggressively to build Arab support for Trump, capitalizing on disaffection among some Democratic supporters over the Biden-Harris administration's continued support for Israel's war in Gaza.

Fabrizio had long been seen as a realist in the polling world. Some consultants liked to give their clients happy talk—Boris Epshteyn was literally known within the campaign as "Mr. Good

News"—but Fabrizio had a reputation for giving it straight. Sometimes Trump took it smoothly, and sometimes he didn't. After Trump's failed reelection campaign in 2020, Fabrizio wrote an autopsy in which he argued Trump had been damaged by voter perception he had mishandled the coronavirus pandemic and wasn't seen as trustworthy. Trump, Fabrizio argued, had also lost significant support from white voters, a group that had helped propel him to the White House. Trump was livid when he found out about the autopsy and confronted the pollster about it over the phone. But Fabrizio, who'd worked for Trump dating back to his days as a New York builder, had long maintained the former president's respect, not to mention that of Wiles and Chris LaCivita. That was illustrated over the summer, when Fabrizio moved from his perch at a pro-Trump super PAC to become a senior strategist on the official campaign.

"Are you sure we're doing that good?" Trump asked, after Fabrizio gave him his read on the race earlier in the fall.

"Sir, when did I become the optimist and you become the pessimist?" Fabrizio said.

Trump laughed.

———

As the election hurtled into its final stretch, Trump was doing three or four rallies a day, a pace that left his much younger aides exhausted. When he wasn't onstage, he was often in Trump Force One doing tele-rallies. After being evicted from the White House four years earlier, there was nothing he wouldn't do to get back. Trump was campaigning so hard he was losing his voice, eating soup to soothe his throat.

Trump was overbooking and massively overstretching himself. Onstage, his rallies were routinely running to around ninety minutes, as he rambled about everything from his aversion to teleprompters to the attacks he was facing from former First Lady Michelle Obama.

To keep Trump's schedule resembling something close to manageable, his team hatched a plan to rein in the length of his speeches. On the teleprompter, they would note when he hit the forty-five minute mark and then when he hit one hour. Trump signed off on the plan—yeah, yeah, fine—but when it was put into motion, he had other ideas. When the forty-five minute warning hit during a rally close to Election Day, Trump picked up the pace, as was the plan. But then the sixty-minute mark appeared. Trump paused, cocked his head and launched into a verbal assault on the iconic CBS News program *60 Minutes*, announcing to the crowd he was suing the network for allegedly manipulating a recent interview it had conducted with Kamala Harris.

Stephen Miller looked at his fellow aide, Jason Miller. "We just committed the biggest self-own in the history of American politics," Stephen Miller said.

To Trump's lieutenants, something bigger was at work. Trump was pushing back against their efforts to control him. *No one programs me*, he seemed to be saying. The way he'd paused before laying into *60 Minutes*, they could tell there was something mischievous about it. It felt calculated.

Trump's plane was packed during the final week. Wiles had been responsible for determining who got on Trump Force One, but handed the task off to LaCivita after growing tired of it. LaCivita knew he had to rein it in. At one point during the final week, LaCivita booted a kid who helped run the campaign's TikTok account. The staffer hadn't been on the flight manifest but had gotten on anyway.

"Where do you think you're going?" LaCivita told the kid. "You're off at the next stop and you're going home commercial."

With Trump nearing a possible return to the White House, everyone was trying to be in proximity to him. That, of course, included Natalie Harp. Harp had been playing more nicely with the campaign leadership as of late. But she still operated as if she answered to no one but Trump, and she still ruffled feathers. Unbeknownst to campaign leaders, she at one point reached out to Mike Johnson with stories she had flagged from the conservative website Breitbart News that were about the House speaker's staffers. One of the articles was about a Johnson aide who, according to the story, harbored anti-Trump views. Another article was about a Johnson policy aide who, the piece said, formerly worked as a lobbyist for companies that had a financial interest in providing funding for Ukraine in its war with Russia. Harp told Johnson that Trump wanted to know why he had those people working for him. Johnson—surprised by Harp's outreach—later contacted campaign officials and said the stories were inaccurate.

Boris Epshteyn was also hovering close. He had always seemed obsessive about being near the boss, but now things were at an eleven on the Richter scale. Epshteyn would linger by Trump's desk, blocking the way of the flight attendant who was trying to serve people food.

Epshteyn was in peak "Mr. Good News" form. During an off-the-rails rally in Lititz, Pennsylvania, on November 3, Trump said he wouldn't "mind" if an assassin shot through journalists to hit him. No one thought it was a great moment for Trump—

except Epshteyn, who was there to greet him and tell him he'd done a terrific job.

Beyond Trump, it was hard to find many people who liked Epshteyn. If there was an unpopularity contest among the staff, he'd very possibly win it. Other aides could recite eye-rolling moments from months, if not years, earlier. One classic came from early the previous year. During a Zoom meeting one day, Epshteyn accidentally turned his camera on and, to the shock of his coworkers, didn't have a shirt on. Realizing what had happened, Epshteyn quickly panned his camera toward the ceiling. Some found it funny. Others found it disrespectful.

"Oh God, Boris, put your shirt back on! Jesus Christ!" one person said.

Trump's inner circle had grown exhausted of Epshteyn, but Trump kept him around, recognizing he had quarterbacked the legal strategy that had kept the former president out of prison. As the race wound down, Epshteyn had an idea for an eleventh-hour gambit. He suggested suing a reporter who said Trump had been found liable of raping E. Jean Carroll, which the jury had not actually said.

"I don't want to be talking about rape in the last forty-eight hours of the election," LaCivita said.

Epshteyn backed off.

——

For Trump, Election Day began as it had eight years earlier: With a rally in Grand Rapids, Michigan, his seventy-eighth of the campaign. Trump somberly thanked his staff before emerging to the stage from behind an American flag that served as a curtain.

"This is a sad occasion in certain ways because I think we did like 930 rallies from the very beginning. That's a lot of rallies," Trump said.

He finished up at around 2 a.m.

It had been a good night for Trump. After kicking the crap out of the Trumpers over MSG, Megyn Kelly showed up to a rally in Pittsburgh to lend her support. The team, meanwhile, had gotten word Rogan would be endorsing the former president. Yes, it was late in the game, but it was a massive development. Rogan's superfans drank in every word he spoke, and he appealed to nontraditional voters who didn't always cast ballots. Trump's team rushed to insert a line into the teleprompter, and the ex-president announced it live onstage in Pittsburgh. By this point, Rogan was becoming increasingly immersed in Trump's orbit. He'd become texting buddies with Vance, who had a few days earlier appeared on Rogan's show. Calley Means, Robert Kennedy Jr.'s aide, invited Rogan to Trump's election night event, but the podcast star couldn't make it.

By the time he made it back to the plane in Grand Rapids, it was 2:30 a.m. Trump was still going strong. He put "Rest in Peace" on full blast, and chatted with former ESPN anchor Sage Steele and ex-NASCAR star Danica Patrick, both of whom had joined him on the trail. Howard Lutnick, now leading the transition, was milling about, as was investor Scott Bessent, who was rumored as a possible pick to run the Treasury Department. At one point, Trump playfully tested Bessent on his knowledge of the music of Elvis Presley, one of the former president's favorite artists. Others on the plane were exhausted and eager to get some shut-eye. A bunch went to the front of the plane and passed out. When they landed in West Palm Beach, it was nearly 6 a.m. A long day was ahead.

—

Karoline Leavitt called Trump soon after she woke up on Election Day. The campaign spokeswoman, considered a shoo-in for the White House press secretary job if Trump won, was about to do an interview with Fox News and wanted to know if he had thoughts on what she should say. Reporters, cable news talking heads, and the betting markets were predicting a close race, with polls in each of the seven battleground states neck-and-neck. It was possible that a winner would not be known for days.

Listening to Trump, Leavitt could tell he was confident. Trump asked if she thought he would win. I do, sir, she replied.

Leavitt had noticed throughout the campaign how Trump appeared to be drawing support in traditionally Democratic neighborhoods. She'd seen crowds line the streets to greet him in deep-blue parts of New Jersey and noticed how excited people had been to see him during visits to parts of New York City and Atlanta that were mainly home to minorities. Trump's push to win over working-class voters beyond his largely white base, it was clear to Leavitt, was working.

Trump told Leavitt he'd been hearing positive reports about how voting was going. Things, he said, were looking up.

Trump's lieutenants combed over the early vote numbers and concluded he was in strong shape. Despite the razor-thin margins being hyped by the media, it was already clear to many of them he was on his way back to Washington. Trump had been quizzing folks like LaCivita and Wiles over the last week about his prospects, and he had been asking about polling and early vote numbers. They were all bullish. Now, with a fuller reading of the numbers, the picture was becoming even clearer.

After voting with Melania at a Palm Beach recreation center later in the morning, the ex-president visited the campaign's West Palm Beach headquarters. Fabrizio told him he was going to win Georgia and North Carolina and that things were looking good in Pennsylvania, the granddaddy of the swing states. If he captured all three, he was golden.

"Good, keep it up," Trump said.

Trump had lost the popular vote in 2016 and 2020 and asked Fabrizio if it was possible he'd get it this time. Tougher, Tony said, but it was possible depending on how he performed in California and New York, two highly populated Democratic states.

Trump spent the afternoon at Mar-a-Lago, where aides had converted the dining room into a mini war room. Jason Miller approached Trump with more good news. They had gotten exit poll data. Among the findings: Trump was performing well with Hispanics, and more than two-thirds of voters believed the country was on the wrong track. If people felt that way, it was hard to see them voting for the party occupying the White House.

"Is there anything you're not happy about?" Trump asked.

"No," Miller said with a big smile. "You're going back to the White House."

Trump had long been worried the rug would be pulled out from him, that the election would be stolen. He'd instructed his team and the RNC to pour vast efforts into deploying tens of thousands of lawyers and poll watchers around the country to make sure there would be no funny business. When news broke that Milwaukee was recounting more than thirty thousand absentee ballots because the machine tabulating them hadn't been properly closed, Trump's fears were stirred. He dashed upstairs to his office, where the lieutenants had set up another makeshift war room. LaCivita had anticipated that people would be sending Trump reports of voting problems throughout the day and warned the team not to highlight unsubstantiated rumors on social media. He didn't want the boss getting concerned about something he didn't need to be concerned about.

Look, everything's fine in Milwaukee, LaCivita said. We're the ones who caught it. It's under control. They're going to be counting the ballots again, and we're going to be monitoring them while they do it. Got it, Trump said.

Trump had invited an all-star list of loyal MAGAites and celebrities to join him in Mar-a-Lago's gold-hued ballroom that night. Hockey great Wayne Gretzky was there, as were golfers Bryson DeChambeau and Dustin Johnson. Steve Wynn made it, and so did Elon Musk and Robert Kennedy Jr. Federico Castelluccio, who played a starring role in HBO's hit series *The Sopranos*, was spotted. A buffet was set up, and a big-screen TV was tuned to Fox News. Secret Service agents dotted the room, a reminder of the tight security apparatus that surrounded the former president. Mar-a-Lago was a fort. Guests' cars were scanned and dog-sniffed at the entrance.

"Things are looking good," Doug Burgum said upon greeting Trump in the ballroom. After falling short in the veepstakes, Burgum had become one of the ex-president's most aggressive surrogates and was regarded as a likely cabinet choice. Trump introduced the governor to Musk, whom Trump wanted to tap for a role aimed at cutting government spending.

Vance, meanwhile, was watching returns in a small house on the Mar-a-Lago property where he was staying with his wife, Usha. He was joined by his tight-knit inner circle, including his chief of staff Jacob Reses, as well as advisers Andy Surabian, Luke Thompson, and Jai Chabria, each of whom had helped Vance win his 2022 Senate race and guided his vice presidential candidacy. Vance had also invited a handful of high school friends.

Upstairs, Wiles and LaCivita were joined by James Blair, Taylor Budowich, and Tim Saler, the campaign's data whiz, to pore over returns. Fox News was on, and people scrolled X. While the mood in the room was optimistic—Blair was picking up positive signs in swing counties, in Philadelphia, and among Black male voters in Georgia—there was also an undercurrent of anxiety and a recognition that judgment hour had arrived. It was a far cry from the frenzied election night operation four years earlier, when an allegedly drunk Rudy Giuliani was bopping around and Jared Kushner was calling Rupert Murdoch to ask why Fox News had called Arizona for Biden. Trump himself was calm, so much so that he only made one trip up to the office to confer with Saler before returning to the ballroom. The rest of the night, the team sent Steve Witkoff updates, which Witkoff then relayed to Trump. It was yet another illustration of the faith he had placed in the Wiles crew. At the campaign's moment of climax, he left it in their hands.

At 11:43 p.m., Fox News called North Carolina for Trump. Five minutes later, Bret Baier announced Trump had won Georgia. The former president's swing state wins were piling up, with a speed few had prepared for. Other states were moving in his direction. It wouldn't be days or weeks before the election result was known; it would be hours. The clock had not even struck midnight when Trump said he was ready to make the fifteen-minute drive with Melania to the Palm Beach County Convention Center, where thousands of supporters had gathered for his victory party. Wiles, LaCivita, Fabrizio, and Dan Scavino would be in their own car. A larger group of aides and donors would ride over on a bus.

At 1:19 a.m., Fox News said Pennsylvania had gone for Trump, all but clinching it. With its nineteen electoral votes, the Keystone State was widely seen as the most consequential of the seven battleground states. Budowich was on a bus with a large group of aides and donors headed for the victory party when the network made its declaration. "Holy fuck, they just called Pennsylvania," Budowich said. The bus broke out in cheers.

Vance was in his holding room at the convention center with Tucker Carlson, Omeed Malik, Don Jr., and Don Jr.'s kids when Pennsylvania was called. The place exploded.

At 1:21 a.m., NewsNation became the first TV network to call the race for Trump.[3] Miller phoned the former president to inform him of the news. Trump was less surprised than relieved. It was over. His quest to reclaim the White House was complete. Without a clear-cut call, Trump had been planning to go onstage and say the results pointed to a win. Now he could declare victory, without any ambiguity. Harris still hadn't called to concede to Trump, as Hillary Clinton had done in 2016. It was a move that Trump had never afforded Biden in 2020.

Trump fans at the convention center were going nuts. People cheered and yelled "USA! USA!" The alcohol had been flowing all night, and at one point an evidently drunk woman started vomiting near the press risers, just out of sight from a bank of cameras broadcasting live around the world. Trump, Vance, and a raft of family, friends, aides, and allies flooded the backstage area. It was mayhem. People were hugging, crying.

Corey Lewandowski, stripped of his role but not his access, approached LaCivita to offer his congratulations. LaCivita stared him down. A few weeks earlier, the *Daily Beast* had published a story alleging LaCivita had made an astronomical $22 million in the two years he'd worked for Trump. Many suspected

Lewandowski's fingerprints were on the piece, and he was retaliating for his downgrade. When Trump—who abhorred the idea of people getting rich off him—found out, he went ballistic. The next day, LaCivita caught a 6 a.m. flight from Virginia to meet up with Trump on the trail. After LaCivita walked him through the numbers, Trump agreed the piece was incorrect and urged his aide to sue the outlet. Of Lewandowski, Trump said, "He's a bad guy." LaCivita was infuriated—and now, with Trump about to accept victory, he let Lewandowski know it.

"Fuck you, fuck you, and fuck you," LaCivita told Lewandowski. Lewandowski, he added, would not be joining the other aides onstage.

"The boss said I could go up," Lewandowski protested.

"No, he didn't," LaCivita said.

When Trump took the podium at around 2:30 a.m. to loud cheers, Lewandowski moseyed his way onto the back of the stage anyway. Melania and Barron stood to Trump's left. Eric and Lara were to his right.

Trump wasn't planning to use a teleprompter but changed his mind after it became clear he would be giving a victory speech. While Trump liked to riff, he recognized that important speeches required him to be on message. This was no time to discuss the heat Arnold Palmer was packing. In a nod to the key role his staff played on the campaign, he gave shout-outs to LaCivita and Wiles and invited both of them to speak. The restrained Wiles declined by vigorously shaking her head, leading Trump to jokingly refer to her as an "ice maiden." He also lavished praise on Vance, the forty-year-old senator Trump had crowned as the future of the Republican Party. "I took a little heat at the beginning, but . . . I knew the brain was a good one, about as good as it gets," Trump said. Trump invited UFC bigshot Dana White to the mic, who thanked a number of bro podcasters for their support, including "the mighty and powerful Joe Rogan."

"America has given us an unprecedented and powerful mandate," Trump told the crowd, pointing to the victories Republicans were scoring up and down the ballot. With the Senate in its grip and the House seeming to head that way as well, the party would have unified control of Washington when Trump entered office in January. He had become the first Republican to win the popular vote in two decades, had swept all seven battleground states, and had succeeded in making gains among minority and other traditionally Democratic groups. While Trump's 2016 win was based upon his appeal to blue-collar white voters, he had tapped into a new vein of working-class supporters who saw Trump as a vessel to take out their dissatisfaction with a system that wasn't working for them.

Trump had promised to take a bulldozer to the federal government, to enact sweeping change for his legions of supporters, and to take on the establishment. There would be little standing in his way. He would be able to reshape the country's law enforcement agencies and nominate loyalists to cabinet posts.

He had shown the mainstream Republicans who wanted to get rid of him after January 6, his critics in the media, and the prosecutors who had pursued him. Four years after leaving the White House in disgrace, he'd regained power.

On this warm South Florida night, he'd gotten the revenge he'd hungered for.

EPILOGUE

Two days after his decisive win in the 2024 election, Trump got a call from New York Congresswoman Elise Stefanik, one of his staunchest loyalists on Capitol Hill. Stefanik, who had joined Trump onstage at his victory party, had an ask. She wanted to be Trump's ambassador to the United Nations. Stefanik had spent a decade on the House Armed Services Committee and had her eye on the job for a while, relaying her interest to officials on Trump's transition team before the election had even taken place.

Trump didn't commit right away, but said it sounded like a great idea. The president-elect was riding high and was eager to get his cabinet into place. Gone was the chaos of 2016, when virtually no one thought he would win. This time, it would be different.

The following day, a Friday, the president-elect rang Stefanik back.

"The job is yours," he told her. "I wanted to call to let you know."

With that, Stefanik became the first person chosen to serve in Trump's cabinet.

The pick illustrated a key dynamic shaping Trump's vision for a second term. He wanted to surround himself with loyalists.

Stefanik was the first member of Congress to endorse Trump's 2024 bid and was a member of his defense team when the House of Representatives impeached him in 2020. Soon, three other members of that team—former Texas Congressman John Ratcliffe, former Georgia Congressman Doug Collins, and former New York Congressman Lee Zeldin—would also be nominated for positions, Ratcliffe to the CIA, Collins to the Department of Veterans Affairs, and Zeldin to the Environmental Protection Agency.

They would soon be joined by Elon Musk, who ended up spending more than $250 million to help Trump win.[1] In the days following the election, Musk was a constant presence at Mar-a-Lago, and Trump tapped him to co-lead, alongside Vivek Ramaswamy, a newly formed advisory body devoted to slashing government spending.

After the 2016 election, Trump had nominated a range of people to his cabinet, from people widely respected in their field, like James Mattis for secretary of defense, to oil executives like Rex Tillerson to secretary of state. None were close with Trump previously, and many would eventually clash with him. After being fired from his post, Tillerson described Trump as a "pretty undisciplined" president who "doesn't like to get into the details of a lot of things."[2] Not long after resigning, Mattis called Trump "the first president in my lifetime who does not try to unite the American people."[3]

Then there was his vice president, Mike Pence, who refused his demands to overturn his 2020 election loss.

This time, Trump was picking people who would not criticize him, obstruct his governing agenda, or push back on his wishes. He wanted free rein.

By mid-December, Trump's post-election honeymoon was in full swing. Final results showed he had won the popular vote by more than two million votes, or 1.5 percent. Canadian Prime Minister Justin Trudeau had made a pilgrimage to Palm Beach to kiss his ring, as were corporate behemoths like Meta executive Mark Zuckerberg and Apple CEO Tim Cook. He was feted at the New York Stock Exchange, and *Time* named him "Person of the Year"—an award the media-obsessed president-elect coveted. ABC News, an outlet that Trump loved to hate, also fell in line. In December, the network agreed to pay $15 million to settle a defamation lawsuit Trump had filed against it.

Trump's power was at its peak.

"We really do have a mandate," Trump told a group of allies at Mar-a-Lago in mid-December. "You know, I never really understood that word before, but I understand it now and it feels different this time. It's better."

The political world was waking up to that reality, too. While there had been resistance within the congressional wing of Trump's party after the 2016 election, that wasn't the case this time around. Republicans—especially those who knew they would be running for election in two years' time—recognized that by taking on Trump, they risked the wrath of the president-elect and his movement. Exhibit A: The pressure Republican senators were facing to confirm Trump's cabinet picks. Nearly all the staunch loyalists Trump nominated for administration posts—including the most controversial ones like pro-Trump activist Kash Patel, whom he'd picked to lead the FBI, and Robert F. Kennedy, Jr., who he'd selected to run the Department of Health and Human Services—appeared on glide paths to confirmation. There had been one hiccup—Matt Gaetz was forced to withdraw his nomination for attorney general after widespread outrage, including from within the party, over his allegations of sexual misconduct. Trump had let that one go, but he wasn't about to let Congress run this process, and that meant standing behind the guy who had the rockiest go of it: Pete Hegseth, Trump's Pentagon nominee.

Hegseth was a surprise pick to run the biggest government agency with a budget of over $800 billion and nearly three million employees, given that he was mainly known for being a cable news personality. But Trump had a twinkle in his eye for the forty-four-year-old *Fox and Friends* host, who was an Afghanistan and Iraq war veteran. Trump had floated the idea that Hegseth serve at the Pentagon or the Department of Veterans Affairs after Hegseth interviewed him at Bedminster earlier in the year. Now that Trump had tapped him, all hell was breaking loose. There were a flood of reports about Hegseth engaging in extramarital affairs, about an alleged drinking problem, about accusations of financial mismanagement at a veterans group he had run. A police report detailing allegations he'd sexually assaulted a woman in a Monterey, California, hotel in 2017 was made public, a charge Hegseth adamantly denied. Some of the stories were shockingly personal, as when the *New York Times* got its hands on an email Hegseth's mother had sent her son in which she called him "an abuser of women." (She would later recant the remarks.)

Trump's allies mounted an intense pressure campaign aimed at keeping Republican senators onboard, especially Joni Ernst of Iowa, a former military officer who had previously spoken of sexual harassment in the military and voiced skepticism over the choice of Hegseth. A cavalcade of MAGA influencers, including

Donald Trump Jr. and Charlie Kirk, took to social media to warn Ernst she'd suffer political consequences if she voted against Hegseth.[4] Iowa Attorney General Brenna Bird, a staunch Trump backer, wrote an op-ed piece in Breitbart News attacking "D.C. politicians" who "think they can ignore the voices of their constituents."[5] An Elon Musk–financed political group, meanwhile, ran ads in Iowa encouraging voters to call Ernst and urge her to support Hegseth.

The bombardment was unrelenting, and there were signs it was working. Ernst was facing reelection, and if she opposed Hegseth she could face a Trump-backed primary challenge. A few days after saying that Hegseth had "his work cut out for him," Ernst described a meeting she had with him as "encouraging" and said she would "support Pete through this process." Congressional Republicans were on notice: If they dared to get in Trump's way, they would face a well-organized and well-financed online MAGA mob that could end their political careers.

Hegseth, meanwhile, pressed forward. He traversed the Senate halls, going from meeting to meeting with lawmakers, including those who'd been lukewarm on him.

Trump stood by his side. "Pete's a fighter. He's done a good job," Trump told his allies at Mar-a-Lago. "Last week I thought he was dead. But now I think he's going to make it, and I think he's going to be good."

———

And then there was Susie Wiles.

To everyone who served with her on the campaign, it was obvious what was next for Wiles, the only person who'd managed to run a functional Trump political operation for a sustained length of time: White House chief of staff.

Wiles had waved away questions about her interest in the job in the months before the election. She wanted to help out, get the right people in place. But she'd been running the show for over three years now, and she needed a breather. She felt that particularly acutely back in September, during the height of the knife fight with Lewandowski. Watching him try to dismantle the organization she'd created had been disheartening. Who needed this anymore?

After Lewandowski was exiled, things brightened again. During the Madison Square Garden rally, Wiles joined JD Vance, Donald Trump Jr., Howard Lutnick, Taylor Budowich, and a former Trump White House official named Cliff Sims for a huddle in Vance's holding room. Look, they told her, you're the only person who can do this job. They said they were planning to make a full-court press the day after the election to ensure she got it. Wiles still hadn't decided whether she wanted the position, but she was touched by the overture. A few nights later, a group of senior lieutenants, including LaCivita, Fabrizio, Wiles, and campaign aide Robert Gabriel had dinner at Trevini Ristorante in Palm Beach, when the subject came up again. Everyone was in agreement. Susie, they told her, you need to push for this. By the weekend before the election, Wiles had decided that she wanted to be chief of staff.

Soon after the election, Wiles met with Trump. He wanted her to do the job, too. She had a few requests—mainly that the team she had surrounded herself with during the campaign join her. The conversation went smoothly—the only real hiccup coming when Boris Epshteyn popped in and inadvertently interrupted them. Trump and Wiles hammered out a statement and made it official.

The few people in Trump's orbit who were not fans of Wiles were coming to grips with her power and the fact she was here to stay. That included former Marvel Entertainment executive Ike Perlmutter, the billionaire Trump friend and Ron DeSantis ally who had been critical of her. Shortly after the election, Trump, Perlmutter, and Wiles met at Mar-a-Lago to hash things out.

"We're all on the same team. Let's move on," said Perlmutter, who, with his wife, Laura, contributed $25 million to elect Trump.

Perlmutter and Wiles shook hands as a glad Trump looked on. "Wow, that's great," Trump said.

Since Trump entered politics in 2015, no one had survived for as long a time and at such a senior level as Wiles. She had developed an intuitive understanding of how to read him, how to allow him to be himself while also keeping him as disciplined as possible, and how to give him advice without being overbearing. When Hegseth came under fire in early December, Trump considered replacing him with his old nemesis, DeSantis. That didn't sit well with Wiles, who DeSantis had tried to destroy. She let it be known to Trump that she disapproved, but she told him that if DeSantis was what he wanted, then she would make it work.

Along with Wiles, Trump had also empowered Vance. The vice president–elect was playing a key role in the transition, sitting in on meetings with Trump. Several of his favorites for cabinet positions—including Kennedy and Gabbard—had been nominated. While Vance would potentially face competition for the Republican nomination in 2028—Stefanik, among others, harbored presidential ambitions—he had emerged as a leader of the MAGA movement. And he had an army of powerful allies in his corner, including Tucker Carlson and Donald Trump Jr., ready to propel him.

—

Trump would be going into office with a governing mandate, a team of loyalists by his side, and a surge in public support—things he did not have in 2016. He also had a lineup ready to carry out his thirst for revenge, especially at the FBI and Department of Justice, two of the agencies he cared about most. Patel had once promised to "go out and find the conspirators, not just in government but in the media . . . who lied about American citizens, who helped Joe Biden rig presidential elections." Pam Bondi, who had succeeded Gaetz as Trump's attorney general nominee, had once said that once Trump won, "the prosecutors will be prosecuted" and the "investigators will be investigated."[6]

Trump and his allies got to work quickly. Two days after the ABC settlement was announced, Trump filed suit against Ann Selzer and her polling firm, as well as the *Des Moines Register* and its parent company Gannett, over the Iowa poll that had so angered him. The following day, House Republicans released a report saying Liz Cheney should face an FBI investigation for her work on the committee investigating January 6. Trump responded to the report by posting that "Liz Cheney could be in a lot of trouble." His quest for revenge appeared underway.

ACKNOWLEDGMENTS

Writing a book, I learned early on in the process, isn't a one-person job.

I am grateful to Matt Latimer, who, along with Keith Urbahn at Javelin, are the best Washington book agents in the business. I owe a huge debt to Amar Deol at Grand Central Publishing, who did an amazing job of shepherding this book through the finish line. Thank you to Sean Desmond, now at Harper, for his early interest in this project.

Miriam Elder is a brilliant editor, and I couldn't have done it without her. Miriam is a calm, steady hand at the wheel who offered advice, helped sharpen my narrative and writing, and was always there to take my (many) phone calls.

Maggie Rhoads was an indispensable research assistant. Maggie helped keep me organized, transcribed my many interview recordings, managed the compiling of source notes, and so much more. She has a bright future in journalism.

I am grateful to Hilary McClellen, a terrific fact-checker who helped ensure the accuracy of the manuscript.

Thank you to the leadership at *Politico* for their generosity and flexibility in allowing me to pursue this project over the last two years. I am also grateful to Meridith McGraw and Natalie Allison, my partners in crime on the Trump campaign beat.

I am especially appreciative of my sources, who recognized the importance of documenting history. You know who you are.

This book is dedicated to my mom, Catherine, and brother, Joey. It is also dedicated to my dad, Lester, who passed away in September 2024. I miss him every day.

NOTES

PROLOGUE

1 Caitlin Huey-Burns, "At Trump's N.H. Rally, True Believers and Big Fans," *RealClearPolitics*, last modified on June 18, 2015, https://www .realclearpolitics.com/articles/2015/06/18/at_trumps_nh_rally_true _believers_and_big_fans_127030.html.

2 MJ Lee and Pat St. Claire, "Trump Draws Thousands in Phoenix, Continues Immigration Theme," CNN, last modified on July 12, 2015, https:// www.cnn.com/2015/07/11/politics/donald-trump-phoenix-rally /index.html.

3 Noah Gray and Theodore Schleifer, "30,000 Turn Out for Trump's Alabama Pep Rally," CNN, last modified on August 21, 2015, https://www .cnn.com/2015/08/21/politics/donald-trump-rally-mobile-alabama/index .html.

4 "Speech: Donald Trump Holds a Campaign Rally in Grand Rapids, Michigan—November 4, 2024," Roll Call, last modified on November 4, 2024, https://rollcall.com/factbase/trump/transcript/donald-trump-speech -campaign-rally-grand-rapids-michigan-november-4-2024.

5 "Election 2024: Exit polls," CNN, last modified on November 25, 2024, https://www.cnn.com/election/2024/exit-polls/national-results/general /president/0; "Exit Polls," CNN, last modified on November 23, 2016, https://www.cnn.com/election/2016/results/exit-polls.

1: "YOU'RE NOT GOING TO BELIEVE THIS"

1 Josh Dawsey and Michael Scherer, "Trump Jumps into a Divisive Battle over the Republican Party — with a Threat to Start a 'MAGA Party,'"

Washington Post, last modified on January 23, 2021, https://www
.washingtonpost.com/politics/trump-republican-split/2021/01/23
/d7dc253e-5cbc-11eb-8bcf-3877871c819d_story.html.

2   Allie Griffin, "Eric Trump Alerted His Dad to FBI Raid, Said Agents
'Ransacked' the Ex-President's Office," *New York Post*, last modified on
August 9, 2022, https://nypost.com/2022/08/09/eric-trump-alerted-his-dad
-to-the-mar-a-lago-raid.

3   Michael Balsamo and Eric Tucker, " Trump Says FBI Searched Estate in
Major Escalation of Probe," Associated Press, last modified on August 9,
2022, https://apnews.com/article/donald-trump-mar-a-lago-government
-and-politics-9e8d683afe87389407950af7ccfdbdd6.

4   "Here's Donald Trump's Presidential Announcement Speech," *Time*, last
modified on June 16, 2015, https://time.com/3923128/donald-trump
-announcement-speech.

5   Alex Isenstadt, "DeSantis Draws Contrast with Trump as Party Hunts for
2024 Alternative," *Politico*, last modified on November 16, 2022, https://
www.politico.com/news/2022/11/16/desantis-trump-2024-election
-00067834.

6   *Inside Edition*, "Former Trump Aide Reveals Details about Dinner with
Kanye," YouTube, last modified on December 2, 2022, https://www.youtube
.com/watch?v=QwTvzfpI33s.

7   Adam Gabatt, "Milo Yiannopoulos Claims He Set Up Fuentes Dinner 'to
Make Trump's Life Miserable,'" *The Guardian*, last modified on November
30, 2022, https://www.theguardian.com/us-news/2022/nov/30/milo
-yiannopoulos-nick-fuentes-donald-trump-dinner.

8   Jill Colvin and Kevin Freking, "Pence Calls on Trump to Apologize for
Dinner with Antisemite," Associated Press, last modified on November 28,
2022, https://apnews.com/article/2022-midterm-elections-kanye-west
-entertainment-3bf5238639d0fd45c287be036420dcb2.

9   Rebecca Shabad, "McConnell after Trump-Fuentes Dinner: Anyone
Meeting with Antisemites 'Unlikely to Ever Be Elected President,'" NBC
News, last modified on November 29, 2022, https://www.nbcnews.com
/politics/congress/mcconnell-rebukes-trump-dinner-white-supremacist
-rcna59241.

10 Matthew Boyle, "Exclusive—Trump Denounces Fuentes: 'Nobody' That Embraces Antisemitism Has a Place in American First Movement or GOP," Breitbart News, last modified on December 16, 2022, https:/www.breitbart.com /politics/2022/12/16/exclusive-trump-denounces-fuentes-nobody-that -embraces-antisemitism-has-a-place-america-first-movement-gop.

2: FNG

1 Kristen Holmes, "Trump Calls for the Termination of the Constitution in Truth Social Post," CNN, last modified on December 4, 2022, https://www .cnn.com/2022/12/03/politics/trump-constitution-truth-social/index.html.

2 Ted Johnson, "Donald Trump's Major Announcement: Digital Trading Cards of Himself for 'Only $99 Each,'" Deadline, last modified on December 15, 2022, https://deadline.com/2022/12/donald-trump -announcement-digital-trading-cards-1235200212.

3 Michael C. Bender, Matt Flegenheimer, and Maggie Haberman, "DeSantis Tried to Bury Her. Now She's Helping Trump Try to Bury Him," *New York Times*, last modified on April 18, 2023, https://www.nytimes.com/2023/04 /18/us/politics/susie-wiles-trump-desantis.html.

4 Ted Johnson, "'Florida Man Makes Announcement': New York Post Buries Donald Trump's 2024 Announcement as Others in GOP Shun Mar-A-Lago Event," Deadline, last modified on November 16, 2022, https://deadline .com/2022/11/donald-trump-2024-new-york-post-ivanka-trump -1235173748.

5 "Trump Attacks Rupert Murdoch and Fox News—Again—Claiming 'Destruction of America' amid Defamation Lawsuit," *Forbes*, last modified on March 1, 2023, https://www.forbes.com/video/6321511736112/trump -attacks-rupert-murdoch-and-fox-newsagainclaiming-destruction-of -america-amid-defamation-lawsuit.

6 Alex Isenstadt, "This mornings program at the DeSantis retreat includes a 'fireside chat' between DeSantis and Fox News host Laura Ingraham," X, last modified on February 26, 2023, https://x.com/politicoalex/status /1629884414455889920.

7 Ewan Palmer, "Donald Trump Doubles Down on Rupert Murdoch Attack as Fox News Rift Widens," *Newsweek*, last modified on March 2, 2023,

https://www.newsweek.com/trump-rupert-murdoch-fox-news-2020
-election-1784696.

3: "EMBRACE THE SUCK"

1 Aaron Navarro, "DeSantis Gathers Donors, GOP Politicians at Event as He
Considers 2024 Presidential Run," CBS News, last modified on February 27,
2023, https://www.cbsnews.com/news/desantis-donors-gop-retreat
-considers-2024-presidential-run.

2 David Smith, "'I Am Your Retribution': Trump Rules Supreme at CPAC as
He Relaunches Bid for White House," *The Guardian*, last modified on
March 4, 2023, https://www.theguardian.com/us-news/2023/mar/05/i-am
-your-retribution-trump-rules-supreme-at-cpac-as-he-relaunches-bid-for
-white-house.

3 Alex Griffing, "'This Is a Huge Development': Fox News Reports Trump
Could Be Handcuffed after Indictment Next Week," Mediaite, last modified
on March 17, 2023, https://www.mediaite.com/news/this-is-a-huge
-development-fox-news-reports-trump-could-be-handcuffed-after
-indictment-next-week.

4 Jonah E. Bromwich, Alan Feuer, Maggie Haberman, Ben Protess, and
William K. Rashbaum, "Trump Claims His Arrest Is Imminent and Calls
for Protests, Echoing Jan. 6," *New York Times*, last modified on April 4,
2023, https://www.nytimes.com/2023/03/18/us/politics/trump-indictment
-arrest-protests.html.

5 "Trump Makes Statement from Mar-a-Lago Following NY Arraignment
Transcript," Rev, last modified on April 4, 2023, https://www.rev.com/blog
/transcripts/trump-makes-statement-from-mar-a-lago-following-ny
-arraignment-transcript.

6 Jake Lahut and Zacharcy Petrizzo, "The GOP Campaign Trail Is Already
Getting DeSantis-Proofed," *Daily Beast*, last modified on March 16, 2023,
https://www.thedailybeast.com/the-republican-2024-presidential
-campaign-trail-is-already-getting-gov-ron-desantis-proofed.

7 Bess Levin, "Ron DeSantis Swears He's Never Eaten Pudding with Three
Fingers as an Adult," *Vanity Fair*, last modified on March 25, 2023, https://
www.vanityfair.com/news/2023/03/ron-desantis-chocolate-pudding
-denial.

8 Jake Holter, "DeSantis Says He Has No Experience with 'Paying Hush Money to a Porn Star,'" WFLA News, last modified on March 21, 2023, https://www.wfla.com/news/florida/desantis-says-he-has-no-experience -with-paying-hush-money-to-a-porn-star; Gary Fineout, "DeSantis Calls Trump Indictment 'Un-American' and Says He Won't Assist in Extradition," *Politico*, last modified on March 30, 2023, https://www .politico.com/news/2023/03/30/desantis-trump-indictment-00089865.

9 Jonathan Allen, Dasha Burns, Henry J. Gomez, and Allan Smith, "Ron DeSantis' Donors and Allies Question If He's Ready for 2024," NBC News, last modified on March 24, 2023, https://www.nbcnews.com/politics/2024 -election/ron-desantis-donors-allies-question-ready-2024-rcna76246.

4: YOU'RE EITHER WITH ME OR AGAINST ME

1 Jared Gans, "Trump Widens Lead over DeSantis to 33 Points in New Survey," *The Hill*, last modified on April 11, 2023, https://thehill.com /homenews/campaign/3944123-trump-widens-lead-over-desantis-to-33 -points-in-new-survey.

2 Julia Mueller, "Haley: Manhattan DA Case against Trump 'More about Revenge Than It Is about Justice,'" *The Hill*, last modified on March 21, 2023, https://thehill.com/homenews/campaign/3909990-haley-manhattan -da-case-against-trump-more-about-revenge-than-it-is-about-justice.

3 "Highlights and Analysis: Donald Trump Indicted in Hush Money Probe," NBC News, last modified on March 31, 2023, https://www.nbcnews.com /politics/donald-trump/live-blog/live-updates-manhattan-grand-jury -indicted-donald-trump-rcna75172.

4 Rebecca Shabad, "McCarthy: 'I Don't Know' If Trump Is the Strongest Candidate to Beat Biden in 2024," NBC News, last modified on June 27, 2023, https://www.nbcnews.com/politics/2024-election/mccarthy-dont -know-trump-strongest-candidate-beat-biden-2024-rcna91379.

5 Rachel Bade, Eugene Daniels, and Ryan Lizza, "Playbook: Inside Trump World's Fury at McCarthy," *Politico*, last modified on May 28, 2023, https:// www.politico.com/newsletters/playbook/2023/06/28/inside-trump-worlds -fury-at-mccarthy-00103979.

6 Tina Daunt, "Trump Threatens 'If You Go After Me, I'm Coming After You' Day after Court Warns Him Not to Issue Threats," Yahoo Entertainment,

last modified on August 4, 2023, https://www.yahoo.com
/entertainment/trump-threatens-m-coming-day-233448930.html.

7   "United States of America v. Donald J. Trump, Waltine Nauta, and Carlos
De Oliveira," U.S. Department of Justice, last modified on July 27, 2023,
https://www.justice.gov/storage/US-v-Trump-Nauta-De-Oliveira-23-80101
.pdf.

8   "Former President Donald Trump Responds to Indictment at Georgia GOP
Convention Transcript," Rev, last modified on June 12, 2023, https://
www.rev.com/blog/transcripts/former-president-donald-trump-responds
-to-indictment-at-georgia-gop-convention-transcript.

9   Alex Isenstadt, "Trump Vows to Stay in the Race Even If Convicted,"
Politico, last modified on June 10, 2023, https://www.politico.com/news
/2023/06/10/trump-vows-to-stay-in-the-race-even-if-convicted-00101403.

5: BORIS AND THE HUMAN PRINTER

1   Letter provided by source.

2   Letter provided by source.

6: "IS THAT LADY FROM THE RNC GONE YET?"

1   Shane Goldmacher, "Trump Leads in 5 Critical States as Voters Blast Biden,
Times/Siena Poll Finds," *New York Times*, last modified on November 5,
2023, https://www.nytimes.com/2023/11/05/us/politics/biden-trump-2024-
poll.html.

2   Shane Goldmacher, "Voters Doubt Biden's Leadership and Favor Trump,
Times/Siena Poll Finds," *New York Times*, last modified on March 2, 2024,
https://www.nytimes.com/2024/03/02/us/politics/biden-trump-times
-siena-poll.html.

3   "Speech: Donald Trump Holds a Political Rally in Hialeah, Florida -
November 8, 2023," Roll Call, last modified on November 8, 2023, https://
rollcall.com/factbase/trump/transcript/donald-trump-speech-political
-rally-hialeah-florida-november-8-2023/.

4   Nick Robertson, "Trump Knocks DeSantis after Reynolds Endorsement,"
The Hill, last modified on November 7, 2023, https://thehill.com/homenews
/campaign/4297057-trump-knocks-desantis-after-reynolds-endorsement.

5   Nick Robertson, "Trump Gets Mixed Reactions in Haley's South Carolina,"
    The Hill, last modified on November 25, 2023, https://thehill
    .com/homenews/campaign/4327393-trump-gets-mixed-reactions-in
    -haleys-south-carolina.

6   "'This Race Is Far from Over,' Haley Says after New Hampshire Defeat,"
    New York Times, last modified on January 23, 2024, https://www.nytimes
    .com/video/us/elections/100000009279771/nikki-haley-new-hampshire
    -primary.html.

7: "A NASTY TITLE"

1   Joseph Biden, "Remarks of President Joe Biden — State of the Union
    Address As Prepared for Delivery," The White House, last modified on
    March 7, 2024, https://www.whitehouse.gov/briefing-room/speeches
    -remarks/2024/03/07/remarks-of-president-joe-biden-state-of-the-union
    -address-as-prepared-for-delivery-2.

2   Lalee Ibssa and Soo Rin Kin, "Trump Claims Liz Cheney and Jan. 6
    Committee Should Be Jailed," ABC News, last modified on March 18, 2024,
    https://abcnews.go.com/Politics/trump-liz-cheney-jan-6-committee
    -members-jailed/story?id=108257827.

3   Maegan Vazquez, "Trump Says on Univision He Could Weaponize FBI,
    DOJ against His Enemies," *Washington Post*, last modified on November
    10, 2023, https://www.washingtonpost.com/politics/2023/11/09/trump
    -interview-univision.

4   Sarah Fortinsky, "Trump Warns Haley Donors Will Be 'Permanently
    Barred from the MAGA Camp,'" *The Hill*, last modified on January 24,
    2024, https://thehill.com/homenews/campaign/4428148-trump-warns
    -haley-donors-will-be-permanently-barred-maga-camp.

5   Gary Fineout, "Trump Calls on Republicans to Challenge DeSantis' Lone
    Florida Supporter in Congress," *Politico*, last modified on March 25, 2024,
    https://www.politico.com/news/2024/03/25/laurel-lee-trump-primary
    -desantis-00148789.

6   Emma Barnett and Jillian Frankel, "Trump Says There Will Be a
    'Bloodbath' If He Loses the Election," NBC News, last modified on March
    16, 2024, https://www.nbcnews.com/politics/donald-trump/trump
    -bloodbath-loses-election-2024-rcna143746.

7   Chris Michael, "Trump Says He Will Be a Dictator Only on 'Day One' If Elected President," *The Guardian*, last modified on December 5, 2023, https://www.theguardian.com/us-news/2023/dec/06/donald-trump-sean -hannity-dictator-day-one-response-iowa-town-hall.

8   Christian Hall, "Biden, Trump in Dead Heat for 2024, While Kennedy Gains Traction, Poll Shows," Bloomberg, last modified on December 20, 2023, https://www.bloomberg.com/news/articles/2023-12-20/biden-trump -in-dead-heat-while-kennedy-notches-22-poll-shows.

9   Rebecca Falconer, "Graham 'Worried about 2024' If Trump Focuses on 2020 Election," Axios, last modified on December 24, 2023, https://www .axios.com/2023/12/24/lindsey-graham-trump-2024-presidential-election.

10   Ginger Gibson, "Trump Says Immigrants Are 'Poisoning the Blood of Our Country.' Biden Campaign Likens Comments to Hitler," NBC News, last modified on December 17, 2023, https://www.nbcnews.com/politics/2024 -election/trump-says-immigrants-are-poisoning-blood-country-biden -campaign-liken-rcna130141.

11   Jared Gans, "More Than Half of Voters Think Trump Will Act Like a Dictator If Elected: Poll," *The Hill*, last modified on December 18, 2023, https://thehill.com/homenews/campaign/4366724-more-than-half-of -voters-think-trump-will-act-like-a-dictator-if-elected-poll.

12   Isaac Arnsdorf, "Trump Warns of 'Bedlam,' Declines to Rule Out Violence after Court Hearing," *Washington Post*, last modified on January 9, 2024, https://www.washingtonpost.com/national-security/2024/01/09/trump -comments-violence-bedlam.

13   Karine Jean-Pierre and John Kirby, "Press Briefing by Press Secretary Karine Jean-Pierre and NSC Coordinator for Strategic Communications John Kirby, January 10, 2024," The White House, last modified on January 10, 2024, https://www.whitehouse.gov/briefing-room/press-briefings/2024 /01/10/press-briefing-by-press-secretary-karine-jean-pierre-and-nsc -coordinator-for-strategic-communications-john-kirby-january-10-2024/.

14   Joseph Biden, "Remarks by President Biden at a Campaign Event | New York, NY," The White House, last modified on March 29, 2024, https://www .whitehouse.gov/briefing-room/speeches-remarks/2024/03/29/remarks-by -president-biden-at-a-campaign-event-new-york-ny.

15 Victoria Balara, "Fox News Poll: Record Number Say Abortion Should Be Legal," Fox News, last modified on March 27, 2024, https://www.foxnews .com/official-polls/fox-news-poll-record-number-say-abortion-should-be -legal.

16 Domenico Montanaro, "Most Americans Say Criminalizing Abortion Is Wrong—and are Divided on Deportation," NPR, last modified on April 3, 2024, https://www.npr.org/2024/04/03/1242285012/biden-trump-2024 -election-poll.

17 Liz Hamel, Audrey Kearney, Ashley Kirzinger, Shannon Schumacher, and Isabelle Valdes, "KFF Health Tracking Poll March 2024: Abortion in the 2024 Election and Beyond," KFF, last modified on March 7, 2024, https:// www.kff.org/womens-health-policy/poll-finding/kff-health-tracking-poll -march-2024-abortion-in-the-2024-election-and-beyond.

18 Kellyanne Conway and Marjorie Dannenfelser, "Opinion: If They Want to Win, Republicans Need to Go on Offense on Abortion," Washington Post, last modified on August 24, 2023, https://www.washingtonpost.com /opinions/2023/08/24/abortion-politics-2024-campaign-republican-message.

19 "Graham Introduces Legislation to Protect Unborn Children, Bring U.S. Abortion Policy in Line with Other Developed Nations," U.S. Senator South Carolina Lindsey Graham, last modified on September 13, 2022, https://www.lgraham.senate.gov/public/index.cfm/2022/9/ graham-introduces-legislation-to-protect-unborn-children-bring-u-s- abortion-policy-in-line-with-other-developed-nations.

20 Burgess Everett, Sarah Ferris, and Marianne Levine, "Graham's Abortion Ban Stuns Senate GOP," Politico, last modified on September 13, 2022, https://www.politico.com/news/2022/09/13/grahams-abortion-ban-senate -gop-00056423.

21 Jonathan Allen and Rebecca Shabad, "Trump Calls on Alabama Lawmakers to Protect IVF after Court Ruling," NBC News, last modified on February 23, 2024, https://www.nbcnews.com/politics/2024-election /trump-calls-alabama-legislature-take-action-protect-ivf-services -rcna140259.

22 Anthony Adragna, "Graham 'Respectfully' Breaks with Trump on Abortion," Politico, last modified on April 8, 2024, https://www.politico .com/live-updates/2024/04/08/congress/graham-breaks-with-trump-on -abortion-00151056.

23 Anthony Adragna, "Trump Slams Graham's Conservative Abortion Stance as 'Handing Democrats Their Dream,'" *Politico*, last modified on April 8, 2024, https://www.politico.com/live-updates/2024/04/08/congress/trump -graham-abortion-attack-00151159.

8: "FUCK THIS, WE'RE GOING TO FIGHT"

1 Jordan Rubin, "Trump's Lawyer May Be Losing His Most Valuable Asset: Credibility in the Courtroom," MSNBC, last modified on April 23, 2024, https://www.msnbc.com/deadline-white-house/deadline-legal-blog/trump -gag-order-trial-judge-merchan-todd-blanche-rcna148977.

2 Taiyler S. Mitchell, "Donald Trump Denies Falling Asleep during Trial," *HuffPost*, last modified on May 2, 2024, https://www.yahoo.com/news /donald-trump-denies-falling-asleep-210911105.html.

3 Shayna Jacobs, Tom Jackman, Devlin Barrett and Marianne LeVine, "Looking Trump in the Eye, the N.Y. Judge Warns He May Jail Him," *Washington Post*, last modified on May 6, 2024, https://www .washingtonpost.com/politics/2024/05/06/trump-hush-money-trial -merchan-new-york.

4 James Liddel, "Trump Finally Offers Explanation for Why He Backed Out of Testifying in Hush Money Trial," *The Independent*, last modified on May 23, 2024, https://www.the-independent.com/news/world/americas/us -politics/trump-testify-hush-money-trial-past-b2550234.html.

11: A "NEVER TRUMP" GUY

1 Emily Crane and Steven Nelson, "SD Gov. Kristi Noem Having 'Absurdly Blatant and Public' Affair with 'Handsy' Trump Aide Corey Lewandowski, Sources Say," *New York Post*, last modified on September 15, 2023, https:// nypost.com/2023/09/15/kristi-noem-corey-lewandowski-affair-shakes-up -trump-running-mate-stakes; Laura Collins and Ken Silverstein, "Exclusive: Married South Dakota Governor Kristi Noem and Trump Advisor Corey Lewandowski Have Been Having a Years-Long Clandestine Affair," *Daily Mail*, last modified on September 15, 2023, https://www .dailymail.co.uk/news/article-12509093/Kristin-Noem-Corey -Lewandowski-secret-affair.html.

12: TOUR OF SELF-DESTRUCTION

1 Maggie Haberman and Katie Rogers, "The Day John Kelly and Corey Lewandowski Squared Off Outside the Oval Office," *New York Times*, last modified on October 22, 2018, https://www.nytimes.com/2018/10/22 /us/politics/john-kelly-lewandowski-fight-secret-service.html.

2 Mike DeWine, "I'm the Republican Governor of Ohio. Here Is the Truth about Springfield," *New York Times*, last modified on September 20, 2024, https://www.nytimes.com/2024/09/20/opinion/springfield-haitian -migrants-ohio.html.

13: "SOMETHING'S UP"

1 "Read the Prosecutors' Detention Memo," *New York Times*, last modified on September 23, 2024, https://www.nytimes.com/interactive/2024/09/23 /us/routh-detention-memo.html.

2 Elaina Plott Calabro, "The Accidental Speaker," *The Atlantic*, last modified on April 22, 2024, https://www.theatlantic.com/politics/archive/2024/04/ mike-johnson-speaker-ukraine-trump/678108/.

3 Jon Passantino and Liam Reilly, "News outlets Were Sent Leaked Trump Campaign Files. They Chose Not to Publish Them," CNN, last modified on August 13, 2024, https://edition.cnn.com/2024/08/13/media/trump -campaign-hack-news-media-report-iran-wikileaks/index.html.

4 Maggie Haberman, Rebecca Davis O'Brien, and Jonathan Swan, "How Donald Trump and Robert F. Kennedy Jr.'s Unlikely Partnership Took Shape," *New York Times*, September 2, 2024, https://www.nytimes .com/2024/09/02/us/politics/donald-trump-robert-kennedy-jr-partnership .html.

14: BRAT SUMMER, BRO FALL

1 Rachel Treisman, "JD Vance Went Viral for 'Cat Lady' Comments. The Centuries-Old Trope Has a Long Tail," NPR, last modified on July 29, 2024, https://www.npr.org/2024/07/29/nx-s1-5055616/jd-vance-childless-cat-lady -history.

2 American Moment, "The Hillbilly Has a Moment (feat. J.D. Vance)," YouTube, last modified on September 20, 2021, https://www.youtube.com /watch?v=ohqaH3ABiHg.

3   Anna Betts, "JD Vance Attacks Childless Teachers in Newly Resurfaced Remarks," *The Guardian*, last modified on August 28, 2024, https://www .theguardian.com/us-news/article/2024/aug/28/jd-vance-attack-childless -teachers.

4   "Trump Aide Defends Vance's 'Childless Cat Lady' Comment," Newsmax, last modified on July 25, 2024. https://www.newsmax.com/newsfront /karoline-leavitt-donald-trump-jd-vance/2024/07/25/id/1174001.

5   Matthew Impelli, "Meghan McCain's New Warning for Conservatives," *Newsweek*, last modified on July 26, 2024, https://www.newsweek.com /meghan-mccain-conservatives-warning-jd-vance-2024-election-donald -trump-1930745.

6   Paul Krugman, "JD Vance's 'Cat Ladies' Riff Has Serious 'Handmaid's Tale' Vibes," *New York Times*, last modified on July 25, 2024. https://www .nytimes.com/2024/07/25/opinion/kamala-harris-jd-vance.html.

7   Amit Chaturvedi, "JD Vance Couch Story: How a Joke Turned into Trending Topic and Was Fact-Checked," NDTV, last modified on August 7, 2024, https://www.ndtv.com/offbeat/jd-vance-couch-story-how-a-joke -turned-into-trending-topic-and-was-fact-checked-6282160.

8   Hannah Demissie, "Vance Responds to 'Childless Cat Ladies' Backlash, Claims Democrats Are 'Anti-Family,'" ABC News, last modified on July 26, 2024, https://abcnews.go.com/Politics/vance-responds-childless-cat-ladies -backlash-claims-democrats/story?id=112310494.

9   "*State of the Union:* Interview with Rep. Ro Khanna (D-CA); Interview with Gov. Josh Shapiro (D-PA); Interview with Sen. J.D. Vance (R-OH)," CNN, last modified on September 15, 2024. https://transcripts.cnn.com /show/sotu/date/2024-09-15/segment/01.

10   Elon Musk, "I will be there to support!" X, last modified on October 3, 2024, https://x.com/elonmusk/status/1842048755169690103.

11   Hyunjoo Jin and Alexandra Ulmer, "Elon Musk Endorses Trump in Presidential Race, Calls Him 'Tough,'" Reuters, last modified on July 13, 2024, https://www.reuters.com/world/us/elon-musk-says-he-fully-endorses -tough-trump-posts-photo-2024-07-13.

12   Dana Hull, "Musk-Funded Ad Pitches Trump as 'American Badass' to Young Men," Bloomberg Government, last modified on September 27,

2024, https://news.bgov.com/bloomberg-government-news/musk-funded
-ad-pitches-trump-as-american-badass-to-young-men-1.

13 "NPR/PBS News/Marist Poll National Tables September 27th through
October 1st, 2024," NPR/PBS News/Marist Poll, last modified on October
1, 2024, https://maristpoll.marist.edu/wp-content/uploads/2024/10/NPR
_PBS-News_Marist-Poll_USA-NOS-and-Tables_202410021120-1.pdf.

14 Sareen Habeshian, "Trump Hits Back at Joe Rogan over RFK Jr. Nod,"
Axios, last modified on August 9, 2024, https://www.axios.com/2024/08/09
/trump-joe-rogan-rfk-jr.

15 Dominick Mastrangelo, "Trump, Rogan Interview Tops 38 Million Views,"
The Hill, last modified on October 29, 2024, https://thehill.com/homenews/
media/4959974-joe-rogan-trump-interview.

16 Rob Bailey-Millado, "Tony Hinchcliffe Dropped by Agents after Slur
against Comic Peng Dang," New York Post, last modified on May 13, 2021,
https://nypost.com/2021/05/13/tony-hinchcliffe-dropped-by-agents-after
-using-asian-slur.

17 Monica Alba, "Harris' Campaign Launches Ad Seizing on Trump Ally's
Racist Comments about Puerto Ricans," NBC News, last modified on
October 28, 2024, https://www.nbcnews.com/politics/2024-election/harris
-campaign-launches-new-ad-seizing-trump-allys-racist-comments
-rcna177686.

18 Ashley Carnahan, "Trump Denies Knowing Comedian Who Told Crude
Joke about Puerto Rico: 'I Have No Idea Who He Is,'" Fox News, last
modified on October 29, 2024, https://www.foxnews.com/media/trump
-denies-knowing-comedian-who-told-crude-joke-about-puerto-rico
-i-have-no-idea-who-he-is.

19 Charlie Nash, "Megyn Kelly Rips Trump's 'Bro-Tastic' Madison Square
Garden Rally: 'Do They Have No Women Advising Their Campaign?'"
Mediaite, last modified on October 28, 2024, https://www.mediaite.com
/politics/megyn-kelly-rips-trumps-bro-tastic-madison-square-garden-rally
-do-they-have-no-women-advising-their-campaign.

15: REVENGE

1 Brianne Pfannenstiel, "Iowa Poll: Kamala Harris Leapfrogs Donald Trump
to Take Lead near Election Day. Here's How," Des Moines Register, last

modified on November 2, 2024, https://www.desmoinesregister.com/story
/news/politics/iowa-poll/2024/11/02/iowa-poll-kamala-harris-leads-donald
-trump-2024-presidential-race/75354033007.

2   Marc Levy and Michelle L. Price, "Trump Works the Fry Station and Holds
a Drive-Thru News Conference at a Pennsylvania McDonald's," Associated
Press, last modified on October 21, 2024, https://apnews.com/article/trump
-harris-mcdonalds-2024-presidential-election-pennsylvania-73e55c8c1db4
adc2a547b62bd5142be3.

3   Andrew Dorn and Tulsi Kamath, "Here's How NewsNation/Decision Desk
HQ Called the Presidential Race First," NewsNation, last modified on
November 6, 2024, https://www.newsnationnow.com/politics/2024
-election/how-newsnation-decision-desk-hq-called-pennsylvania-for
-trump.

EPILOGUE

1   Jason Lange and Tim Reid, "Musk Spent Over a Quarter of a Billion Dollars
to Help Elect Trump," Reuters, last modified on December 6, 2024, https://
www.reuters.com/world/us/musk-spent-over-quarter-billion
-dollars-help-elect-trump-2024-12-06.

2   Anthony Zurcher, "How Trump Feud with 'Dumb as a Rock' Tillerson
Erupted," BBC, last modified on December 7, 2018, https://www.bbc.com
/news/world-us-canada-46407993.

3   Paul LeBlanc and Barbara Starr, "Mattis Tears into Trump: 'We Are
Witnessing the Consequences of Three Years without Mature Leadership,'"
CNN, last modified on June 4, 2020, https://www.cnn.com/2020/06/03
/politics/mattis-statement-trump/index.html.

4   Jill Colvin, Hannah Fingerhut, and Lisa Mascaro, "Pressure on Iowa
Senator Shows Consequences for Republicans who Oppose Trump," PBS
News, last modified on December 12, 2024, https://www.pbs.org/newshour
/politics/pressure-iowa-senator-shows-consequences-for-republicans-who
-oppose-trump.

5   Brenna Bird, "Exclusive—Iowa AG Brenna Bird: Iowans Made Their Voice
Clear, the Senate Must Confirm Trump's Cabinet," Breitbart News, last
modified on December 6, 2024, https://www.breitbart.com/politics/2024

/12/06/exclusive-iowa-ag-brenna-bird-iowans-made-their-voice-clear-the-senate-must-confirm-trumps-cabinet.

6   Peter Stone. "'Incredibly Harmful': Why Trump's FBI and DoJ Picks Scare Civil Liberties Experts," *The Guardian*, last modified on December 10, 2024, https://www.theguardian.com/us-news/2024/dec/10/trump-fbi-kash-patel-justice-department-pam-bondi.

ABOUT THE AUTHOR

ALEX ISENSTADT is a national political reporter at *Politico*, where he has covered Donald Trump since 2015. He has appeared on TV outlets including CNN, Fox News, and MSNBC. He lives in Washington, D.C. You can follow him @politicoalex.